One-Act Plays for Acting Students

An anthology of short one-act plays for one, two or three actors

Edited by
NORMAN A. BERT

MERIWETHER PUBLISHING LTD.
Colorado Springs, Colorado

Meriwether Publishing Ltd., Publisher
P.O. Box 7710
Colorado Springs, CO 80933

Editor: Arthur L. Zapel
Typesetting: Sharon E. Garlock
Cover design: Anne Kircher

© Copyright MCMLXXXVII Meriwether Publishing Ltd.
Printed in the United States of America
First Edition

Library of Congress Cataloging-in-Publication Data

One-act plays for acting students.

      Bibliography: p.
      1. Acting. 2. One-act plays, American. 3. American
    drama--20th century.   I. Bert, Norman.
    PN2080.054   1987   812'.041'08   87-42871
    ISBN 0-916260-47-X

6 7 8   02 01 00 99 98

INTRODUCTION

The quality of theatre and of film in this country depends primarily on two groups of people: the actors and the writers. And the **future** of the performing arts is in the hands of new actors and writers who are learning their craft now. Everything we do to increase their inspiration and dedication to their art, everything we do to give them the opportunity to see their work on stage, will directly improve the theatre of tomorrow.

And they need to work together, these actors and writers. They are partners. In spite of the inevitable conflicts between the writers of the words and the doers of the words, and in spite of the continuous negotiations between the actors' unions and the writers' unions, most actors and authors sense a kinship for each other. This relationship needs to be fostered and nurtured in our new artists; student actors need the experience of doing new plays; new playwrights need to see actors engaged in the task of giving their visions flesh and voices. New plays like these offer freedom to explore for both. Be sure to get the rights to use these plays from the authors — they will make it easy for you.

For twenty years, the American College Theatre Festival has been committed to the development of new actors and playwrights. Each year in the ACTF, thousands of theatre students in colleges and universities across the nation prepare plays and perform them for an audience that totals in the millions. Many of these plays are new scripts. The efforts of the best student actors and writers participating in the ACTF are recognized by the Irene Ryan Acting awards and the Michael Kanin Playwriting awards. The work is exciting and challenging. It is what theatre is all about.

You now hold in your hands a book, **One-Act Plays for Acting Students,** which embodies this same vision of actors and playwrights working together. Many of the writers featured in this collection are capable dramatists who have not yet achieved wide reputations; and the book is especially designed for the use of actors who are learning their craft. I hope you will read these scripts, and even more, I hope you will bring them to life through the hard work of exploration and performance. Of course, actors must stir around in the dust of the classics and the glitter of last year's Broadway success. But **dare to take the risk** of working with new material. And, while you do this, I hope you will be consciously aware of the joy of discovery, the satisfaction of creation and the excitement of originality. I hope that you will realize that you are part of something larger than a class project or a mini-play: You are engaged in making our future happen.

David Young, Producing Director
American College Theatre Festival
The John F. Kennedy Center for the Performing Arts
Washington, DC
1987

CONTENTS

Part I

Scripts

Scripts for Two Actors

ANNIVERSARY

by
CONRAD BISHOP

Director of *The Independent Eye* theatre troupe in Lancaster, Pennsylvania, Conrad Bishop has had scripts produced by Jon Jory of the Actors Theatre of Louisville and by Marshall Mason of the Circle Repertory Theatre in New York. This script, *Anniversary,* is part of a cycle of plays titled *Families* which premiered in Lancaster in 1980; broadcast over Philadelphia public radio, *Families* received a 1982 Ohio State Award, a top international radio honor.

Production Suggestions

While *Anniversary* has primarily a realistic, representational style, it also contains moments when the characters break out of their dinner milieu and speak directly to the audience. These transitions may be marked by a sound effect such as bell or a guitar chord, or they can be done just as effectively by sharp, defined transformations on the part of the actors. However you choose to handle these transitions, the juxtaposition of realism and presentationalism makes *Anniversary* an exciting play to perform and watch.

You can handle the telephone ring either as an actual sound effect or as a sound heard only by the characters.

Address all inquiries concerning performances, readings, or reprinting of this work *or any portion thereof* to Conrad Bishop, 115 Arch Street, Philadelphia, PA 19106. For details, see "Part II: Securing Rights for Your Production," pages 223 to 232.

ANNIVERSARY

by
CONRAD BISHOP

The action takes place in the present in the home of a sophisticated young couple celebrating their first anniversary.

Characters:
THE MAN — Chris
THE WOMAN — Chris's wife

Setting: *The room has an intimate dining table and two chairs. A telephone sits on a near-by end table.*

MAN: Terrific meal

WOMAN: For a terrific couple.

MAN: Happy anniversary, honey.

WOMAN: The first of many.

MAN: Many happy returns.

WOMAN: Speaking of returns, do you want to look at the bills?

MAN: This is our anniversary, honey.

WOMAN: There's a final notice.

MAN: Yeh, but . . .

WOMAN: I'll put them on the desk.

MAN: So many things have happened in one year. So many adjustments.

WOMAN: Adjusting, learning to give and take . . .

MAN: Take charge of our lives, face up to our problems and solve them.

WOMAN: And now that we've solved them, it should really be nice.

MAN: Because it has been kind of rough, you know . . .

WOMAN: Well sure, it's hard to grow. We've grown personally.

MAN: We have. Like our quarrels have grown . . . I mean they've matured.

WOMAN: Our anger, we've learned how to deal with it. That magazine article . . .

MAN: "Have Fun with Your Anger."

WOMAN: And you know, when we have kids, I am never going to be angry with them. It's just not necessary. If you love them and raise them the right way, they'll never cause you problems.

MAN: Not many couples could say on their first anniversary that they have solved all their significant problems.

WOMAN: But it's true.

MAN: I think we're way ahead of most couples. Maybe five years ahead of most.

WOMAN: Happy anniversary, honey. *(They kiss and turn front.)* Our marriage, well it's hard to talk about because it really has been this incredible experience . . .

MAN: Incredible but believable. We're more than just married. We're good friends.

WOMAN: Friends, of course we're more than just friends. It's so stimulating, so liberating . . . I've been liberated to do so much. New furniture, new colors, new recipes . . .

MAN: Zulu cookery. We have so many tastes in common. Even colors. Now the brighter end of the chartreuse scale is not often . . .

WOMAN: It's not often found so early in a marriage.

MAN: Really incredible. *(They turn to one another.)*

WOMAN: Honey, before it gets too late and we get involved in something else, could you take out the garbage?

MAN: Huh?

WOMAN: Would you take out the garbage? It's kind of piled up.

MAN: Honey . . . you're gonna laugh.

WOMAN: What?

MAN: The garbage. I just can't cope with the garbage.

WOMAN: Oh. Well, as long as it's out before breakfast.

MAN: No. I don't mean garbage now. I mean garbage always. Garbage forever.

WOMAN: But we agreed: garbage is your province. Do you

think we're making too much garbage, is that it?

MAN: It's not a recycling question, or a question of less garbage or better garbage. It's the fact of garbage.

WOMAN: Well, it's a human fact. We all generate refuse. If you put two people together...

MAN: That's it. That's it. This is our product. Our love, our sensitivity, our relationship results in this...horrible accumulation. Oh, I know it's a petty little thing, but...

WOMAN: It's not petty. There *are* three sacks of it. Honey, this is our anniversary. I would like it to be a garbage-free anniversary.

MAN: And how can we really, truly say Happy Anniversary when there is this external manifestation of our relationship bulging across the kitchen at us? The Johnsons? Two doors down? He goes out once a week with a little plastic thing. It doesn't look like garbage, it doesn't smell like garbage. It's an intense but comprehensible concentration of semi-organic substance, like the Johnsons. But ours...

WOMAN: I don't understand.

MAN: Take out the garbage. Please. *You* take out the garbage

WOMAN: I could take out the garbage.

MAN: Yes.

WOMAN: But I think there's something more basic here.

MAN: Honey...

WOMAN: Why do you want to give *me* the garbage when you hate it so much?

MAN: I'm not giving it to you.

WOMAN: I just don't like the idea of having it thrust into my hands.

MAN: I'm not thrusting.

WOMAN: You are thrusting.

MAN: Why do you use these masculine images? I'm not trying to thrust it, I'm trying to...*share* it!...You've never had the freedom to take out the garbage, and I want that experience *for you*.

WOMAN: Well ... thank ... you ... *(They turn front.)* It is a dilemma, of course, not that it can't be worked out. I have a great concern for the garbage, just as much as Chris does, because it seems to have this place of importance in our lives ...

MAN: It's a kind of focal point for a lot of things, and maybe if we can just focus on the focal point, things will come more into focus.

WOMAN: Because very often, in terms of taking responsibility, Chris has a tendency to ... give it to me. And we thought perhaps we should work this out the way we work things out. He would state what he feels and I would state what I feel. Which we did. I stated that the garbage needs taking out.

MAN: And I agreed. But I stated that I had a very negative reaction to her tone of voice in stating her statement.

WOMAN: So I tried to find a better tone of voice in which to state the needs of the garbage, in order to strike a better balance between Chris's needs and those of the garbage. I tried a plain old "Take out the garbage."

MAN: That's very blunt.

WOMAN: OK. "Honey, I wonder if I might ask you to expel the garbage?"

MAN: It rings false.

WOMAN: OK. "Sweetheart. Dearest. I know you don't like to, because there's a lot on your mind such as solving the nation's balance of payments and also paying our bills, but I really don't know where to put any more garbage. Should I pile it in the bathroom or the closets, or put it in the bed as a helpful hint, or serve it again for dinner? Or maybe we could sleep in the garage and use the house for the garbage but could you *please take it out?*"

MAN: I hate attempts at humor.

WOMAN: "Oh, look at *this!* It's the *garbage!* It would be so much fun to do something with this! But I need a big strong man to do it! And everyone will look out their window and say, "What a big strong man going down those stairs! Doesn't he take good care of her garbage!"

MAN: She really misses the whole point.

WOMAN: "Hey baby, haul my garbage!" ... Not to take away from our anniversary ...

MAN: Because it really is a very happy anniversary, really ...

WOMAN: Really, really, really incredible. *(They turn to one another, and start to laugh.)*

MAN: I don't know how we got into this.

WOMAN: Neither do I.

MAN: I mean I don't think it's really a problem. It's just a new aspect of our relationship.

WOMAN: Though it is an aspect that's beginning to pile up.

MAN: Look, I'm not trying to shove it under the rug.

WOMAN: No way, no way. Let's put it out in the *middle* of the rug. Some people have potted plants, we'll have canned fungus. The mold will just match the color scheme ... Go on. Say something.

MAN: No.

WOMAN: Don't repress it.

MAN: I have to repress it.

WOMAN: You don't have to repress it.

MAN: You make me repress it.

WOMAN: I just said it: Don't repress it. Don't repress it.

MAN: But your attitude is repress it, repress it.

WOMAN: OK then, repress it! Only repress it better!

MAN: Look, we both know that in order to be resolved this has to come out some way, and not destructively, of course, but in a constructive way that will bring us closer together ...

WOMAN: OK then *do it! Do it! Do it!*

MAN: OK. OK. OK. I'm sick of it all and it has nothing to do with the garbage. It's you and the job and the marriage. I want to throw up. I want to break every window in this mousetrap house. I want to get in the car and take off ninety miles an hour to California and forget I ever got in this because I can't stand the thought of fifty more years of the same damn thing. I want to give all the wedding presents to Goodwill and you come at me with this earnest little mousy sarcastic whine and patch it up with one sincere conversation a week and we make a list that we lose under all the garbage. We spew out day and night and I'm sick of it all! . . . Wow. I feel better.

WOMAN: You do.

MAN: Yes. I feel good. Do you feel good?

WOMAN: No.

MAN: We have a better understanding.

WOMAN: Can I react to that?

MAN: I don't need a reaction.

WOMAN: You . . . *insensitive* . . . *insincere* . . . *insecure* . . . *immature* . . . *(Phone rings.)*

MAN: Telephone.

WOMAN: *(She answers it. Total change of tone.)* Hello? . . . Linda, hi! Oh nothing, just celebrating our anniversary. Talking things over, making plans.

MAN: Tell her about the house.

WOMAN: We looked at a new house. It's incredible! Big lawn, carpets, all electric . . . George wants to say Happy Anniversary.

MAN: . . . Yeh, made it through the first. Fifty more to go. Yeh, incredible. Everything is incredible. Appreciate it. Yeh. Bye. *(Hangs up. Silence.)*

WOMAN: Nice of them to call.

MAN: We called them on theirs. *(Long silence.)* When do you want to see the lawyer?

WOMAN: I'll call Monday.

MAN: You use ours. I'll find a new one.

WOMAN: Everything should be fifty-fifty.

MAN: Even the garbage.

WOMAN: It's good we can be mature about things.

MAN: Make a rational judgment before we get . . . too

involved.

WOMAN: You want me to pack you something?

MAN: No, I'll stop by tomorrow.

WOMAN: You know, I think we still are way, way ahead. A lot of couples, it takes, oh, six or seven years before they split. We've saved all those years.

MAN: I wonder what would happen . . . if one of us . . . sort of . . .

WOMAN: Gave in? Compromised?

MAN: Probably . . . set a bad precedent . . . Well, happy . . .

WOMAN: Yes . . . happy . . . *(they shake hands. Silence.)* Incredible.

THE END

INTERVIEW

by

JOANNA H. KRAUS and GREER WOODWARD

Joanna H. Kraus wrote *The Ice Wolf* which has been widely produced by resident, community and college theatre groups in Canada and the United States; she is Professor of Theatre at the State University of New York College at Brockport. Greer Woodward wrote the lyrics for *Sherlock Holmes and the Red-Headed League* produced by Theatreworks/USA; she has taught at Columbia, Rutgers, Queens College, and Kean College. *Interview* comes from *Tenure Track,* a suite of fourteen sketches about university life. *Tenure Track* won the 1983 American Theatre Association Playwright's Workshop and was given a staged reading at the ATA 47th National Convention at Minneapolis in 1983.

Production Suggestions

A convincing production of this interesting, workable play will have to solve two problems. First, you will need to find a quick but clear way to make the transitions between Margaret's and Donald's offices and across the time lapses in the story's chronology; blackouts probably won't work for this purpose because they're too obtrusive and take too much time. Second, you will need to make it clear to the audience which of the lines the characters are speaking to each other and which ones they are thinking to themselves. Solve these problems by experimenting with different solutions, settling on the one you think is best, and then asking your coach to watch and comment.

Address all inquiries concerning performance, readings or reprinting of this work *or any portion thereof* to Joanna H. Kraus, c/o New Plays, Box 273, Rowayton, CT 06853. For details, see "Part II: Securing Rights for Your Production," pages 223 to 232.

For more information about Joanna Kraus and her work, read volume 104, page 252 of *Contemporary Authors* edited by Frances C. Locher and published by Gale Research, Detroit, Michigan, 1982; a critical essay on *The Ice Wolf* by editor Roger Bedard on pages 455-458 of *Dramatic Literature for Young Audiences,* published by Anchorage Press of New Orleans in 1984; page 444 of the second edition of *Twentieth Century Children's Writers* edited by D. L. Kirkpatrick and published by St. Martin's Press, New York City, 1982; and page 55 of the 1984-86 *Writers Directory* published by St. James Press of Chicago.

INTERVIEW

by

JOANNA H. KRAUS and GREER WOODWARD

The action takes place in two university offices on the Eastern seaboard in the present.

Characters:

MARGARET ALEXANDER, 29 — A professor of speech therapy
DONALD GREGGS, 34 — Director of a university speech clinic

Setting:

The stage is divided into two office areas.

Performance Note:

Dialog in lighter type face indicates interior thoughts.

AT RISE: MARGARET ALEXANDER is seated in her study. MARGARET is twenty-nine, capable, and vulnerable. She is reading over a letter she has just typed.

DONALD GREGGS is seatd, back to the audience, perusing the contents of a file folder. DONALD is thirty-four, bright, charismatic and does what is expedient.

Lightface dialog indicates interior thoughts.

MARGARET: *(Reading over her letter.)* ... **am writing to apply for the position of Co-Director of Laramee Clinic of Speech and Hearing at Bricknell University. Damn, I can't type tonight.** *(Fixes error.)* **Bilingual? A hyphen?** *(Consults dictionary.)* **Not according to Random House! Why am I so nervous about this?**

DONALD: *(Turning around in his chair, reads aloud from MARGARET's letter.)* **Bilingual ... Spanish ... five year's teaching ... supervision clinic ... My God, this sounds just like what we wanted! Margaret Alexander. Hm.**

Doctorate from Columbia. Um-hmm. Um-hmm.

MARGARET: *(Reads aloud from DONALD's letter.)* **Please send us a copy of your recent article in *The Speech Teacher* on "The Use of Puppetry in Speech Clinics with Primary School Spanish Speaking Children." Unfortunately the issue indicated is missing from our library. Sincerely yours, Donald Greggs, Director, Laramee Clinic.**

DONALD: *(Finishes reading article.)* **Good! She could get ten articles from our Saturday clinic.** *(He dials a number on the telephone.)* **John? Donald Greggs. Yuh. Yuh. Yuh, we must get together soon. I'm swamped. That's why I'm calling. Yuh. Yuh. Everyone else is in trouble, but the Prez gave me the green light to expand the clinic. Listen, one of your former assistants applied. A Margaret Alexander. Any info?**

MARGARET: *(Talking on telephone.)* **Yes, I could come. Let me check my calender.** *(Flips through empty calendar.)* **Yes, that would be fine. Thanks for calling. Yes, Thursday.** *(Hangs up phone. Jumps up.)* **This is it. This is *it*. It's one of the most prestigious clinics in the country. I wonder if I should bring the videotape.**

(MARGARET and DONALD are walking into DONALD's office.) **And I loved the idea of a tree — a live one — in the middle of the restaurant.**

DONALD: **Well, the service is slow there, but I thought it would give us a good chance to talk.** *(Grins at her.)* **Glad you liked the tree.** *(They sit. DONALD continues, all business now.)* **Margaret, that was an effective method of handling the parent conferences on that videotape. We're interested in doing some public service on cablevision here. Would you be interested in working on that?**

MARGARET: **Certainly. Educational? Fund-raising? What would be the prime purpose?**

DONALD: **Good PR for the clinic.** Sharp. Shoots straight.

MARGARET: Dreams of power. Would he play fair? Is he a gamesman or a jungle fighter?

DONALD: That might be something we could do when you're here — if you come here.

MARGARET: I'd like that, naturally.

DONALD: She sounds scared. She doesn't trust me. What's she frightened about? I'm not going to jump her. *(To MARGARET)* **What do you think of our facilities?**

MARGARET: I like them, but I don't like the concept of the one-way mirror viewing rooms.

DONALD: Why not?

MARGARET: Because it benefits the graduate students. There's no evidence it benefits the patients. In fact, I think it produces tension.

DONALD: Funny. I've always thought that too.

MARGARET: I mean the patients know that you're there. It makes them guinea pigs. A side show. You see all their flaws and they never catch a glimpse of you. There's something unfair about that.

DONALD: A little bit like an interview?

MARGARET: *(Surprised. A smile. Then a warm look between them.)* Well, a bit.

DONALD: A smile. Ten points, Donald. Why don't I just tell her she's my first choice. No, Donald. Unprofessional. You've got to see three other candidates.

MARGARET: Of course, everyone here at the Institute has been very nice.

DONALD: Uh-oh, Miss Prim and Proper's back. *(To MARGARET)* **Margaret, in your article you discussed puppets as a vehicle for oral fluency with non-English speaking students. What kind of feedback did you get on that?**

MARGARET: Oh, that was fantastic. All these shy kids hid behind the stage and out came these character voices. And the amazing thing is that they were speaking English!

DONALD: *(Smiles)* **Goes right back to Dewey, doesn't it? Experiential learning.** Bet she's magic with kids. Wonder if she's got any?

MARGARET: Nice the way his eyes light up when he talks about the clinic. Must be his baby. Wonder if he's got any kids? *(To DONALD)* **Some people think John Dewey is still there at Columbia. But he isn't.**

DONALD: **Shhh! If that ever gets out, Columbia will be out of business.**

MARGARET: **I took an oath not to tell.**

DONALD: **You'd make a lousy spy.** *(A warm look between them.)* Bet she's pretty terrific in other areas. Damn!

MARGARET: **Will there be an opportunity to do research?**

DONALD: **Yes, in fact our office of research prepares a listing of grant opportunities regularly.** *(Grabs a booklet and hands it to her.)* **Take a look at it.**

MARGARET: **Thank you.** *(Takes booklet and leafs through.)*

DONALD: Relax, Margaret. I'm not going to shoot you at sunrise.

MARGARET: I can't concentrate. What's wrong? Margaret Alexander, read the page and say something brilliant. *(To DONALD)* **This looks very interesting.** Oh, that was brilliant. Dr. Alexander, kindly refer to Rule One — Never get involved with someone you're working with. *(Puts glasses on and studies article.)*

DONALD: **Well, you don't have to read it all now. I'll let you take it with you.**

MARGARET: *(Hesitates)* **But can you get another copy?**

DONALD: *(Explodes)* **Frankly, Margaret, if I couldn't, I wouldn't offer it!**

MARGARET: Strange! What did he get so angry for?

DONALD: **Do you have any questions?**

MARGARET: *(Tries to cover increasing nervousness.)* **Yes. Are you planning to focus on any particular constellation of speech disorders?**

DONALD: **Right now, we're generalists. But the person coming in would have input, obviously, into the direction of the program.** Now, let's be analytical. If you study her feature-by-feature, she's not pretty. Hell, she's not even as attractive as my wife. You could work with her. You could work with her — without even wanting her. Best damn qualified candidate you've got.

MARGARET: **Dr. Greggs, I'm very interested in your program. Even at Columbia they said that Bricknell University had one of the best clinics on the whole Eastern seaboard.**

DONALD: **We're getting there! Everyone on the staff works hard.**

MARGARET: But they never warned me about you. Margaret, this sort of thing does NOT happen to professionals. Dr. Greggs, I will not allow you to distract me. I want this job. That tie's exactly the same color as his eyes. Do me a favor, Dr. Greggs, in the next ten seconds turn one-hundred-and-ten and toothless!

DONALD: *(Rising)* **Of course we are interviewing other candidates, but we should make some decisions next month.** If she comes here, you know what will happen, don't you? You just got your life back in order. What about all those promises you made? Wish her credentials weren't so damn good. She uses the whole vocal scale. The patients would love listening to her! Hey, buddy. Rule One. Never mix bed and business. *(To MARGARET, crisply.)* **We are also interested in an expertise in aphasia with older patients. Do you have any expertise in this area?**

MARGARET: **Well, I studied it in graduate school, of course.**

DONALD: *(Sharply)* **Clinical expertise. Not theoretical.**

MARGARET: **No, but I am sure I could handle it.** That wasn't in the job description.

DONALD: **That could be a problem.**

MARGARET: You're in trouble, kid. *(To DONALD)* **Is there any additional information you'd like? Someone you'd like to call? Anything you want me to send?**

DONALD: I better get this over with. *(To MARGARET)* **I think we have everything we need right now. We appreciate your coming on such short notice. Did you drive here?**

MARGARET: *(Sharply)* **No.**

DONALD: **Then would you like a cab to take you to the station? We'll pay for it, of course.**

MARGARET: *(Sharply)* **Yes.**

DONALD: A snapping turtle, who needs that?

MARGARET: C'mon, old girl, put your white gloves back on. You haven't lost yet. **Dr. Greggs, I'd enjoy being part of the clinic.** Now he won't even look at me. *(He avoids looking at her.)* **And it's been a pleasure to meet you and the staff. Goodbye.** *(Extends her hand.)*

DONALD: *(Ignores her hand.)* **I'll ask my secretary to call a cab for you.** If I touch her once, I won't have the guts to vote "no." *(DONALD opens door for her. MARGARET exits, returns to study. MARGARET and DONALD, each in own office, pick up letters.)*

MARGARET: *(Reading DONALD's letter.)* **...though you have unusual qualifications and excellent recommendations...**

DONALD: *(Reading MARGARET's letter.)* **...impressed by the scope of the clinic program... want to thank...**

MARGARET: *(Reading letter.)* **...we have a commitment to serve a growing mature population.... the position has been filled by someone with clinical expertise in the area of aphasia.**

DONALD: *(Reading letter.)* **...a great pleasure to meet you.** *(Folds letter, puts back in envelope. A sigh. A shrug. Turns.)*

MARGARET: *(Reading letter.)* **...a pleasure to meet you... and wish you continued success in your career.** *(Crumples the letter and throws it on the floor. Exits. DONALD exits.)*

THE END

WATERMELON BOATS
by Wendy MacLaughlin

WATERMELON BOATS

by

WENDY MACLAUGHLIN

Wendy MacLaughlin does commentaries and theatre reviews for National Public Radio in Kansas City and has had her plays performed at The Missouri Repertory Theatre and The Actors Theatre of Louisville. *Watermelon Boats,* commissioned by the latter company, was performed in an extended version at The Edinburgh International Festival and televised over Kansas City Public Television.

Production Suggestions

The playwright suggests that the watermelon boats — hollowed-out melon rinds with candle masts — as well as all other props be imaginary and that the actors mime the use of them. In rehearsal, however, you should occasionally use real, physical props (or substitutes) in order to keep the mimed business accurate.

The actors in this play will find it a real challenge to play three different ages believably in the span of ten minutes. To do this successfully, you should carefully observe women of each age (eleven, sixteen, and twenty-one) to find characteristic ways of managing your body and voice. Secondly, you should give careful attention to the transitions. The playwright suggests transitions be marked by a sound effect (foghorn) and a change in hair style. You may create other ways of marking the transitions, but in any case, the transitions must be played clearly and crisply.

Address all inquiries concerning performances, readings, or reprinting of this work *or any portion thereof* to Wendy MacLaughlin, 1103-B West 47th St., Kansas City, MO 64112. For details, see "Part II: Securing Rights for Your Production," pages 223 to 232.

WATERMELON BOATS

by
WENDY MACLAUGHLIN

The action takes place on the shore of a lake at three different moments over a ten-year span of time.

Characters:

KATE — tan, thin, and healthy. She wears one long braid, jeans, and a button-down shirt.

KITTY — rounder, softer, and more feminine. She wears a peasant blouse, a full skirt, and two braids tied with ribbons.

They age from eleven to twenty-one in the course of the play.

Setting: *Two ladders facing the lake, which is located where the audience sits.*

KITTY: *(Face front.)* **How much longer?**

KATE: *(Checking her watch.)* **Twelve seconds. Oh help, your candle went out.** *(Mimes lighting a match on jeans.)*

KITTY: *(Cupping candle.)* **Thank heavens you brought more matches.**

KATE: **Five, four, three, two, one . . . push them off.** *(They each push a boat into the water and watch them sail.)*

KITTY: *(Blows a kiss.)* **Bon Voyage.**

KATE: **Good luck.** *(She waves.)*

KITTY: **Aren't they gorgeous?**

KATE: **The best watermelon boats we've ever made.**

KITTY: **Fabulous.**

KATE: **Fantastic.**

KITTY: **With the candles they look like stars dancing across the water.**

KATE: **Sir Galahad sailing out to sea in search of the Holy Grail. Mine'll be first across I bet.**

KITTY: **Why?**

KATE: **It's smaller. The wind'll pick it up.**

KITTY: They look the same to me.

KATE: The secret's in the cutting.

KITTY: *(Preening)* Kate, notice something?

KATE: No.

KITTY: I'm wearing a bra.

KATE: I'm never going to wear one.

KITTY: My mother says you'll look like a cow if you don't.

KATE: I like cows.

KITTY: Hanging to your knees.

KATE: She just says that to scare you so when you have breasts you'll smash them all down.

KITTY: Ummm. *(Unbraiding her hair.)* Who do you think we'll have for sixth grade?

KATE: Mr. Hawkins I hope.

KITTY: Me too. He has neat eyes. Every time he looks at me I have to go to the bathroom. Did you know I was born nine months after my brother died?

KATE: Exactly?

KITTY: He died January ninth. I was born October ninth.

KATE: *(Incredulously.)* They did it the day he died?

KITTY: I can't believe boys put that . . .

KATE: The whole idea is gross.

KITTY: I wonder what it feels like?

KATE: No boy is ever going to do it to me.

KITTY: Never?

KATE: Well maybe if I get married but I probably won't because of my career.

KITTY: There're still pictures of him all over the house. My father wanted me to be a boy.

KATE: Mine too.

KITTY: Doesn't that just make you furious. *(Frustrated with her hair.)* Why does Mother braid my hair so tight.

KATE: Here, let me help. *(Unbraids KITTY's hair and mimes brushing.)*

KITTY: Thanks. You've been my best friend since first grade. Isn't it amazing we've been coming to this lake for six years? Am I yours?

KATE: My what?

KITTY: Best friend.

KATE: Sure.

KITTY: Do you have a lot of best friends?

KATE: Some.

KITTY: Don't you think it's weird we're best friends and we're both named Katherine?

KATE: Lucky everyone calls you Kitty and everyone calls me Kate.

KITTY: Kitty's a funny name.

KATE: Perfect for you.

KITTY: I like Kate better.

KATE: When I'm a great writer everyone'll call me Katherine.

KITTY: Like Katherine Mansfield.

KATE: Who?

KITTY: "I want by understanding myself to understand others." She wrote that in 1922. In her journal.

KATE: Oh . . . yes.

KITTY: I have total recall. People with high I.Q.'s usually do.

KATE: *(Impressed.)* You know your I.Q.?

KITTY: Ah-huh.

KATE: How?

KITTY: Once I looked it up in Miss Porter's office.

KATE: What's mine.

KITTY: That's not my business.

KATE: But you know it.

KITTY: I might.

KATE: Then tell me.

KITTY: I shouldn't.

KATE: I'll tell Miss Porter if you don't.

KITTY: Weeeeelllllll . . . I don't remember exactly but it's lower than mine. *(A foghorn blows. KATE stops brushing and fixes her hair.)* If this fog ruins everything I'll die. We can hardly see the boats. Oh there they are. Look, Kate. *(No answer.)* Kate? Are you still mad?

KATE: *(Cold)* I'm not, but the rest of the class is furious. We had a chance to win the Drama High School Cup three years in a row.

KITTY: It's just a stupid play. I'm sorry. I know you wrote it and it's very good but . . .

KATE: It would have looked good on my college transcript.

KITTY: I'm sorry. I told you to give me sets. I'm good at art. Why'd you make me be that dumb ol maid?

KATE: Come off it, Kitty. You died to be the maid. The maid got to wear the cute costume.

KITTY: Well no one told me she had any lines.

KATE: Only one.

KITTY: You know I freeze in front of people.

KATE: Four words. Four simple words and you screw them up.

KITTY: My parents must have gone through the floor with embarrassment. God, I wish I had a drink.

KATE: I've told you a million times every ounce of liquor you drink destroys ten thousand brain cells.

KITTY: Who cares about my brain anyway. Boys certainly don't.

KATE: You really make me mad, you know it? When are you going to grow up? Really, Kitty. When?

KITTY: *(Imitating)* Really, Kitty? When? You sound exactly like my parents. Grow up, Kitty, be like Kate. Kate has her feet on the ground. Kate has a head on her shoulders. I don't want to be like you. I want to be me. Anyway I can't be you, can I? Boy am I insecure. Guess it's because I haven't had my period in two months. *(A laugh.)* You don't think I'm pregnant do you?

KATE: Two months isn't very long.

KITTY: I stopped wearing a diaphragm.

KATE: Damn.

KITTY: It's such a bother. Who knows what's going to happen every date.

KATE: You know what's going to happen if you get pregnant.

KITTY: I'll get an abortion.

KATE: Don't be crazy.

KITTY: I don't have the vaguest idea who the father might be. Can't imagine any of the imbeciles we know being a father. Can you?

KATE: You've got to stop sleeping around.

KITTY: I can't. I mean I don't want to.

KATE: Have some respect for yourself.

KITTY: I like it.

KATE: You like being used? That's what they're doing you know. You might just as well be a urinal.

KITTY: It's not like that. When I'm close to a boy . . . really close, I feel important. For a time someone needs me. We're connected. Both a part of the same thing. Afterwards though, at home in bed . . . I feel more alone. Kate, do you think there might be a real person growing inside of me. A little body with fingers and toes?

KATE: Why do I feel responsible for you?

KITTY: Promise you'll come with me if I have to have an abortion.

KATE: I'd do anything in the world for you but that.

KITTY: You have to.

KATE: I can't. It's wrong.

KITTY: I would for you.

KATE: Abortion is wrong.

KITTY: What'll I do?

KATE: I'm sorry, Kitty. I have to follow my conscience.

KITTY: You're really hard, Kate. You know it.

KATE: If having principles is hard . . .

KITTY: Even here . . . in the Spring, at the lake. I'm all relaxed but you're still so strong. Thin, brown . . .

KATE: I wish I could help you . . .

KITTY: Thin . . . brown and hard. Year round.

KATE: So be it.

KITTY: Very dull.

KATE: What?

KITTY: Thin . . . brown and hard. Year round. It's very

dull. Booooooorrrrrrring.

KATE: *(Tight lipped.)* **Sorry.**

KITTY: **Some day you should let go a little. Maybe . . . smile at a guy.**

KATE: **Too disciplined I guess.**

KITTY: **Well brought up.**

KATE: **Probably.**

KITTY: **Or afraid.**

KATE: **Afraid?**

KITTY: **You might spoil the image. Perfect woman. Nobly planned.**

KATE: **Well it's late. I have to go.**

KITTY: **I bet you'll spend the night thinking of lines you won't cross. Perfect stays on one side looking down her nose at the rest of us screwing it up on the other.**

KATE: *(Turns to go.)* **Goodnight, Kitty.**

KITTY: *(Grabs her arm.)* **And you think you're going to be a writer? That's a laugh. Who's going to read you? You don't know the first thing about life.** *(Foghorn blows. They change hair style.)*

KITTY: *(Shivers.)* **Ohhh it's getting cold.** *(They put on sweaters.)* **Not even a moon. But look, the first star is out. Don't you wonder if there aren't people just like us up there thinking we're a star. Oh God, Kate, promise you won't write that in your first book. Everyone'll think I'm psycho.**

KATE: **I doubt I'll write one page, much less a book.**

KITTY: **You're kidding.**

KATE: **No.**

KITTY: **You're going to be a famous writer.**

KATE: **Who says?**

KITTY: **You've always said.**

KATE: **Changed my mind.**

KITTY: **You can't do that.**

KATE: **Stop staring at me.**

KITTY: **I counted on you.**

KATE: Swell.

KITTY: You've always known where you were going and how you'd get there.

KATE: That was grade school.

KITTY: High school too.

KATE: Well college is different. Not only harder but there're lots of people out there smarter. And they don't try to please everyone all the time. You were right, Kitty, I do want to be perfect. Remember when you said that?

KITTY: No.

KATE: Five years ago. Here at the lake. At first I was furious. Then I wanted to cry but I couldn't. Know why? I didn't feel enough.

KITTY: That's better than feeling too much like me.

KATE: You're sensitive.

KITTY: I get hurt.

KATE: You know what I do when I start to feel something? I come on with my holier than thou superior look. Inside I'm dying to experience everything but I never will because I act like I already have. Oh Kitty, what if I die without ever feeling anything?

KITTY: Then you won't feel guilty all the time. That's what makes me want to throw myself in the lake.

KATE: Right now you wouldn't believe how guilty I feel. If I don't become the world's greatest writer my parents won't be proud of me and you'll be disappointed.

KITTY: But you'll make it. You've got talent.

KATE: I'm not as smart as you.

KITTY: But you're stronger.

KATE: No, Kitty, you are. You wouldn't let me change you.

KITTY: Did you want to?

KATE: I thought you wanted me to.

KITTY: All I want is to get married, be a good mother and have you as my friend.

KATE: You don't need me.

KITTY: We need each other. You're my perfect friend. I love you.

KATE: The only thing perfect about me is that. *(Foghorn.)*

KITTY: *(Climbs ladder.)* Look at our boats ... way out. Sailing together, neck and neck.

KATE: *(Climbs ladder.)* We're not across yet.

KITTY: But we're going to make it.

KATE: The trick is the journey.

KITTY: Isn't it hard to believe we're already twenty-one?

KATE: Seems like only minutes ago we were eleven.

KITTY: *(Extends hand.)* Sometimes I wish we didn't have to get any older.

KATE: *(Takes KITTY's hand.)* Wouldn't it be nice if now could be always. *(They hold hands as the light gets blinding bright before fading to black.)*

THE END

DALMATIAN

by
CONRAD BISHOP

Conrad Bishop has written thirty-eight produced plays and has directed more than eighty productions. He collaborates with Elizabeth Fuller in writing and staging plays and in directing *The Independent Eye* theatre company. Their plays have received production awards from the Corporation for Public Broadcasting, American Personnel & Guidance Association, and the American Bar Association. They have been co-winners of Actors Theatre of Louisville's Great American Play contest and have received a National Endowment for the Arts Playwriting Fellowship. *Dalmatian* comes from a cycle of plays called *Families* which premiered in Lancaster, Pennsylvania, in 1980.

Production Suggestions

The realistic action of *Dalmatian* is punctuated by stylized, ritualistic moments when Mrs. Leonard stands on her chair and Kathy kneels. Deciding how best to play these important transitions is part of the challenge of preparing this play.

You can handle the telephone rings either as an actual sound effect or as a sound heard only by the characters. If you choose to go without sound effects, you need to be sure your characters really do "hear" the sound and respond to it.

Address all inquiries concerning performances, readings, or reprinting of this work *or any portion thereof* to Conrad Bishop, 115 Arch Street, Philadelphia, PA 19106. For details, see "Part II: Securing Rights for Your Production," pages 223 to 232.

DALMATIAN

by
CONRAD BISHOP

The action of the play takes place in the present in the office of the assistant principal of a high school.

Characters:

MRS. LEONARD — age unspecified. The assistant principal.
KATHY — a high school student.

Setting: *Mrs. Leonard's office is furnished with her desk and chair, a chair for the students she deals with, and a desk telephone.*

AT RISE: MRS. LEONARD, a trim woman in a business suit, sits at a desk, talking on the telephone.

MRS. LEONARD: **Yes, well I'm sorry, Mrs. Bennett, but we do have state guidelines. If your son hasn't attended classes for the last eight months I really doubt he's ready to graduate ... No, Mrs. Bennett. Our guidelines require that ninth graders be reading at least at sixth grade level and our seniors at least at the third. We have to minimize slippage.** *(KATHY, a student, appears.)* **Come in. Just a minute.** *(On phone)* **Then I suggest you call the principal and tell him what you think of me.** *(Hangs up.)* **What can I do for you?** *(Reflex: MRS. LEONARD stands on her chair. KATHY kneels, covers head with schoolbooks.)*

KATHY: **Miss Henderson sent me.**

MRS. LEONARD: **Oh. Kathy. Have a seat.** *(She sits. KATHY sits in chair opposite.)* **Now let's see. You were here once before. Mr. Bilsing ...**

KATHY: **Mr. Bilsing doesn't like me.**

MRS. LEONARD: **"Disturbing the class."**

KATHY: **He got real snotty and I started to cry, and he said that disturbed the class.**

MRS. LEONARD: **Well, now it's Miss Henderson.** *(Phone*

rings.) **Excuse me.** *(Answers)* **No, I can't take a call now, Phyllis, I've got a student. Who is it, a parent? . . . That's ridiculous. There is no drug problem at this school. His daughter should have absolutely no problem getting any drug she wants.** *(Hangs up.)* **What can I do for you?** *(Reflex: she stands on chair, KATHY kneels.)*

KATHY: Miss Henderson sent me.

MRS. LEONARD: Oh, Kathy. Have a seat. *(They sit.)* Now what is this? It says you were arguing with your teacher in a loud, abusive tone of voice.

KATHY: She was arguing with me.

MRS. LEONARD: About a poem.

KATHY: We had to write a poem. It said, "Write a poem based on a past experience in your life with deep emotional content using the rhyme scheme A-B-A-B."

MRS. LEONARD: So?

KATHY: So I wrote the stupid poem. And she gave me an F.

MRS. LEONARD: Well, Kathy, perhaps if you'd read the instructions more carefully . . .

KATHY: So I ask her, "Why did I get an F, because it all rhymes, I mean." And she says, "Kathy, I cannot pass you on this because you obviously did not write the poem."

MRS. LEONARD: Well, that's a very serious accusation . . .

KATHY: She says, "You are a C student and this is an A poem. And I know you copied it because I remember reading it somewhere." And I said, "I did, I did write it, and I didn't even babysit on Friday, and I had a lot of trouble rhyming some of the words, like 'dalmatian.' "

MRS. LEONARD: Dalmatian?

KATHY: We had a dalmatian.

MRS. LEONARD: So?

KATHY: When my mom and dad broke up, they had this big fight about who got the dog, and finally my dad says, "I'll take the dog, you can have the kid." Dog was a dalmatian. *(Phone rings.)*

MRS. LEONARD: Excuse me. *(Answers.)* Phyllis, I said no calls. A what? A bomb threat? They want the principal. I am the assistant principal, as you know. I handle discipline, counseling, attendance, food service, materials, and absurdity. The principal handles fire drills. Bomb threats come under fire drills. *(Hangs up.)* What is it? *(Reflex: she stands on chair, KATHY kneels.)*

KATHY: I'm Kathy-have-a-seat.

MRS. LEONARD: Oh yes. Have a seat. *(They sit.)* Kathy, my concern with you in this office is that you were arguing with the teacher. Now if your interest is poetry...

KATHY: I don't know that stuff. Last thing was on haiku. I got a C on that one.

MRS. LEONARD: Then you can find a time when she could sit down with you and tell you everything you want to know about poetry. She is a very good teacher, she can help you write good poems, and it's a good way of expressing yourself. Hollering at people is not a good way of expressing yourself. *(Phone rings.)* Hello! Yes! No! No! Yes! Yes! No! OK! Bye! *(Hangs up. Reflex: she starts to stand, halts, sits. Deep breath.)* Now Kathy. I'm sure that Miss Henderson has certainly read a great many poems, and she would certainly be qualified to know...

KATHY: And she said it was good. I wrote a good poem.

MRS. LEONARD: Kathy, you know it is possible that at one time you yourself read this poem somewhere...

KATHY: I don't read poems!

MRS. LEONARD: And then you forgot it, and when you were writing, it re-emerged from your subconscious.

KATHY: Huh?

MRS. LEONARD: It was in your subconscious.

KATHY: No, but we're Catholic.

MRS. LEONARD: I mean you didn't realize it, but the poem had already been written, so in a sense you were correct and Miss Henderson was also correct...

KATHY: When my dad left, he took the dalmatian. Two days later he came back, and I thought he was coming back *home,* **but he came back for the Alpo®.**

MRS. LEONARD: I don't care about the Alpo®.

KATHY: It's in the poem. Does everybody's dad come back for the Alpo®?

MRS. LEONARD: All right, but your scores ... Your test scores are below average in Verbal Synthesis. Not that we're trying to classify you ...

KATHY: You *are* **classifying me! Isn't it classifying me if I never wrote a poem before and now I write one and you classify that I can't?**

MRS. LEONARD: We don't classify you for the sake of classifying you. We classify you so that we have more time to devote to your best interests.

KATHY: My best interests is that I wrote it. *I wrote it, I wrote it, I wrote it! (MRS. LEONARD stands on chair. KATHY kneels, submissively. Silence.)* **I really did.** *(They return slowly to sitting positions.)*

MRS. LEONARD: *(Speaks distractedly, by rote.)* **Kathy, the issue is not the poem. The issue is cooperation. The poem is not for the sake of the poem. The poem is to give you   experience   in   cooperation   ...   fulfilling assignments ... following directions ...** *(Silence. She sits, covering her eyes.)*

KATHY: Mrs. Leonard?

MRS. LEONARD: Does any of this ... make any sense?

KATHY: Uh-uh.

MRS. LEONARD: *(Quietly, without moving.)* **When I first came to work here ... there was a bell that rang at ten-thirty. Now that wasn't for classes to change. Nothing happened at ten-thirty, except that the bell rang. So I asked, "Why does that bell ring at ten-thirty?" And I was told that it was the Ten-thirty Bell. And that we had always had a Ten-thirty Bell. And that it was not my position to question the Ten-thirty Bell. It took me some time to get used to the fact that we had ... a Ten-thirty Bell. I used to get very upset every morning about ten-twenty-five.**

But I came to see at last that it did have a function. It brought us together. It rang, and we all knew we were part of something . . . that nobody understood, nobody knew the purpose, nobody could possibly change . . . but we were *all in it together.* Do you follow me? I understand your problem, I sympathize . . .

KATHY: Then will you tell Miss Henderson to give me a grade? Cause I wrote it, and she says it's good . . .

MRS. LEONARD: No, I will not. Don't you understand? Are you so stuck in your own little pimply problems that you don't think about mine? We have teacher strikes, assaults on teachers, disrespect for teachers, and I am not about to interfere with the best judgment of a teacher because a C-minus student wrote a poem! What about my needs? Who is filling my needs? Where are my strokes? Where are my warm fuzzies? *(Phone rings.)* **Hello!**

KATHY: I don't need an A . . . just anything.

MRS. LEONARD: *(Change of tone.)* Oh honey, hi. Are you all right? What are you doing out of bed? If you're sick, you stay in bed, otherwise you go to school. I told you not to call unless it's an emergency. What's wrong? . . . I don't know if there's peanut butter. You're nine years old, you can look. Honey, I'm busy . . . What? The mailman came? Is there a letter? Connecticut? Can you read it? What do they say? . . . How many applicants? . . . Rats. No, Mommy thought she had a chance. No, we'll stay here another year. OK, I'll be home at four. You get back in bed. Love you. *(Laughs)* OK. Bye. *(Hangs up.)* My little girl said, "My orange juice tastes angry." A child's view of the world is something very precious. *(Silence. KATHY walks out. MRS. LEONARD picks up the phone.)* Phyllis, will you take my calls? I need a potty break.

THE END

MONEY

by
MATTHEW CALHOUN

Show Business has described Matthew Calhoun's work as "somewhere between Buster Keaton and Woody Allen." Written during the playwright's residency at the New York Public Library, *Money* was performed at New York City's Shuttle Theatre in June, 1984, and as part of Mr. Calhoun's *Comic Duets* at New York City's American Theatre of Actors in 1986.

Production Suggestions

If you wholeheartedly accept the off-the-wall, improbable comic style of *Money,* you will find yourselves with a real success on your hands. Be sure to invite some friends to watch your dress rehearsals so you are prepared to handle the laughter during your performance.

Address all inquiries concerning performances, readings, or reprinting of this work *or any portion thereof* to Matthew Calhoun at 23-51 19th St., Basement Apt., Long Island City, NY 11105. For details, see "Part II: Securing Rights for Your Production," pages 223 to 232.

MONEY
by
MATTHEW CALHOUN

The action takes place at the present day in a city.

Characters:

DUNLOP

SAM RYAN

Setting: *Two chairs in an otherwise empty store.*

AT RISE: A man sits, blandly content, on a chair facing an empty chair. Another enters, looking confused.

DUNLOP: Yes?

RYAN: Am I ... uhh ... *(Looks around.)*

DUNLOP: If you have amnesia I'll need to see some identification.

RYAN: It said outside, "Bank."

DUNLOP: If you don't suddenly remember that you're a bank robber, we'll be OK.

RYAN: But there's nothing here to rob! There's nothing *here!* That sign is very misleading — it really makes it seem like there'll be a bank here.

DUNLOP: *(Bored.)* **This is the bank to which the sign referred.**

RYAN: *(Surprised)* **Uh-huh?**

DUNLOP: *(Humming to himself.)* **Dum-de-dum-de-dum-de-dum**

RYAN: Banks have money, plush carpets — *tellers!* This place looks like an abandoned store front.

DUNLOP: It's all done by hidden computers. Safer that way. We've never been robbed. *(RYAN stares around for the hidden computers, sees nothing.)*

RYAN: *(Anxiously)* **I wanted to open a new account, but I'd like to be reassured ...**

DUNLOP: If you don't sit down I'm going to hit you over the head with this chair. Let me reassure you as to that.

– 38 –

RYAN: Perhaps I'd better leave.

DUNLOP: After I just made a friendly crack-the-ice-remove-all-awkwardness joke? What's it gonna cost you to sit down?

RYAN: What *is* it gonna cost me? The last bank I went to charged me just to walk through the door.

DUNLOP: This bank believes in *positive* reinforcement. Sit, Rover, sit, and you'll get a treat.

RYAN: *(Dubiously)* Another of your tension relieving quips, right?

DUNLOP: I'm not merely a banker, sir. I have training in behavioral psychology. What did you say your name was?

RYAN: Mr. Ryan. Sam Ryan.

DUNLOP: I'm Officer Dunlop. Think of me as your father.

RYAN: You're nothing like my father.

DUNLOP: Aren't you glad?

RYAN: I don't know.

DUNLOP   Sit down, son. We'll discuss your allowance.

RYAN: This seems more Freudian than behavioral.

DUNLOP: What do you know about it?

RYAN: Not much. I had just heard that if you maintain a two-hundred dollar minimum balance in a savings account you get free checking, unlimited. And there was something about a free gift, too, I think, with new accounts.

DUNLOP: You heard that, did you?

RYAN: It was this bank, right?

DUNLOP: *(Rising)* Sit, and I may tell you. *(He holds out the chair.)*

RYAN: There's no service charge for sitting, is there?

DUNLOP: Our whole organization is offended that you even ask. *(Gestures to chair.)* We are a caring institution, a compassionate bank. How could we *possibly* charge you for anything? We want to pay you interest!

RYAN: All right, let's get down to brass tacks. *(He sits. DUNLOP pulls out the chair, causing him to sprawl on the floor.)* **Ow! Ow!**

DUNLOP: That was your free gift. A lesson in mistrust. Developing suspicion and even some paranoia can make your assets grow at an unbelievable pace.

RYAN: This is *nuts! Nuts! (He storms off. DUNLOP pulls out a gun.)*

DUNLOP: Hold it right there, sir. *(RYAN whirls.)*

RYAN: What's that, a squirt gun?

DUNLOP: *(Moving in.)* It *looks* like a squirt gun. It shoots real bullets — it's one of those "keep-out-of-reach-of-children" items.

RYAN: *(Tremulously)* You're holding me up, huh?

DUNLOP: Sir, you held *me* up. Your point blank refusal to sit cost me a *lot* of time.

RYAN: This bank is *nothing* like its advertising said it is. I may report you to the FCC. Maybe even to the BBB.

DUNLOP: Better Business Bureau, huh? We're seeking to do a better business. *(Pats gun.)* That's where this little investment comes in. Empty your pockets, please.

RYAN: *(Shaking head ruefully, but emptying pockets.)* I am *not* recommending you to any of my friends. *(Takes out matches, cigarettes, etc. from his pocket.)*

DUNLOP: Don't you have any money, Mr. Ryan?

RYAN: I *did* have five-hundred dollars, but I went to open an account at the bank the next block down. There was a three-hundred dollar charge for the passbook, another one-hundred fifty dollars for the checks, several dozen minor service charges for things like standing in line, paying in cash, use of the bank's air, and then finally a fifty dollar service charge because my initial deposit ended up being less than a hundred dollars. I ended up owing them money.

DUNLOP: So you came here a debtor? Perhaps you'd like to take out a loan?

RYAN: No, I have five-hundred dollars left, but not here. I left it home. I wanted to find out the policy in advance. That's all that's left of my savings. I can't afford to lose it all in service charges.

DUNLOP: I'm going to need some collateral before I give you a lease on life and let you walk out this door, Mr. Ryan.

RYAN: *(Pointing to the cigarettes, etc.)* That's all I have.

DUNLOP: That's not enough.

RYAN: *(Upset)* So what are you going to do, put me in a safe deposit vault?

DUNLOP: The impertinence! You can't afford that! Let's see . . . *(He ponders.)*

RYAN: I'm going to walk right out that door. You're not going to shoot me with that squirt gun.

DUNLOP: *(Thinking)* Collateral, collateral . . . we used to take people's souls, but we found they never came back for them. We lost a lot of money that way. Had to try to raffle them off, cheap. Sold no tickets at all. *(Punctuating with gun.)* Economics and metaphysics do not mix!

RYAN: What about when a robber says "Your money or your life." Isn't he comparing something economic with something metaphysical? Or what about the phrase "Time is money." Or "Money is the root of all evil?"

DUNLOP: *(To himself.)* Collateral, collateral, let's see . . . *(Jumps up.)* Yes! Yes! A brainwave! Brilliant, my dear Dunlop! Superb! For collateral you must leave me your first born son!

RYAN: I never married. I have no son.

DUNLOP: You sly fox — thinking ahead, eh? All right then, all right. Leave me your dignity as a human being. I know that's not worth much nowadays, but it's all we have. It will be promptly refunded upon your deposit of five-hundred dollars into my hand.

RYAN: If I only had the guts not to be afraid of a squirt gun!

DUNLOP: One lady did, God rest her soul. Your dignity and respect as a human being, please.

RYAN: Aren't we getting metaphysical again?

DUNLOP: Metaphysical? What's more concrete than dignity?

Mine's all tied up in my house, cars, and liquid assets.

RYAN: I foresee big problems if I give you my respect and dignity. I might grovel for hours asking for it back, giving you no peace at all. Or I might commit suicide in your lobby.

DUNLOP: *(Losing his temper abruptly.)* I want your five hundred dollars!

RYAN: *(Sensing a possible advantage.)* If that gun really works shoot it into the air. Prove it. Otherwise I'm walkin' outta here.

DUNLOP: We are a frugal bank, Mr. Victim, Ryan, whatever your name is. We do not shoot ammo into the air.

RYAN: Then what would you gain by shooting it into me?

DUNLOP: That satisfaction of a job well done, if nothing else. *(RYAN stares at him, waiting. After awhile.)* I've changed my mind. You can go.

RYAN: *(Surprised.)* Why?

DUNLOP: *(Coldly)* We want you to think of us as your friend.

RYAN: I ain't goin. *(Tautly)* You'd *shoot* me with that thing!

DUNLOP: *(Putting gun away.)* Banks don't shoot people. Tell your friends about us — Citizens Bank, the bank that does *not* shoot the casual enquirer off the street.

RYAN: So I can just walk out of here?

DUNLOP: Certainly, sir! *(RYAN lets out a huge sigh of relief.)*

RYAN: And there's not a service charge?

DUNLOP: Our bank doesn't believe in service charges. Now, if you'll excuse me, I have to sit here and wait for more customers.

RYAN: What if I put five-hundred dollars in. You'd charge me then, right?

DUNLOP: We'd pay you the highest interest rate allowed by law.

RYAN: Yeah, so would the other bank, the one down the block, if I had anything left after they'd got done charging me. *(Brief pause.)* No charge for the passbook?

DUNLOP: There are no charges for anything, sir.

RYAN: Let's say I open a savings account for five-hundred

dollars and take four-hundred dollars out the next day. How much does that cost me?

DUNLOP: Zero.

RYAN: How late are you open? It's going to take me awhile to run home and get back here with my money.

THE END

JUMPING

by
WILLIAM BORDEN

Besides plays for the stage, William Borden has written scripts for radio, film, and television and has published a novel, short stories, poems, and travel articles. He teaches English at the University of North Dakota and is a core playwright with the Playwrights' Center of Minneapolis. *Jumping* was commissioned by the Playwrights' Center and has been performed in New York, Los Angeles, and other cities.

Production Suggestions

Jumping includes a lot of business with costumes and props — taking off shoes, repeatedly putting on and taking off coats, digging through a purse, reading letters, and writing notes. Because these props are so integral to the play's action, you should start using them *early* in your rehearsal schedule. You will find that using actual props early in your rehearsals will help your pacing and will also suggest useful pieces of business.

Address all inquiries concerning performances, readings, or reprinting of this work *or any portion thereof* to the playwright, William Borden, R.R. 6, Box 284, Bemidji, MN 56601. For details, see "Part II: Securing Rights for Your Production," pages 223 to 232.

JUMPING

by
WILLIAM BORDEN

The action takes place on a Minnesota bridge during winter at the present time.

Characters:

JERRY — a man from San Francisco
DENISE — a woman from Minnesota

AT RISE: JERRY, wearing suit coat or sport coat, enters quickly, determinedly, and heads straight for bridge railing. Steps up, gets ready to jump, holds his breath, closes his eyes — comic effect — stops, thinks, steps down, takes off shoes. Climbs up again, gets ready to jump, etc., stops. Unbuttons coat, gets ready to jump, stops. Buttons coat, gets ready to jump, stops. Thinks. Steps down.

JERRY: I can never remember — do you take your coat off when you jump, or leave it on? If you leave it on, you sink faster. That would seem to be the point. But in the movies I think they take their coats off ... *(Ponders. Blows on hands to warm them. Hits his head.)* **Of course! You leave the coat, because you leave some identification in the coat pocket!** *(Looks through coat pockets.)* **Otherwise, no one might even know ... and if no one knows — what's the point?** *(Searching pants pockets.)* **I forgot my wallet. A note! I've got to be sure she knows ...** *(DENISE, bundled in winter coat, mufflers, hat, enters, preoccupied, looking forlorn.)* **Excuse me.** *(DENISE, lost in her own thoughts, doesn't hear him.)* **Excuse me?** *(DENISE walks past him, not noticing him. JERRY touches her shoulder. She jumps.)*

DENISE: Oh! You scared me.

JERRY: I just wondered if you had a piece of paper and a pen or pencil ... *(DENISE looks at him curiously.)* **I want to write a note. Probably just my name ... address ...**

Social Security number ... bank account number ... driver's license number ... telephone number ...

DENISE: Are you cashing a check?

JERRY: No, I'm ... *(DENISE looks through her purse. Looks some more. JERRY waits ... waits ... looks over her shoulder ...)*

DENISE: Could you hold these? I'm sure I have a pen ... *(DENISE loads JERRY up with stuff from her purse. Finds a pen.)* Here's a pen! *(DENISE hands it to JERRY, but his hands are full. DENISE sticks the pen in JERRY's mouth.)* I think I have a notepad ... *(DENISE pulls more stuff from her purse, loads up JERRY, dumps out her purse.)* I was sure I had a notepad ... *(JERRY sees a letter amidst the stuff dumped from her purse, drops the stuff in his hands, and picks up the letter.)*

JERRY: What about this?

DENISE: No! *(Grabs letter.)* Where's your coat? You'll catch pneumonia! Frostbite! *(JERRY laughs.)*

JERRY: *(Grabs letter, tears off a corner, absentmindedly stuffs letter in his pocket, writes on the corner.)* Frostbite? Pneumonia? Those maladies don't scare me anymore, my dear. No more worries about carcinogens for me. Cigarettes, power lines, nuclear reactors — I don't care.

DENISE: You don't care?

JERRY: I'm past caring. *(Hands her pen.)* Here. Thanks a lot. Saved my life. *(Pause)* So to speak. *(JERRY puts corner in coat pocket. Looks around for a place to put the coat.)*

DENISE: You're past caring?

JERRY: Yes.

DENISE: That's despicable.

JERRY: What?

DENISE: No public spirit! No political consciousness! No democratic responsibility!

JERRY: It's not that —

DENISE: You should be ashamed!

JERRY: No, you don't understand — you see, actually, I'm —

I'm a —

DENISE: *(Putting things back into her purse.)* **Haven't you ever stood up for what you believed in? Haven't you ever considered dying for a cause? You probably don't even vote! Are you registered to vote?**

JERRY: **Well, no, I just —**

DENISE: **Would you like to join the Sierra Club? I have an application in here.** *(Looks through purse.)* **Would you hold this?** *(Looks through purse.)* **Could you just hold these again?** *(Loads him with stuff again. JERRY impatient — resigned — impatient — edges toward railing.)*

JERRY: **Maybe you could mail it to me.**

DENISE: **You won't regret it.** *(DENISE beams at him. He smiles back, waiting for her stuff, which she seems to have forgotten about.)* **Well?**

JERRY: **Well?**

DENISE: **Give me your name and address, so I can mail you the application form.**

JERRY: **Oh! Sure. Do you have a piece of paper? Pen?** *(DENISE looks in empty purse. They look at each other. Laugh. JERRY holds out stuff.)*

DENISE: **Oh!** *(Puts stuff back in her purse.)* **I'm not myself tonight. I'm a little upset, in fact. I get politically involved when I'm upset . . . about personal matters . . . When I was younger, I became a socialist . . . after my fiance left me at the church. It takes my mind off my own troubles. If we had more personal problems, people would get more interested in politics, that's what I think. We could have a real democracy if everybody's personal life was a mess. Do you agree?**

JERRY: **Could you hold this?** *(His coat.)*

DENISE: **Not until I get your name and address and your solemn promise to join.**

JERRY: **The Socialists?**

DENISE: **Sierra Club. I'm not *that* upset. I've had these rejections before.**

JERRY: Um — listen, could you just join for me?

DENISE: Oh, I couldn't do that. That's not democracy.

JERRY: I'm really cold.

DENISE: Well you silly goose! It's Minnesota! Where do you think you are, Florida?

JERRY: Actually, I just moved from San Francisco a few months ago. This is my first winter. And my last.

DENISE: Don't you like it here?

JERRY: It's not that. It's . . . personal problems.

DENISE: *(Pause)* I could arrange for you to get in contact with the Socialist Workers Party. If it's a serious personal problem. If it's not too serious, probably volunteering for the Republicans would do the trick.

JERRY: It's too serious for the Socialist Workers Party.

DENISE: *(Long look. Looks around. Whisper.)* I cannot take you there myself, but I know a man who knows a man who can put you in touch with the underground group . . .

JERRY: No, no . . .

DENISE: Left wing or right wing, whichever you prefer, it works the same, your personal problems melt away, you give yourself to a higher cause . . .

JERRY: Just sign me up with the Sierra Club . . . What did you say your name was?

DENISE: Denise.

JERRY: My name's Jerry. With a J.

DENISE: *(They shake hands.)* Your hand's so cold!

JERRY: Yes, I've been trying to — Would you hold this? *(His coat. She takes it.)*

DENISE: Put your coat on, for heaven's sake, Jerry! *(JERRY edges toward railing. DENISE rushes to him, wraps his coat around him.)* Listen to me! I've lived here all my life, I know what winter's like! You Californians, you live in a dream land. *(JERRY fends her and the coat off.)*

JERRY: I've got to leave the coat here! It's got my name and address in it!

DENISE: Then you're serious about this.

JERRY: You're damn right I'm serious about this!

DENISE: I'm so glad.

JERRY: *(At rail)* I've never been so serious about anything ... *(Doubletake)* **What?**

DENISE: The Sierra Club will really have some clout, once it gets a few members like you! *(JERRY starts to climb onto railing.)* **Wait!**

JERRY: What is it?

DENISE: You don't have to leave the whole coat with me! Just give me the slip of paper ... *(Going through pockets, finds it.)* and put your coat back on.

JERRY: Oh. *(Gets down.)*

DENISE: You Californians! *(JERRY puts on coat. Starts for railing. Stops.)*

JERRY: No, I think I should take it off. *(Starts to take it off. Finds note he tore corner from. Reads it.)*

DENISE: Oh! Don't — read that ...

JERRY: *(Reads)* **My sweetheart Harley ...** *(Reads. Eyes wide. Closes note in embarrassment.)*

DENISE: Pretty graphic, isn't it?

JERRY: Who's Harley?

DENISE: He was my husband. Until this morning.

JERRY: Did you get divorced this morning?

DENISE: I found that note this morning.

JERRY: *(Reads, cautiously.)* "All my love, breathlessly, passionately ... "

DENISE: Don't read the rest.

JERRY: " ... LouEllen."

DENISE: Can you imagine? LouEllen? What kind of a name is LouEllen? From the East Coast, he says. Very sophisticated, he says. Very cosmopolitan, he says. Knows how to dress, he says. Knows what's happening, he says. Well, Jerry, I'll tell you, this gal from Minnesota knows what's happening, you better believe me! She's only nineteen! But her make-up! Her clothes! She thinks she's living in Cosmo magazine, but I'll tell you where she's living —

JERRY: Harley ran off with —

DENISE: Don't speak her name!

JERRY: — What's her name.

DENISE: That's right.

JERRY: We've got a lot in common, I guess . . .

DENISE: *(Ignoring him.)* But I'll tell you, Jerry with a J, he's not even worth the Sierra Club! If I'm not sophisticated enough for old Harley — what's wrong with my clothes? I've got to dress warm! I hope she freezes her little — off! *(JERRY, freezing, grabs his coat and puts it on.)* You poor goose, you're blue! Here, put on my coat. *(Takes off her coat — she has another on underneath it — and wraps it around JERRY, despite his protests.)*

JERRY: Please — no — really — Denise — *(Throws it at her.)* Don't! *(She's hurt.)* I appreciate your concern . . . but it's . . . too late. *(DENISE looks at JERRY's hands, ears, cheeks.)*

DENISE: Frostbite?

JERRY: Suicide.

DENISE: I see. *(JERRY starts for railing. Takes off his coat.)* You Californians! Always exaggerating! Minnesota winters are cold, but they're not that —*(JERRY on the railing, ready to jump.)* Jerry! *(Startled, JERRY starts to lose his balance. Tries to catch himself. Can't.)* Jerry! *(DENISE rushes to him, catches him, pulls him back.)* Jerry.

JERRY: Let me go, Denise. Tell her I hope she's happy with her damn lumberjack —

DENISE: What are you doing, Jerry?

JERRY: She was happy enough with me when we lived in San Francisco — I'm a college professor —

DENISE: Oh, really?

JERRY: — and I was afraid she wouldn't like it here — she's used to warm weather, fresh fish, abalone —

DENISE: What do you teach?

JERRY: — artichokes, avocados — political science — the

-51-

surf, Fisherman's Wharf —

DENISE: **Political science?**

JERRY: **But then, what does she do? She meets a lumberjack — runs off with him — cooks pancakes for him at a lumber camp near the Boundary Waters — wherever they are — named Sven or Ole or Knut.**

DENISE: **Political science?**

JERRY: **So I'm doing the only thing I can do, Denise! Give me that coat!** *(Grabs her coat, puts it on.)* **And that one!** *(JERRY pulls her next coat off of her, puts it on.)* **And that!** *(Muffler, hat, gloves, etc.)* **And that!**

DENISE: **Jerry! Jerry!**

JERRY: **I'll sink for sure now! Straight to the bottom, Denise! They'll find my poor, bloated, waterlogged, drowned body . . . She'll be sorry! Even Sven will be sorry. Or Knut.** *(Climbing onto railing.)*

DENISE: *(Calmly)* **Jerry?**

JERRY: **Don't try to talk me out of it, Denise, my mind's made up.**

DENISE: **I really like that hat, Jerry. Would you mind leaving the hat?**

JERRY: **Oh. Of course, I'm sorry.** *(Getting down, bringing her the hat.)* **I was carried away.**

DENISE: **I understand.**

JERRY: **It was really thoughtless of me.**

DENISE: **It's all right. You're under a lot of pressure.**

JERRY: **Yes. Yes, I am.** *(Starts for railing, stops.)* **You know, I've always admired people who could get involved politically. I just stand on the sidelines . . . analyze . . . observe . . . the scientific approach . . . nonpartisan . . . objective . . .** *(DENISE nods. JERRY reluctantly heads for railing.)*

DENISE: **You were planning on drowning?**

JERRY: **This is a bridge, isn't it? Boy, in San Francisco — the Golden Gate, the Bay Bridge, the San Rafael Bridge, the San Mateo . . . Constant reminders of the ultimate choice!**

The fearful plunge, hundreds of feet into the dark, shark-infested waters below ...

DENISE: *(Looking over the railing.)* **It *is* dark.**

JERRY: **Well, it's night.**

DENISE: **Sharks?**

JERRY: **It's not a pretty death.**

DENISE: *(Looking over railing.)* **Maybe a few Northerns.**

JERRY: **Northerns?**

DENISE: **Northern pike.** *(Holds up her hands to indicate size.)* **Under the ice.** *(JERRY starts to jump.)*

JERRY: **I'm not going to say goodbye, Denise. I don't like goodbyes. So ... Goodbye.** *(Poised. Stops. Doubletake.)* **Ice?**

DENISE: **It's about two feet deep by now.** *(JERRY gets carefully down.)*

JERRY: **That would hurt.**

DENISE: **You could aim for an ice fishing hole.**

JERRY: **I hadn't really paid any attention — I was so upset by the lumberjack — it got so cold so quickly —** *(DENISE shivers.)* **Oh, you're freezing!** *(JERRY takes off coats, puts them on DENISE. They find themselves with their arms in the same coat. They laugh. They look into each other's eyes, grow serious.)*

DENISE: **I know where we could get a cup of hot chocolate.**

JERRY: *(Glances at bridge railing.)* **Well, I am pretty cold. I could probably think this through until spring ...** *(The two of them walking off.)* **Where is this place with the hot chocolate?**

DENISE: **My place.**

THE END

CHECKERS

by

DALE DOERMAN

Dale Doerman lives in Cincinnati where he has served on the steering committee for the Cincinnati Theatre Festival. He has also served on the Ohio Arts Council Theatre Panel. *Checkers* has been performed by the Broad Ripple Theatre Company at the Michigan Theatre Festival in Lakeside and in Cincinnati by the Stable Players and Ensemble Theatre Company.

Production Suggestions

In order to perform the roles of Henry and Lillian believably, the actors will need to observe some real senior adults. Watch for voice and movement patterns, gestures, and other behaviors that you can adapt to your characters. Avoid a generalized stereotype of senility.

Address all inquiries concerning performances, readings, or reprinting of this work *or any portion thereof* to Dale Doerman at 2740 Enslin St., Cincinnati, OH 45225. For details, see "Part II: Securing Rights for Your Production," pages 223 to 232.

CHECKERS

by

DALE DOERMAN

The action takes place in a park during the early evening at the present time.

Characters:

HENRY — an elderly man
LILLIAN — his wife

Setting: *Two chairs, a table, and a checkers game.*

AT RISE: *A park. An elderly lady and gentleman are playing checkers. There are several moments of silence while concentrating on the next move. Then the lady moves, jumping three or four of her opponents pieces and removing them from the playing board.*

HENRY: **Wait! Wait! Let me see that again.**

LILLIAN: **All right, Henry.** *(She repeats the move.)*

HENRY: **Just wanted to make sure.**

LILLIAN: **Satisfied?**

HENRY: *(Nods in agreement.)* **You weren't cheating. My move.**

LILLIAN: **What do you mean?**

HENRY: *(Louder as though she couldn't hear.)* **It's my move.**

LILLIAN: **I heard you. You said I was cheating.**

HENRY: **No. Said you weren't cheating.**

LILLIAN: **But you thought I was.**

HENRY: **Just checking. That's all.**

LILLIAN: **Henry, I'm surprised at you. You have known me for fifty-two years. I waited for you through two wars.**

HENRY: **Second don't count. I was a civil defense warden. I stayed home for that one.**

LILLIAN: **What about that night you were out with Tom Davis doing God knows what till all hours of the morning?**

HENRY: **For Pete's sake, Lillian. Those were practice drills.**

Blackouts! Hell, the whole county knew it!

LILLIAN: Who knows what really went on that night? Everything was so dark.

HENRY: That's the whole point of a blackout, Lillian.

LILLIAN: But you were out there with Tom Davis.

HENRY: Probably. He was the only other warden in the county.

LILLIAN: And Tom Davis left his wife.

HENRY: When? Lillian, have you lost a screw or something?

LILLIAN: He did so.

HENRY: I can't think when you're talking, Lillian. *(Pause)*

LILLIAN: He left her in fifty-eight. That's right, it was fifty-eight.

HENRY: What?

LILLIAN: Tom Davis left his wife in fifty-eight. It was the same year we got that new Oldsmobile.

HENRY: Oh, the Oldsmobile. *(Pause)* Tom didn't leave her.

LILLIAN: Did so.

HENRY: He put her in that home. He couldn't take care of her anymore.

LILLIAN: I think he was running around. Had been since the war.

HENRY: He had the gout so bad they had to deliver his groceries. He wasn't running anywhere.

LILLIAN: He still left her.

HENRY: He put her in the home where she could get the care she needed.

LILLIAN: Don't believe it.

HENRY: She outlived him seven years.

LILLIAN: Maybe.

HENRY: We went to both their funerals!

LILLIAN: You don't know what goes on in those homes.

HENRY: Whose move is it?

LILLIAN: Yours. *(Pause)*

HENRY: Oh ... oh! I'm sorry, Lillian.

LILLIAN: What?

LILLIAN: What?

HENRY: I let you down again.

LILLIAN: How? What did you do now, Henry?

HENRY: It's not what I did. It's what I didn't do.

LILLIAN: What didn't you do, Henry?

HENRY: I forgot to take out the garbage.

LILLIAN: Garbage collection is Friday, Henry.

HENRY: That's right.

LILLIAN: This is Thursday. You didn't forget, Henry. You just remembered too soon. Remember it again later tonight.

HENRY: All right. *(Pause)* I thought I forgot. *(Pause)*

LILLIAN: You were confused.

HENRY: Who was confused?

LILLIAN: You were. You said I was cheating. I wasn't cheating, Henry.

HENRY: Never said you were. Said I checked the move and you weren't cheating.

LILLIAN: What's the difference?

HENRY: *(Makes move capturing one of her pieces.)* There.

LILLIAN: Where?

HENRY: *(Repeats move.)* There.

LILLIAN: Oh. *(Pause)*

HENRY: You never did explain those letters.

LILLIAN: Which letters?

HENRY: The ones I missed in Paris during the war.

LILLIAN: You were home during the war.

HENRY: Not the second war. The first war.

LILLIAN: Oh. I didn't know you were in Paris.

HENRY: I wasn't sightseeing. They had me in a ward with twenty, maybe thirty other fellas. All gassed.

LILLIAN: I don't think that you ever mentioned it.

HENRY: Sure I did. I was there for nearly two months. Never got a letter from you all that time.

LILLIAN: Maybe that was when I was with my grandmother in Indiana.

HENRY: Your grandmother?

LILLIAN: She took the flu. Mother and I went to help out.

HENRY: I always wondered why I never got a letter from you.

LILLIAN: What were the nurses like?

HENRY: Where?

LILLIAN: In Paris. In the hospital in Paris.

HENRY: For Pete's sake, Lillian. How should I remember?

LILLIAN: Well, were they helpful? *(Pause)* Did they speak English?

HENRY: Don't remember.

LILLIAN: Were they very pretty?

HENRY: Couldn't tell. They were all nuns.

LILLIAN: Oh. *(Pause)* You never got the letters?

HENRY: Not a one.

LILLIAN: I wrote better than once a week. You should have gotten some of them.

HENRY: You did write?

LILLIAN: Certainly.

HENRY: Well, there was a war going on.

LILLIAN: Of course, Henry. That's why you were there.

HENRY: I mean they were probably lost.

LILLIAN: Lost?

HENRY: German U Boat might have sunk the mail boat.

LILLIAN: Oh, Henry. Do you think so?

HENRY: Could be. Either that or they sent them on to my old outfit at the front.

LILLIAN: You mean someone else may have gotten those letters and read them?

HENRY: Maybe.

LILLIAN: Your letters from me?

HENRY: Or they may be somewhere under the ocean.

LILLIAN: Henry, why didn't you tell me? All this time ... *(Pause)* It doesn't change anything does it, Henry?

HENRY: Change what?

LILLIAN: The missing letters. I mean ... you still care for

-59-

me don't you?

HENRY: Of course, Lillian. *(Pause)* **Your move.** *(Pause)* **As long as you sent the letters.**

LILLIAN: Oh, I did, Henry.

HENRY: Well then ... your move. *(Pause)*

LILLIAN: I always wondered about those nurses in Paris.

HENRY: I thought you didn't remember that I was in Paris?

LILLIAN: It's just that you always heard those terrible things about French women. And there were all those romances in the movies then ... soldiers falling in love with nurses after they were wounded in the battlefield ... so far away from home ... where their sweethearts were waiting ...

HENRY: They were all nuns.

LILLIAN: Are you sure?

HENRY: White-winged bonnets, long robes, rosaries. Couldn't even see an ankle.

LILLIAN: Oh! So you looked!

HENRY: Sure I looked! How else would I know they were nuns?

LILLIAN: Oh, Henry!

HENRY: Well I had to do something all that time. You couldn't expect me to lie there flat on my back for two months, coughing my lungs out, with my eyes closed.

LILLIAN: Well ...

HENRY: Two months, Lillian?

LILLIAN: No, I suppose not.

HENRY: It wouldn't be fair.

LILLIAN: You're right, Henry. It wouldn't be fair. Besides, you would never know if you had gotten a letter from me, if your eyes were closed the whole time.

HENRY: That's right!

LILLIIAN: There! *(She jumps the remaining pieces.)* **Game!**

HENRY: Game? Already?

LILLIAN: I'm afraid so, Henry.

HENRY: *(Refers to watch.)* **We've got time for one more.**

LILLIAN: All right, Henry. As long as there's time.

HENRY: *(Resetting the board.)* I loved that Oldsmobile. First car we ever owned without running boards.

LILLIAN: What about the Pontiac? It had running boards.

HENRY: We never had a Pontiac.

LILLIAN: Did so. Got it the year Frank went to college.

HENRY: That was a Hudson.

LILLIAN: The blue one with the hood ornament?

HENRY: Maroon. It was deep maroon with black interior.

LILLIAN: *(She moves her piece.)* Oh yes! The one with the radio!

HENRY: *(Moves his piece.)* First car we owned with a radio.

LILLIAN: *(Moves and jumps his piece.)* Pay attention to the game. You're losing again.

HENRY: You're not cheating again, Lillian?

LILLIAN: Henry, I'm surprised at you. You have known me for fifty-two years! I waited for you through two wars!

HENRY: Just checking, Lillian. *(Lights begin a slow fade.)* Besides I didn't go away for the second war. It doesn't count.

LILLIAN: I'm still not certain about Paris.

HENRY: You never went to Paris, Lillian. What are you talking about?

THE END

THE AFFIDAVIT

by
JANET S. TIGER

Janet S. Tiger writes for stage and screen. Her plays have been performed in Los Angeles, San Francisco, Dubuque, San Diego, and New York. *The Affidavit* took first prize in the 1983 Dubuque Fine Arts Society playwriting competition and was subsequently produced off-Broadway in New York by the American Theatre of Actors as well as in Dubuque, San Diego, and San Francisco.

Production Suggestions

Accurate, believable accents will strengthen the performance of *The Affidavit*. To research these accents, listen to *English with an Accent* (A BBC recording available from Drama Book Publishers), or use David Allen Stern's tapes *Acting with an Accent: German* and *Acting with an Accent: Yiddish,* available from Dialect Accent Specialists, Inc., P.O. Box 44, Lyndonville, VT 05851.

If you are doing *The Affidavit* as an acting class project, focus on the acting, not the technical details of set and props. You need a telephone, a trash basket, a few simple touches can suggest the pawn shop milieu. If you don't have a ringing telephone, the actor of Hilda can provide the sound effect using a bicycle bell or, in a class project setting, by saying,"Ring . . . ring . . . ring."

The playwright provides the following historical note: "In the late 1930s, and early 1940s, an affidavit was required of a person wanting to enter the United States as a permanent resident. The affidavit was used to obtain a visa from the United States, which then entitled the visa holder to apply for an exit visa from his home country. A fee of $650 was needed to hold the affidavit open, and if the affidavit was not used within a certain amount of time, it had to be renewed. In Nazi-controlled countries, each time an exit visa was applied for, both the affidavit and the U.S. visa had to be handed over to the Nazis. Even if the exit visa was denied, the affidavit and U.S. visa were not returned. It was not unusual for the exit visa to be denied many times. In other words, the affidavit was no guarantee of survival for European Jews, but without it, there was no chance at all."

Address all inquiries concerning performances, readings, or reprinting of this work *or any portion thereof* to Janet S. Tiger at 4489 Bertha St., San Diego, CA 92117. For details, see "Part II: Securing Rights for Your Production," pages 223 to 232.

THE AFFIDAVIT

by
JANET S. TIGER

The action takes place in a New York pawnshop on a Friday afternoon in the early 1940s.

Characters:

LOUIS MEYER, 42 — A pawnbroker
HILDA GRUENBERG, mid-20s — An immigrant

Setting: *The interior of Meyer's Pawn Shop and Emporium is fur-nished with tables and display cases loaded with jewelry, toast-ers, cameras, and the like. The front door opens onto a city sidewalk complete with an overflowing garbage can.*

Note: *No words in **The Affidavit** may be changed, modified, or altered without the express prior written consent of the playwright.*

AT RISE: As the lights go up, we see LOUIS MEYER at the front door, waving goodbye to a customer. LOUIS is forty-two, but looks about fifty-five, graying, with a definite paunch that he doesn't bother to hide. LOUIS doesn't enjoy that his store has become a pawn shop, but on the other hand, he accepts the twists of fate that are shown to him. He treats life as if it were a poker game with a marked deck — he knows he's going to lose, but he's trying to see how long he can hold out.

LOUIS closes the door, and we see him smiling as he starts to count some money. The phone rings, but LOUIS continues to count methodically, even a little slower perhaps, until the ringing stops. At this, LOUIS stops counting the money and counts to himself, mimicking a person dialing a number. He speaks with a Yiddish accent.

LOUIS: ... **seven, three, nine** ... *(The phone rings again, and this*

time, LOUIS picks it up. Businesslike.) **Meyer's Pawn Shop
and Emporium** ... *(He holds the phone away from his ear.
Calm.)* **I answered on the third ring, as God is my witness,
Ida ... You must have dialed the wrong number then,
because it only rang three times ... I *was* just about to
call you, dear, but you beat me to it ... Yes, he bought
something ... All right, I'll tell you.** *(Slowly, relishing the
story.)* **He came in about twenty-five minutes ago. Wait,
maybe it was thirty, no it was twenty-five ... I'm getting
to it, Ida ... I knew he was a buyer because he had on a
new suit from Goodman's still with the tags showing. A
brown suit, a little too tight, but you know what a goniff
that Goodman is.** *(Reflective)* **I wonder how he does it, you
think he tells them it'll stretch like leather ...** *(Holds the
phone away from his ear.)* **I'm getting to it, I just wanted to
tell you the whole story. You know, Ida, a good story is
like a nice dinner, you don't want to rush and spoil it
and get indigestion. So anyhow, he walks in, Mr.
Bernstein, his name was and ... I'm not sure I noticed
what color shoes he was wearing, I never liked dealing
in shoes. Maybe they were brown, let me think ... How
did I know you were joking? ... Now where was I? ... So
he walks in the store ...** *(Quickly)* **Ida, I have to go, there's
a customer.** *(He hangs up quickly as we see the door open.
HILDA GRUENBERG enters. She is a nice-looking woman in
her mid-20s wearing clothing that was once expensive, but has
seen better days. She is smiling, but it's clear that she has a
heavy weight on her shoulders.)*

LOUIS: *(Polite)* **Ah, Mrs. Gruenberg, how are you today?**

HILDA: *(Nervous, with slight German accent.)* **I'm all right, I
suppose.**

LOUIS: **Things could always be worse, that's the way I look
at it.**

HILDA: *(Doubtful)* **Maybe.**

LOUIS: **I figure if I'd been born with a middle name like
Baruch or Benjamin, I'd be in Hollywood right now.**

(HILDA looks surprised at this.) **With Baruch or Benjamin, my name would be Louis B. Meyer, just like the movie king. And I'd be sitting in the sunshine, surrounded by beautiful actresses, not answering the phone every twenty seconds to hear my wife ask if I've made enough money to take her to the Catskills this summer ...**

HILDA: *(Cuts in.)* **I'd love to talk, but I'm in a bit of a rush today, Mr. Meyer.**

LOUIS: **I'm sorry, I like to talk too much. It gets lonely here this time in the afternoon. In fact, since it's Friday, you're lucky to catch me here. I should have closed ten minutes ago ... Now, what can I get you? Do you need a scarf? It's getting a little chilly out there.** *(He pulls out a box of scarves to show her.)*

HILDA: **They're very nice, but today I didn't come to buy.**

LOUIS: *(Slight pause.)* **Oh, I see.**

HILDA: *(Hesitant, this is difficult for her.)* **Do you remember last month when I brought in that ring?**

LOUIS: *(Evasive)* **I see so many things every day. People bring me bracelets and necklaces and ...**

HILDA: *(Cuts him off.)* **The one I showed you last month, with the rubies.** *(He tries to remember, shakes his head.)* **This one.** *(She opens her purse and removes a small bag, from which she removes a ring wrapped in cotton.)* **It was my mother's. My father gave it to her on their first anniversary, and when she died, he kept it for me. You looked at it last month, remember?** *(He looks at it cursorily, he remembered it.)*

LOUIS: *(Uncomfortable)* **A true family heirloom.**

HILDA: **You told me it was worth $10,000.**

LOUIS: **No, *you* told me it was worth $10,000, and I didn't disagree.**

HILDA: **I need to get some money very quickly.**

LOUIS: **Doesn't everyone?**

HILDA: **This isn't a joke. My father's affidavit expires tonight, and I need $650 to keep it open.**

LOUIS: **I didn't know your father was back there still.**

HILDA: He wouldn't come with us last year, and so now ...

LOUIS: *(Finishes for her.)* **Now he's stuck.**

HILDA: *(Quick)* **Don't say that.**

LOUIS: **I'm sorry, I'm sure you'll get him out.**

HILDA: **I have to get to the Post Office before they close to get a money order. That's why I'm in a rush — I must get it stamped in today's mail.**

LOUIS: **Talk about waiting until the last minute, what about your sponsor?**

HILDA: **He's already put up all the other money, he told us we would have to do it this time.**

LOUIS: **I thought he was that rich fellow, Steinwalt ...**

HILDA: **I'm desperate, Mr. Meyer, I'll pay you any interest you want.**

LOUIS: **To be very honest, I'm not interested in loaning you anything against the ring.**

HILDA: *(Stunned)* **Oh.**

LOUIS: **But I will make an offer to buy it from you.**

HILDA: *(Relieved)* **Oh.** *(Realizes what this means.)* **But the ring has been in our family for years. It has sentimental value.**

LOUIS: **Then you won't sell it to me?** *(She picks up the ring and looks at it carefully, then puts it down.)*

HILDA: *(Resigned)* **How much?**

LOUIS: **Well, let me look at it a little more carefully.**

HILDA: **It's the same ring as before, you can see that.**

LOUIS: **The difference is, if it's going to be my ring, then I look at it a little more closely.** *(He takes out a loupe and proceeds to scrutinize the ring while HILDA slowly becomes impatient. He looks up.)* **Oh, you can sit down if you want.**

HILDA: *(Trying to be polite.)* **I'd rather stand.**

LOUIS: **Suit yourself.** *(He turns back to the ring and continues his scrutiny as HILDA becomes more and more impatient. Finally, as she is about to say something, he puts down the loupe and turns to her.)* **I'll give you $650.** *(She is so stunned that she has to grab the counter to keep from falling over.)*

HILDA: **Are you joking? You told me that ring is worth**

thousands!

LOUIS: What something is worth and what you'll get for it is two completely different things.

HILDA: *(Furious)* Then I'll take it elsewhere, that's all. *(She takes the ring angrily and turns to leave, then stops and looks at her watch. Furious, but now with the edges of defeat creeping in.)* You kept me here on purpose, looking at the ring, so there's nowhere else to go to. It's too late. *(He shrugs.)* I thought you were a friend.

LOUIS: You know what they say — never do business with friends.

HILDA: What you are is a bastard.

LOUIS: Flattery will not improve my offer.

HILDA: *(Quiet)* What kind of a man are you?

LOUIS: Is this a quiz?

HILDA: You live off the sorrows of poor people, your own people, how can you look yourself in the face?

LOUIS: It won't work. Your words aren't going to change my offer. I'm a businessman, that's what kind of man I am. And as for poor people, you had your chance to leave Europe years ago, like my family did — in the hold of a ship, packed in like sardines. But your families wouldn't leave, no, things were too nice for all of you. That coat you have on, maybe it's a little threadbare, but when it was new it probably cost more than my wife's entire wardrobe. Then you people come over here, bringing your diamonds and jewelry, taking any price, then expecting us to pay top dollar. *You* were the ones that flooded the markets, *you* were the ones who depressed the prices! Now, you have to live with it.

HILDA: *(On the edge of pleading.)* You said it was worth $10,000, give me at least ten percent — that's only $1,000.

LOUIS: *(Firm)* $650.

HILDA: *(Desperate)* Then $900 ... $700. My baby is only two years old, I can't even afford an orange for her.

LOUIS: An orange? What a luxury! My son died during the

Depression because we didn't have enough money for medicine.

HILDA: I'm sorry.

LOUIS: Six hundred fifty dollars. It's my final offer.

HILDA: *(Can't hold back any longer, yells.)* **My God, what kind of a man are you?**

LOUIS: *(Lets the air quiet.)* **But it's not *my* father.** *(This stops her cold, and she looks like she's trying not to cry. He hands her a handkerchief.)*

HILDA: *(Amazed, more to herself.)* **I'm bargaining with my father's life. Every day I watch and pray my letters to him won't come back with that horrible stamp on it —** "Addressee unknown, moved — no forwarding address." **Every day I watch and yet now I argue over a few dollars. May God forgive me.** *(Quiet, but strong.)* **Mr. Meyer, I'll take your offer.**

LOUIS: **Very smart woman.** *(He takes out the money from his pocket and starts counting.)*

HILDA: *(Trying to stay in control.)* **Maybe when you sell this, you can take your wife on that vacation.**

LOUIS: **If I tell her. You know, sometimes I don't tell her everything.** *(Returns to counting the money.)*

HILDA: **Don't you have any nicer-looking money?**

LOUIS: **You could always iron it, but I don't think you have the time. Here, 648, 649, 650.** *(He hands her the money.)* **And you can have this, too.** *(He holds out two singles to her, and she looks surprised.)* **It's for the cab, so you can get to the Post Office on time.** *(She doesn't take it at first, then reaches out for the money.)*

HILDA: **I wish I had the strength to throw this in your face.**

LOUIS: **I'm glad you're not on the Yankees, then.** *(She doesn't laugh at this, but turns and walks to the door.)* **Goodbye, Mrs. Gruenberg.** *(She stops, then turns back to him.)*

HILDA: **As God is my witness, I'll never set foot in this store again.**

LOUIS: You've seen *Gone With the Wind,* too! Wasn't that a wonderful movie? I love that Scarlett person, she's just beautiful . . .

HILDA: *(Ignores him.)* You make jokes, Mr. Meyer, but God will spit on you for what you're doing to us.

LOUIS: *(Cheery)* You have a nice Sabbath, too, Mrs. Gruenberg. *(She shakes her head, then leaves, shutting the door firmly behind her, but resisting the urge to slam it. LOUIS watches her leave, then goes to the door and turns the "Open" sign to "Closed." As he's doing this, the phone starts to ring, and we see him debate for a moment, then walk over and pick up the phone.)* Meyer's Pawn Shop and Emporium . . . Yes, Ida, I'm still here. I answered the phone, didn't I? . . . I'm on my way now . . . Nothing. Just looking . . . One of those fancy immigrants — she had a ring full of red glass she thought was rubies. You know these refugees, always another story. *(As he listens, he looks at the ring, holding it up to the light, and smiling to himself.)* Of course I didn't give her any money against it — she'd come back and get it out of hock, then complain I switched it on them. No, I sent her away . . . The other one? I never did finish that story, did I? . . . Well, he came in and . . . *(Holds phone away from ear.)* All right, all right. He bought that ring in the window, on the left, no the left side next to Sam's store. The one with that emerald in it . . . I can't show it to you, it's sold. If you came to the store once in awhile . . . How much? Let me check. *(He reaches into his pocket, and checks the remaining cash from the first sale.)* Fifty dollars, no forty-eight . . . I paid the tax, that's why it was forty-eight dollars . . . Of course, I'm sure . . . Why would I want to hold out on you? . . . I haven't gambled in months, well, weeks, but . . . I'll bring the money straight home. See you soon, dear. *(He hangs up phone, and we can hear Ida still yelling. LOUIS gets his coat, and goes to the door. The phone rings again, and this time, he just lets it ring, but talks to it.)* Don't worry, I won't forget the garbage. *(He gets the wastebasket out and puts the contents into a bag, then replaces the basket behind the counter. As he does he spots the ring MRS. GRUENBERG sold him. To phone, mechanical.)* **I'll be on the five-twenty-four, Ida, same as always.** *(He looks at the ring once more, then drops it into the bag with the other garbage and sighs heavily. He then turns out the light, and as the phone stops ringing, he takes the bag with him, and walks through the door. We see him drop the bag into the trash receptacle and exit.)*

THE END

THE SPLIT DECISION

by
WILLIAM MOSELEY

William Moseley has had his plays produced on stage and on radio. In 1982 he and five other playwrights were chosen by Edward Albee to join him in a three-week workshop at the Atlantic Center for the Arts in Florida. *The Split Decision* is a revised version of Moseley's segment of a collaborative play which resulted — *Scenes from a Non-Marriage,* directed by Albee at the Atlantic Center in November, 1982. In May 1985, a radio adaptation of *The Split Decision* was produced and broadcast by WNYU-FM in New York City as part of their *On Cue* radio drama series.

Production Suggestions

The Split Decision presents the male actor with a real challenge. In the words of the playwright, "I think there's a danger in this play of David's appearing a one-dimensional, insensitive bore — which would make us wonder why a woman like Ginger would ever hook up with him to begin with." While realizing that David is a less attractive character than Ginger, the actor should avoid playing him as a villain or as a complete fool. Instead, the actor should try to see the world from David's viewpoint and should seek out his positive, human qualities.

Address all inquiries concerning performances, readings, or reprinting of this work *or any portion thereof* to William Moseley at 102 Highview Drive, Cocoa, FL 32922. For details, see "Part II: Securing Rights for Your Production," pages 223 to 232.

Read about William Moseley in *A Critical Survey of Short Fiction* edited by Frank N. Magill (Salem Press, 1981), volume 7, page 2736.

this is it

THE SPLIT DECISION

by
WILLIAM MOSELEY

The action takes place in an apartment in a Midwestern university town in the present time.

Characters:
DAVID — in his twenties
GINGER — in her twenties

Setting: *The living room of Ginger and David's apartment. One half of the room is **hers**. Its low, comfortable sofa, framed needlework and macrame wall hanging, soft drapes, and throw rugs give it a warm, home-like atmosphere. The other half of the room is **his**. More like a lab than a home, its steel desk with a home computer, its tile floor without carpets, its chrome and plastic furniture, and modern, abstract graphics on the walls create an effect of cold practicality and efficiency.*

AT RISE: Lights up on DAVID, seated at his desk, facing the audience, typing at the keyboard of his computer. After a few moments, GINGER enters, carrying a serving tray with coffee pot, cups, saucers, and spoons. She stops unhappily when she sees DAVID working. Then she crosses to set the tray on the coffee table in front of the couch.

DAVID: *(Hearing the dishes rattle, but not looking up.)* **Ginger —?**

GINGER: *(Only half serious.)* **Know what, David? Some evening you're going to be all absorbed in that machine, and call out "Ginger?" — and it *won't* be me.**

DAVID: *(Barely listening, continuing to work.)* **Hmm? And who'll it be?**

GINGER: **Oh . . . maybe nobody.**

DAVID: **Yeah, well — Have to put this in memory, so I can boot it up for Harris tomorrow morning.**

GINGER: **You *gave* me a full report — all through dinner. While *I* was hoping we'd have time to talk about —**

DAVID: *(Interrupting)* **I'm nearly finished — final details on that conversion job for the city libraries. Gotta get the data from their card catalog system into MARC Records. Harris generates these broad concepts, then can't see the trees for the forest. Me, though — I'm good with —**

GINGER: *(Overlapping)* **"Good with details"** ... *(As she sits on sofa.)* **So you've said — in detail — ever since you got home from work. I'd been hoping we could talk about our —**

DAVID: *(Continuing, over her.)* **Harris depends on me — to blaze a trail through his forests. Nobody on the committee ever thinks** *I* **might be smart enough to invent a marketable concept.** *(Finishing, he turns off computer and pushes his chair back, as GINGER begins pouring coffee.)*

GINGER: **I made the kind you like — we got the beans in fresh at the shop today.** *(She holds out cup on saucer to him. He rises and crosses to take cup, leaving her holding saucer. She shrugs and sets it back down.)*

DAVID: *(Sipping coffee, musing.)* **"Concept"** — *that's* **all I need.** *(Turns away, lost in thought.)* **Something really different —** *creative* ...

GINGER: *(She hesitates, then tries.)* **I — now and then** *I* **get ideas. If it's a new idea you need,** *I* **might ... I could help —** *(But he cuts her off with a scornful look and a derisive "Ha!" Rebuked, she goes on after a couple of beats.)* **Anyway ... I thought you** *like* **the detail work.**

DAVID: **Oh I do ... usually. You can get lost in it, though — get lost in the trees. You keep asking yourself when you'll raise a forest of your** *own.* *(Sinking onto sofa.)* **Now walking into a committee meeting with an original project proposal — software to sell hardware — well, it'd make me feel — feel more** *real,* **I guess. It'd** *prove* **something ...**

GINGER: *(After a moment, tentatively.)* **Maybe — maybe if you stopped** *thinking* **about it for a while —**

DAVID: **Now Ginger, I don't need more of your donut-shop philosophy —**

GINGER: **No, listen. Lots of university people come into the**

shop, right? And *they* say that when a person has a problem to solve, best thing is to switch your mind to some *other* problem, totally unrelated, and —

DAVID: Yeah, yeah — and suddenly your subconscious comes up with a solution to your *first* problem. The "eureka" process.

GINGER: The —?

DAVID: *(Condescending)* "You--*reek*--ah." Greek.

GINGER: Oh. Whatever. All I know is, one of the professors will be sitting at the counter, dunking a Krispy-Kreme and bitching about his car's transmission — when all at once he'll jump up, yell "I got it!" — and go running straight out the door . . . no check, no tip, no nothing. *(A beat.)* That's why I tell the girls to always collect from university people in advance.

DAVID: My transmission is fine . . . I don't *have* another problem to kick around, while my subconscious comes up with an original program to sell.

GINGER: Yes you do. You have another problem. *(A beat.)* *We* have another problem. *(Short pause. DAVID sighs and pushes himself to his feet.)*

DAVID: *(Moving to his side of the room.)* But it's a closed system, dammit, whenever we try to *discuss* it! We go through scene after scene, nothing conclusive, around and around like — like —

GINGER: Around and around like — a donut? *(DAVID snorts a "Ha!" but she goes on.)* A donut . . . that's what it's turning into, this — this non-marriage of ours.

DAVID: "Non-marriage" —?

GINGER: They used to call it "shacking up" — I like "non-marriage" better. Or would you prefer "trial marriage"? But how many trials run for *five years*, David? *(A beat — no response from him.)* All right, how about "living together"? — that's pretty non-committal. Or maybe "free-style relationship"? with your "spouse equivalent"?

DAVID: Ginger, come off it —

GINGER: "Relationship," then. After five years, my spouse equivalent, this "relationship" of ours is turning into a donut.

DAVID: *(Dropping into a chair at his desk.)* Damn I hate it when you're frivolous!

GINGER: You're always saying I don't have imagination. *(Rising)* But this afternoon, making a-a--special donut for a lady — it really did cross my mind that our living together's getting more and more like a donut. *(Crossing to him.)* A comfortable shape that's soft and light enough — sweet, too, on the outside. But it gets a little sticky if you hold onto it too tight, or for too long a time —

DAVID: *(Turning away.)* And I hate it when you're so illogical —

GINGER: — and at the center? At the center, there's nothing. Just a great big empty *hole.*

DAVID: *(After a short pause.)* You want to talk about donuts, or you want to talk about us?

GINGER: Us. Are we going to get married, or not? Do we split up? We have to decide!

DAVID: *(Rising, his back to her.)* "Decide" — you've made me loathe that word! All we ever decide is that we have to decide — but we never *decide.*

GINGER: *(Ironic.)* Yeah ... maybe we should let one of your *computers* decide. *(Moving to couch.)* Computers don't waste energy on frivolous, illogical things like caring, or love, or — *(DAVID suddenly darts after her and grabs her shoulder.)*

DAVID: Wait —! *(Turning her around.)* Say that again!

GINGER: Uh — "Frivolous, illogical things like caring, or love —"

DAVID: No, no: let the computer decide! Eureka! *(As a puzzled GINGER watches, he rushes to his desk.)* I've found my forest! Oh this is gonna be great — gr-r-*reat*! *(Grabs up a legal pad and pencil and starts scribbling notes.)* OK: first, outline proposal, with profit potential —

GINGER: *(Sighing)* **Back to the old keypunch board** ... *(At the coffee table, she begins placing dishes back onto the tray.)*

DAVID: *(In his own world.)* **I'll do the systems and operations flow charts myself, to hell with Harris. We can lease at our standard rates, plus residuals at, say, ten percent of gross** ...

GINGER: **Been nice talking with you.** *(As she starts off, carrying tray waitress-style.)* **You needn't bother leaving me a tip** ...

DAVID: *(Suddenly noticing her.)* **Wait!** *(Going after her.)* **Don't go — I need you!**

GINGER: *You* **need** *me?*

DAVID: *(Leading her to couch.)* **Need your reaction — a quick marketing poll. Just — here, just sit back down for a minute.**

GINGER: *(Placing tray on coffee table.)* **All right** ... **but I'll warn you —** *(As she sits on couch.)* **The donut's getting sticky** ...

DAVID: *(Leaning in to her, pad in hand.)* **Now: you've seen the ads for those companies that use computers to match up people, right? What're they called — uh —**

GINGER: *(Uninterested, shrugging.)* *I* **don't know — Computer dating services?**

DAVID: **That's it — with catchy names, like — like what?**

GINGER: *(As before.)* **Oh, "Dateline"** ... **and "Date-a-Mate"** ... **Debby used one last week named "The Mating Call." But why would you —**

DAVID: *(Rushing on.)* **So — since somebody's made a program to determine who should be** *together* ... **why can't** *I* **create a program to decide who'd be better off** *apart?* **Instead of computer match-ups, we'll have —**

GINGER: *(Can't believe it.)* **Computer** *divorce?*

DAVID: **Of course divorce — if you're married. If you're** *not* **married, it'd be — uh — what?**

GINGER: *(Hard)* **Splitting up.**

DAVID: *(Pacing, his side of room.)* **Good enough: divorce or splitting up. Think how much pain and anguish the computer can eliminate! The destructive arguments, the**

heartache and tears! The — the —

GINGER: *(Not sharing his enthusiasm.)* The *scenes,* that go around and around . . .

DAVID: Yes! Why, the savings in detective and lawyer fees *alone*'ll far outweigh what we'll charge for — for — What'll we call it?

GINGER: *(Trying to get a word in.)* David —

DAVID: No, no, we can't call it "David." Gotta be a catchy trade-name or slogan — like "The Mating Call," only the opposite.

GINGER: *(Rising)* David, I *won't* turn this decision over to a *machine!* To split up or not to split up — how can you even —

DAVID: *(Crossing to her.)* Wait. Say that again.

GINGER: *(Turning away.)* I'm never saying *any*thing again to *you!*

DAVID: Decision . . . to split or not to split . . . Got it! We'll name it — *(Writing)* "The Split Decision." That's from boxing, the fights — lots of couples can relate to that.

GINGER: I don't doubt it . . .

DAVID: *(Returning to his desk eagerly.)* The committee'll love it — we can develop the whole package and lease the master . . . maybe to the same outfits that run the computer *matching.* That way, see, they can offer *both* services.

GINGER: *(Sarcastic.)* Get you coming and going . . .

DAVID: *(Making notes again.)* Good point! — repeat business. Now the variables here . . . what'll we call — Ah, this is too slow! *(Throws pad and pencil impatiently onto desk.)*

GINGER: *(As before.)* Oh surely you can communicate better with your *computer.*

DAVID: That's right! *(Sitting at computer.)* I've got the word processor disk, and the printer . . . *(Turns on computer, makes a few entries.)* OK — the in-put data: the variables. What can we —? Ah! N.C.F.s, we'll call 'em: Non-Compatibility Factors. Feed these in, with appropriate weights —

GINGER: David! Are you actually figuring out how people are going to break *up*? *(She crosses slowly to him on his next lines.)*

DAVID: *(More to himself, occasionally making entries.)* N.C.F.s'll be things like — umm — changes in sexual attitudes and frequency . . . maybe assorted "irritability factors" — yes — such as hair in the bathroom sink, or odd and excessive noises during eating, sleep, or sex . . . What else? Things that've *changed* during the relationship . . .

GINGER: Such as bringing your work home every night? Or being willing to talk — *two-way* talk?

DAVID: Nah, these Non-Compatibility Factors have to be *measureable* — on a scale of — *(Breaks off, sensing her mood, and looks up at her.)* Oh now Ginger . . . Don't stand in my light — this is my big break! *(Rises, touches her.)* Let me get it finalized tonight — then *tomorrow* we can have this — uh — "two-way talk," or whatever.

GINGER: Shouldn't it be the other way? Us first — the machine tomorrow?

DAVID: You gotta go with the flow! This "Split Decision" idea of mine — the committee'll eat it up! They're always pushing creativity — creative technology, creative computer science . . .

GINGER: And I guess you don't believe *my* work could ever be creative.

DAVID: Creative donut science? Hah! *(Sitting again.)* Let's see . . . need some more N.C.F.s — enough to form a reliable base . . . May have to calculate probability . . . *(He takes a small, credit-card-size calculator from his shirt pocket as GINGER returns to the couch and sits. While she is speaking, he'll work with the calculator and computer.)*

GINGER: *(After a short pause, aware that DAVID isn't really listening.)* I — I created something today. You don't think I can, but I did. This older woman came in the shop and asked if we made birthday cakes. Her grandson was going to be six, and she said he loved the taste of our Krispy-

– 80 –

Kremes better than anything. Debby told her no, we don't make cakes . . . and the lady was about to leave, when I stopped her. I had an idea. *(Picking up a cup from the tray.)* I — I didn't know it was a "you-*reek*--ah." I just went back to the kitchen — it was the baker's off-shift — and I created a birthday donut. *(She takes a sip from the cup — but the coffee's cold, and she puts it down with a grimace.)* **David?**

DAVID: *(Busy at the computer.)* **Huh? Yeah, that's . . . nice . . .**

GINGER: **A birthday donut, David — a foot wide! I planned it all by myself: rolled out a batch of our regular dough; cut the outer and inner circles with a sharp knife; put it through the riser and into the fryer . . . then glazed it with chocolate. That's our special chocolate icing, you know** — another idea of mine — *(Tilting the coffee pot and looking into it.)* **thinning it with strong, black, end-of-the-pot coffee, instead of water. Everybody brags on our chocolate icing.** *(She looks to DAVID — no response.)* **Then I put six birthday candles around the top of the giant donut . . . Oh, you should've seen the grandmother's eyes light up when I brought it out! "But don't leave the hole empty," I told her. "I won't," she said; "I'll fill it with chocolate ice cream — his favorite." The little boy tomorrow, David: can you imagine how *his* eyes will light up?**

DAVID: *(Mumbling, absorbed in his figures.)* **Yeah, uh . . . tomorrow . . . yeah . . .**

GINGER: **The biggest donut in the world — candles all around — made especially for him —** *(Rising)* **created for him — by *me* . . . something to bring people *together,* not split them apart.** *(With a few steps toward him.)* **And the hole — the hole in the middle of the birthday donut, David: that hole will be *filled* . . . filled with a lot more than ice cream!** *(She waits for a response from him, a last chance. But he continues working. She grabs up the tray and starts off, then stops and turns back.)* **Know what? I've just *made* my decision — and without the help of your**

damned computer! *(She walks out. DAVID makes a final entry on his computer, then turns it off.)*

DAVID: **Ginger, would you** — *(Breaks off; rises, looking around the room.)* **Ginger . . .?** *(Crosses slowly to couch, sees the tray is gone, and glances toward exit. A bit louder.)* **Ginger?** *(When there is no reply, he looks from her side of the room to his and back again, frowning — as though it's just begun to dawn on him that he's lost something, but can't think what it is.)*

THE END

COMING FOR A VISIT

by
BEN JOSEPHSON

Ben Josephson's plays have been produced in Los Angeles and Berkeley. His comedy *Horace Whirley's Woe* won the 1985 Jacksonville University Playwriting Competition. The premier of *Coming for a Visit* was presented by the New One-Act Theatre Ensemble at the Attic Theatre in Hollywood in 1982.

Production Suggestions

The actress playing Mrs. McNulty has the double challenge of portraying upper middle age and producing an effective Irish accent. Both problems can be solved by research. The actress should watch some fifty-year-old women to catch the appropriate rhythms and physical movement patterns. For the accent problem, she might use David Allen Stern's tape *Acting with an Accent: Irish* available from Dialect Accent Specialists, Inc., P.O. Box 44, Lyndonville, VT 05851. Along with these technical approaches, she should immerse herself in all that she can discover and imagine about Mrs. McNulty's character and also focus on the verbal rhythms Mr. Josephson has so carefully scripted into Mrs. McNulty's lines.

Address all inquiries concerning performances, readings, or reprinting of this work *or any portion thereof* to Ben Josephson at 286 East Second Street, Benicia, CA 94510. Performance royalty checks for *Coming for a Visit* should be made payable to Stephen W. Kalkstein. For details, see "Part II: Securing Rights for Your Production," pages 223 to 232.

COMING FOR A VISIT

by
BEN JOSEPHSON

The action takes place in early September, 1966, in Mrs. McNulty's house in Galway City, Ireland.

Characters:

MRS. McNULTY — in her fifties
TIMOTHY WAGNER — 19, an American

Setting: *Left, Mrs. McNulty's kitchen with a table, two chairs, a kettle on the stove, a picture of the three Kennedy boys and another of Pope John XXIII. Right, her sitting room with an overstuffed chair, an electric fire, and a chest.*

AT RISE: MRS. McNULTY, alone, opens the oven, looks in, shuts it. Checks her watch, puts on a raincoat, and exits by way of the sitting room.

MRS. McNULTY: *(Pause. Offstage.)* **Go on inside, I'm tellin' ya!**
TIM: *(Offstage)* **Thank you, but ...**
MRS. McNULTY: *(Offstage)* **I'll be back in a flash.**
TIM: *(Offstage)* **But lady, I ...**
MRS. McNULTY: *(Offstage)* **Into the house! I will not have ya stay outside in the pourin' rain!** *(Sound of the door slamming. TIM, nineteen, enters the sitting room. He wears a pack on his back, under a poncho, and his jeans are soaked from the knees down. He looks about suspiciously, takes off his poncho and pack and then, after a moment's reflection, puts them back on and makes for the door.)*
MRS. McNULTY: *(Offstage)* **You might drown on the way to the corner and back!** *(Door slam. She enters, wet.)*
TIM: **Look, lady, I ...**
MRS. McNULTY: *(Extracts a newspaper from under her raincoat, brandishes it as a trophy.)* **But I did keep my paper from gettin' the least bit wet!**
TIM: **I really appreciate this, but ...**
MRS. McNULTY: *(Turns the fire on.)* **Is it waitin' for me to undress ya, you are?**

TIM: Uh ... I, uh ...

MRS. McNULTY: Will you have some tea now, or ... ?

TIM: Tea? No, I ...

MRS. McNULTY: Or will you put it off till after you've had your bath?

TIM: I have to go.

MRS. McNULTY: *(Stops him, pulls off his poncho.)* Don't you be drippin' on my floor. Now, set your boots by the fire and come into the kitchen. *(Exits to the kitchen, hangs up the poncho and her raincoat, and makes tea. TIM takes off his pack, his boots, and his socks.)* There's a loaf in the oven and two kippers in the fridge. Where in the blessed world were you goin' on a day like this?

TIM: South.

MRS. McNULTY: Then you'd be comin' from the north, I expect.

TIM: From Donegal.

MRS. McNULTY: Well, *that's* a good thing! At least Donegal is a *place.* Empty it may be, and lonely, but it's right there where it belongs. If it's only "south" you're headin', how will you know when it's time to stop?

TIM: I stopped.

MRS. McNULTY: You surely did. You're lucky it was Mrs. McNulty came upon ya, and you sloggin' southward through a Galway flood. I've four rooms you can choose from, but only one catches the mornin' sun. Are you a late sleeper, or do ya like to wake up with the dawn's first gleam? *(Pause)* Do ya sleep late, I said? *(Pause)* For it's a bright mornin' often follows a rainy day.

TIM: I'll be leaving when the storm lets up.

MRS. McNULTY: You'll find Brian Lynch's bathrobe in the lower dresser drawer. And they'll none of 'em be back for three weeks, if you're worryin' you'll be driven out in the night. What's your name?

TIM: *(Appears barefoot at the kitchen door.)* Tim.

MRS. McNULTY: Then have ya no dry socks? *(Sits him down,*

and wraps dish towels around his feet.) **Tell me your full name.**

TIM: Timothy Wagner.

MRS. McNULTY: **But ya can't sit around in these soggy trousers!**

TIM: Is the tea ready yet?

MRS. McNULTY: **And your mother's side: would *that* be Irish?**

TIM: Some of it, I guess.

MRS. McNULTY: **You *guess*?**

TIM: She's got some Polish, some Greek, some Cherokee . . .

MRS. McNULTY: **Are you from Oklahoma, then?**

TIM: Huh?

MRS. McNULTY: **Indian territory!**

TIM: What do you know about . . . ?

MRS. McNULTY: **I spent last August on a Greyhound bus! From sea ta shinin' sea, and back again. It makes no sense you wanderin' about the bleakest part of Ireland.**

TIM: I'm from New Jersey.

MRS. McNULTY: **Then have ya never heard of Brian Lynch? He lives in Hackensack.** *(Pause)* **Ah, *'tis* a big place. Brian was the first of my boys to leave.**

TIM: What "boys?"

MRS. McNULTY: **Why, for twenty years I've been lettin' rooms to the University lads. In the summers I have an empty house.** *(The energy which has been driving her drains. She gets the tea and some biscuits, and sits with TIM at the table.)* **Read the paper. I'll not blather any more.**

TIM: I don't read newspapers.

MRS. McNULTY: **Is that how you drink your tea?**

TIM: What . . . ?

MRS. McNULTY: **Not a drop of milk? Nor any sugar at all? Well, have a biscuit, at least.**

TIM: Thank you.

MRS. McNULTY: **Will ya be votin' for Bobby Kennedy for President? He's going to run some day. I'm sure he will.** *(Pause)* **And why didn't ya stay in Donegal, if you're so** determined to be hidin' your head in the sand?

TIM: *(Re: the biscuits.)* **May I have another?**

MRS. McNULTY: *(Pushes the plate to him.)* **Must ya even ask?**

TIM: **I was well brought up.** *(Pause. Warm and cozy.)* **Get away every summer, do you?**

MRS. McNULTY: **I had never left the twenty-six counties before last year. Will ya be wantin' one egg or two with your kippers?**

TIM: **Two. And a glass of Guinness.**

MRS. McNULTY: **Aha! He's got a taste for it!**

TIM: **Been living on the stuff.**

MRS. McNULTY: **And you so well brought up.**

TIM: **You thumb a ride, you get three or four miles down the road, and then part company.**

MRS. McNULTY: **In a pub.**

TIM: **And I can't resist your Irish hospitality.**

MRS. McNULTY: **Then you will be stoppin', after all!**

TIM: **I want to . . . I have to . . .**

MRS. McNULTY: **To what?**

TIM: **It's time I started . . .**

MRS. McNULTY: **. . . time you started south again, is it? It's time you . . . !**

TIM: **I'm going east from here.**

MRS. McNULTY: **. . . time you went runnin' again, spinnin' with the dial of a crazy compass, reelin' through the storm! My boys go off — oh, yes they do — but it's a better life, at least, that *they* go lookin' for!**

TIM: **I'd trade places with them if I could.**

MRS. McNULTY: *(As if to say "gotcha!")* **Then you *do* know what you want!**

TIM: *(Ironic, yet passionate.)* **I want to be a Donegal Irishman! To be a potato-eating, sheep-shearing simpleton who lilts away his life in Gaelic! To free myself forever from that . . . that *world* out there you find so glorious!**

MRS. McNULTY: **And when I've saved enough, I'll be off again. Donegal, indeed!**

TIM: It ain't exactly Hackensack.

MRS. McNULTY: My next trip is to the Holy Land.

TIM: *(No irony.)* You'll like it there.

MRS. McNULTY: Have you been to Jerusalem, then?

TIM: I've been doing the Grand Tour. This is my last stop. I was heading for Shannon when . . .

MRS. McNULTY: Oh, well, if it's a plane you have to catch, then . . . !

TIM: No. No hurry.

MRS. McNULTY: Have you been away long?

TIM: Over a year.

MRS. McNULTY: Ah, Brian is so happy now. *(Pause)* You've changed your plans, have you?

TIM: You're proud of Brian.

MRS. McNULTY: He's a fine man! And what a house! With a swimmin' pool, and divin' boards, and . . . !

TIM: I'm going to Sweden.

MRS. McNULTY: But not until tomorrow, surely?

TIM: Is he ever coming home?

MRS. McNULTY: For a visit. "One day," he promised me last summer, "I'll be comin' for a visit."

TIM: I was just at the post office. I got a letter. *(Puts the letter on the table.)*

MRS. McNULTY: From Sweden, is it?

TIM: From my mother.

MRS. McNULTY: But she must want you home. Surely she does.

TIM: Surely.

MRS. McNULTY: Yet you turn . . . you turn and run off and you leave her? You're selfish, Timothy! You're an unfeelin' boy . . . unfeelin', and selfish, and cruel! *(TIM gets up, goes into the sitting room, and starts putting on his socks. MRS. McNULTY follows.)* You close off your heart, and you run off to the ends of the earth without a thought for . . . Oh, dear Lord, the bread is burnin'! *(Rushes back into the kitchen, takes the bread out of the oven.)* Have you ever tasted home-baked soda bread? *(TIM stops putting on his soggy socks. He contemplates them for a moment, then takes them off. While MRS. McNULTY, assuming he's dressing to leave, talks in the kitchen, TIM takes off his pants, gets Brian's robe from the chest, and puts it on.)* **Let's see ... let's see. A little dark, maybe. No ... no, it isn't charred a bit! You are not to leave till it's cool enough to ...! Ha! But *I* have no right to keep ya. 'Tis a fine loaf, though, a perfect loaf. You'll never taste a better. You dressin' to go and ... oh, wasn't it I myself that drove you out? Mmmm ... with some butter melted in ...! Surely it was ... it was myself. The butter's fresh, and I have apricot preserves.** *(Picks up the letter.)* **A grand place, America, grand and prosperous. With back-yard pools and ... But you'll not find soda bread the likes of *this* in any of your fifty states! Your mother has a graceful hand. And there's feelin' in it. You can see there's feelin'. Brian told me when he left he would be comin' home again, he would be comin' home to stay. "When I've made my fortune," he said. His "fortune," is it! Ah, those years away ... all those years have changed him.** *(Reads the letter idly.)* **". . . an order to report . . ." A graceful hand, she has. "To report for induction into . . ."** *(Realizing)* **A graceful and a feelin' hand. No, Brian isn't ...! But can it really be he isn't Irish any more? One day ... maybe one day he'll be comin' for a visit.** *(TIM, in Brian's robe, enters the kitchen and slices himself a piece of bread; MRS. McNULTY smiles.)*

THE END

AULD LANG SYNE
or, I'LL BET YOU THINK THIS
PLAY IS ABOUT YOU
by Beverly Creasey

AULD LANG SYNE
OR, I'LL BET YOU THINK THIS
PLAY IS ABOUT YOU

by
BEVERLY CREASEY

Beverly Creasey, actor, choreographer, and playwright, has performed with the Repertory Four of New York and is now president of Playwrights' Platform of Boston. *Auld Lang Syne* premiered at the Playwrights' Platform Marathon Workshop Festival in May, 1984, and was subsequently presented by the Outer Cape Performance Center of Cape Cod.

Production Suggestions

You will have a lot of fun playing these two characters who have vastly different personal tempos. The actor who plays Charles has the fewer lines but the more difficult role. The challenge of the role is to play an "aloof, disassociated, disconnected" character without boring or alienating the audience. A positive approach to solving the problem is to discover what Charles *does* care about — and what he *does* connect with — and then let him concentrate on those obsessions so completely that Anna must practically assault him physically to get his attention.

Address all inquiries concerning performances, readings, or reprinting of this work *or any portion thereof* to Beverly Creasey at 164 Brayton Road, Brighton, MA 02135. For details, see "Part II: Securing Rights for Your Production," pages 223 to 232.

AULD LANG SYNE
OR, I'LL BET YOU THINK THIS PLAY IS ABOUT YOU

by
BEVERLY CREASEY

The action takes place at the present in late afternoon in front of a museum in Boston.

Characters:
ANNA — a fashionable woman
CHARLES — a well-dressed man

Setting: *The script demands no scenery.*

AT RISE: CHARLES has just left work and is waiting in front of the museum. ANNA walks by, hesitates, decides to recognize him, and speaks.

ANNA:　Charles, I thought you lived in New York. Last I saw your mother, she said you had taken a position in the city, fundraising or endowments or something, but that was last year when I saw her. You're here! What a surprise!

CHARLES:　Anna, I wouldn't have recognized you. Oh. Oh yes, I moved back four weeks, maybe a month ago. I didn't like New York.

ANNA:　But it was your dearest wish to be in New York. And you didn't like it?

CHARLES:　No. I um didn't um like ... it. It didn't ... work out.

ANNA:　Howard Rader moved to New York. I bumped into his wife at a matinee not long ago. He moved his whole family to White Plains so he could do research at Mt. Sinai and instead of finding a cancer cure, he had a coronary. She said the pace was maddening. Her blood pressure couldn't stand it either so back they came. They had to start completely over, making connections, setting up another house. Did you find it difficult moving back?

CHARLES: Rader?

ANNA: Howard Rader. Catherine Rader, and the three little Raders. There are probably more by now. Charles, we used to go to the theatre together all the time.

CHARLES: Oh. I guess...

ANNA: Charles, the four of us saw the *Man of La Mancha* where Don Quixote fell into the orchestra pit. They stopped the performance and Howard went backstage to offer medical assistance. Howard, who does DNA research and knows nothing about broken bones... you thought he was a pompous... oh never mind.

CHARLES: Umhh. I guess I know who you mean. Where do they live now?

ANNA: Wayland, not far from me, but that's not important. Where they live is neither here nor there. This conversation isn't about the Raders... I, I thought of you today, at breakfast. I think I had a premonition... of meeting you this afternoon. A precognition I mean, I'm sure of it. I have them all the time... but you know that. You always made fun of me when I warned you about a premonition.

CHARLES: I don't remember.

ANNA: Charles! We fought round and round about it. I wouldn't want to drive because I'd have foreseen an accident, or I'd insist you change your route to work. Charles, are you in there? No. No. I am sorry I said that. It's wonderful to see you again. There's absolutely no point in bringing up these things. I'm glad you've let it go. I've hoped for years that if we met again, you'd have left all the terrible fights behind.

CHARLES: Well I have. I remember very little actually. I wish I could recall last year or last week even but I seem unable to retain things... you're remarried? Someone told me you were, my mother, I think.

ANNA: No, I almost did but... No, I'm not remarried. Are you?

CHARLES: No. Actually no. I'm afraid, as you well know, I'm

not good at marriage. But . . .

ANNA: No. You mustn't think that. You were good at it. It was the marriage that wasn't good. Don't blame yourself at all.

CHARLES: I don't blame myself. I don't even think about it. I try to live apart from the rest of the world. It's insane out there. I just don't care.

ANNA: You weren't so cynical before.

CHARLES: I'm older.

ANNA: Well I'm not . . . cynical I mean. I'd be afraid to miss something if I shut myself away like you. It's cowardly to hide . . .

CHARLES: It's all right. You can call me cowardly. I don't let anything bother me.

ANNA: Fidge.

CHARLES: Come again?

ANNA: Fidge. It just came to me. I used to call you "Fidge."

CHARLES: You did?

ANNA: Charles! Don't you remember anything? I called you "Fidge" because you always fussed and fidgeted so at concerts and plays.

CHARLES: I don't go to many concerts, and plays are for babies. I imagine I do fidget at times but I never think about it. You see Anna, when you've adjusted to a life, you know what's right for you; you know what's comfortable. You don't notice the things another person might. You become accustomed to your bad habits, and you even grow fond of them.

ANNA: I wish I had understood then about you. I wish I had understood a lot of things. I'm so sorry for what happened to us. *(Starts to cry.)* **Please forgive me.** *(Holds CHARLES.)*

CHARLES: *(Extricates himself.)* **Anna, for what? For heaven sake. It's all forgotten.** *Literally* **forgotten! . . . I can't see that there's anything to forgive. It's not important. Really.**

ANNA: Please, Charles. I do remember, and it is important

to me. Maybe we have met today for a reason. I did foresee it after all. Maybe this is our chance to undo something, my chance to tell you something.

CHARLES: Hey, there's nothing to undo. Anna, you're making more of this than there is. We've met purely by accident. We live near the same city, we were bound to meet sooner or later. It's nothing more than coincidence.

ANNA: You can believe it's coincidence if you want, but I needed to see you. I've wanted to for a long time. I've been thinking about us, about what happened. I need to tell you something.

CHARLES: Tell me something?

ANNA: Yes.

CHARLES: Now?

ANNA: Yes.

CHARLES: After all these years what could be so important? Did you find my Swiss Army knife.?

ANNA: Aghhh!

CHARLES: Little joke. You're too sensitive, Anna. You should have forgotten long ago, about whatever it is you think is so important now. You shouldn't let memories hurt you. Just let them go.

ANNA: *Like you?* Like you let memories go? You C-O-W-A-R-D! You let life go. You let me go. You could have tried to stop me but you didn't care enough. Is nothing worth keeping to you?

CHARLES: My Swiss Army knife.

ANNA: You're making this a joke because you don't want to hear what I have to say.

CHARLES: Please, someone will hear us and think we're still married.

ANNA: Oh, please let me start over again. I'm sorry. I don't want recriminations. I just want to tell you something. It's I who has to apologize. *(She is practically on top of CHARLES.)*

CHARLES: Hey. You're making me very uncomfortable. In fact, I can't really stay... Actually I'm meeting some friends . . . they're meeting me. If they saw this . . . they don't know about you . . . oh, they know I was married but I'd rather keep it uncomplicated. I don't want to hurt your feelings but I can't do this. I don't know what to say. This is so awkward.

ANNA: For God's sake, Charles. I'm not going to embarrass you in front of your friends. It's not like I'm going to shoot you. After two long years, I just want you to listen for one short minute. Can you give me one minute?

CHARLES: Couldn't you just shoot me?

ANNA: You always winced at my little talks, didn't you. You're afraid of the strangest things.

CHARLES: I try to keep an open mind.

ANNA: Open at both ends.

CHARLES: I remember things.

ANNA: What things?

CHARLES: Lots of things.

ANNA: I can see that I'm not being fair to you. It wasn't fair before either to push and push for what I wanted.

CHARLES: Sure it was.

ANNA: No. When I didn't get it, I condemned you for my disappointment.

CHARLES: I never felt condemned.

ANNA: What did you think happened then?

CHARLES: I thought you were bored.

ANNA: Bored? That's all you thought it was? No questions, no protests, no feelings?

CHARLES: I had feelings.

ANNA: Did you? I couldn't tell.

CHARLES: Well it doesn't matter now anyway.

ANNA: It does. Because I thought you didn't care for me. I left because of it. Why didn't you care for me?

CHARLES: I did.

ANNA: Then why didn't you ever come to school? You never even knew what I did there. You hated socializing with the faculty and every time you saw my boss you'd extend your hand and you'd ask, "Have we met?"

CHARLES: It didn't seem important. It was just your boss.

ANNA: What about my father?

CHARLES: What about Lloyd?

ANNA: Floyd, Charles, Floyd! Oh Charles, it's been an obsession with me lately. I see you on the street. I see you in the morning on the train. It's not you of course.

CHARLES: It's just one of your precognitions.

ANNA: It was not. I phoned your mother this morning I was so desperate. She said you came back to Boston to work at the museum and I might catch you after work today. I thought of phoning you first but I wouldn't have known what to say. Not that I'm doing so well face to face. *(She drops her bag.)*

CHARLES: But here you are. What a surprise.

ANNA: What a shock you mean. Why do things never work out as planned?

CHARLES: What do you do at school?

ANNA: I plan class reunions.

CHARLES: I hope they come off better than this one.

ANNA: Yes they do . . . It seems so futile now. It's lost it's . . .

CHARLES: Meaning?

ANNA: No.

CHARLES: Patina?

ANNA: No.

CHARLES: Luster?

ANNA: No. No. Charles. No. My feelings haven't changed about what happened. They've just changed about what's happening now. I simply wanted to say I'm sorry for misjudging you, for misplacing my trust. I thought words were so important and they aren't at all. I wanted to hear the words . . . and I did hear them from someone else . . . When I finally heard them, they didn't mean anything because it was too late. That's all. Do you see?

CHARLES: Not really.

ANNA: Naturally you don't see. You couldn't see the entire

-97-

Morman Tabernacle Choir if they marched into your bedroom and sang the "Ode to Joy" directly into your ear.

CHARLES: How does that go?

ANNA: You dullard. I'm sorry Charles, I always forget that under this aloof, disassociated, disconnected exterior is an aloof, disassociated, disconnected interior! You're so disconnected, you didn't even notice I was gone until I came back to get my things. You didn't even notice I was missing. All you missed was your precious Swiss Army knife. And I'll tell you something. It wasn't for you, it was for Howard. I didn't get it for you, I got it for Howard . . . Howard Rader. You see, I'm spelling it out for you now. Howard and me. Howard and I . . . Please remember me to your mother. It's been lovely bumping into you. Have a good life and be well. *(Exit)*

CHARLES: Howard Rader has my Swiss Army knife?

THE END

WIDOWS

by
STEPHEN GRECCO

Steve Grecco, who teaches drama and creative writing in the English Department at Penn State, has won the Shubert Playwriting Award, two Earplay Awards, and two NEA writing fellowships. He writes for radio and the stage. *Widows* was given a reading at the Tyrone Guthrie Theatre's Noon Series in 1978 and was broadcast by the National Radio Theatre in 1982.

Production Suggestions

Widows presents its performers with the problem of acting old age. Young actors should avoid the generalized, senile decrepitude which too often passes for "old age." To play Mrs. Watts and Agnes believably, you should study the script carefully to learn about the specific physical, vocal, and personality characteristics of the two women. You should also observe some women in their late fifties and seventies in order to find actual behaviors to imitate or adapt.

Address all inquiries concerning performances, readings, or reprinting of this work *or any portion thereof* to Stephen Grecco at 1103 S. Garner Street, State College, PA 16801. For details, see "Part II: Securing Rights for Your Production" pages 223 to 232.

WIDOWS

by
STEPHEN GRECCO

The play's action takes place on an autumn evening in the present in a secluded area of a small city park.

Characters:
MRS. WATTS — in her late seventies
AGNES — in her late fifties

Setting; *A park bench.*

AT RISE: MRS. WATTS can be seen sitting on a park bench, absently nibbling on a cookie. A small brown paper bag rests in her lap. Presently AGNES enters. She spots the bench and decides to sit down opposite MRS. WATTS.

AGNES: *(Exhaling audibly.)* **Feels so darn good to sit down.** *(Short pause, turns to MRS. WATTS.)* **You know, you get the best view of the river from this here bench. My name's Agnes; what's yours?**

MRS. WATTS: **Mrs. Watts.** *(Proffers bag.)* **Have a cookie.**

AGNES: **Why, thank you, Mrs. Watts.** *(Chews)* **Mmmm. Delicious. Something tells me you made these yourself.**

MRS. WATTS: **Nope. Store bought. Never baked so much as a muffin in all my seventy-seven years.** *(Short pause.)* **Hubby used to take care of the bread and cakes — 'fore he passed away.**

AGNES: **So — you're a widow, too.**

MRS. WATTS: **Been one for over fifty years.**

AGNES: **Fifty years. My, that's a long time. Uh ... how did your husband ... pass away?**

MRS. WATTS: **Well, can't rightly say he passed away. He ... jumped off a viaduct during an unexpected snowstorm. Don't suppose I ever met another person with such a tender set o' nerves.**

AGNES: Snow made your husband nervous?

MRS. WATTS: Snow, rain, sunshine. You name it. The slightest disturbance would send him leaping to his feet. One day I came back to the apartment and found him locked up in the linen closet. Told me there was a strange buzzin' sound comin' from the bathroom. *(Slight pause.)* Turned out the handle on the john didn't work properly and the water kept on flushin'.

AGNES: I knew a man like that. He had a stroke one morning when his alarm clock went off.

MRS. WATTS: Roland — that was my late husband's name — Roland had a special fondness for talking birds. Gave him such a heap o' pleasure to hear them recite the short poems he wrote. At one point we had six parakeets, two myhna birds, and one parrot in our living room. Trouble was, he was too scared to go near them and I had to clean the cages myself. *(Sighs)* But, when you're in love, you don't mind the inconvenience.

AGNES: Were there any children?

MRS. WATTS: No, we didn't have time for that. Rolly ... expired six weeks after the ceremony. *(Short pause.)* He never should have gotten married. Some people just ain't cut out for it. Poor dear. Often wonder about him and try to imagine how my life might have been if he wasn't so ... so ...

AGNES: Jumpy?

MRS. WATTS: That's a good word. Rolly had an unusually small funeral. Bein' so nervous and all, it was difficult for him to make friends. Still, the minister had some kind words to say about him. Said that if it wasn't for his nervous affliction, Rolly would have made an outstanding watchmaker. That's what he wanted to do — make watches. He even went to watchmaking school, but for obvious reasons that didn't work out.

AGNES: Why do you suppose he was so nervous?

MRS. WATTS: That's always been a mystery to me, 'though I

suspect it had something to do with the snoring problem he had as a child. Seems his family tried to break him of the habit by locking a stray dog in his room at night, a mangy German shepherd that became vicious whenever it heard strange noises.

AGNES: My late husband had trouble sleeping when he first became a policeman. He'd often lie awake nights, waiting for an emergency call. Thank God, no call ever came. The station had orders not to put him on the night beat anymore unless martial law was declared. He suffered somewhat from night-blindness, which more or less meant he couldn't shoot too straight once the sun went down.

MRS. WATTS: We both agreed to have my border collie put to sleep before we tied the knot. Rolly had this amazing fear of large dogs. Small ones, too.

AGNES: During his first Christmas on the force, Bruno accidentally shot an elderly woman on her way home from midnight mass. Grazed her on the right hip. Nothing serious.

MRS. WATTS: Had that collie dog for well over ten years. Cried myself to sleep for the next three nights.

AGNES: He was almost suspended from the force after that incident. Third time it happened. The woman threatened to sue if action wasn't taken.

MRS. WATTS: As we were walkin' out of the vet's office, tears started streamin' down Roland's face, faster 'an you could count 'em.

AGNES: Lucky for her the chief put Bruno in another precinct. Swore he'd go after her if he lost his job.

MRS. WATTS: Tears o' joy, more 'an likely. Missy made him a total wreck whenever he came to my house accourtin'. Took me forever to figure out his knees was wobblin' out o' dread of that innocent creature than from some cripplin' palsy or the St. Vitus dance.

AGNES: How was Bruno supposed to know the woman was

running home to shut off her oven? You'd be suspicious too if you noticed somebody darting from the side door of a church at one in the morning with poinsettia plants under both arms.

MRS. WATTS: Rolly offered to pay the cost of the ... visit. A lovely gesture, I thought, for someone who was on unemployment. I declined his generosity, of course. In them days the charge for the ... service was one dollar and seventy-nine cents, plus tax. *(Slight pause.)* Doctor never mentioned what the tax was for.

AGNES: The woman turned out to be one of those religious fanatics you're always reading about. Prided herself on being the only person in Philadelphia whose potted plants were blessed by a cardinal.

MRS. WATTS: He promised to buy me a stuffed rabbit for my birthday to make up for the loss. I told him it wouldn't be the same. *(Brief sigh.)* Father strongly advised me against marrying Roland. So did mother and her four maiden sisters.

AGNES: My family was overjoyed when I married Bruno because they heard his people had seven illegal wine presses in their basement.

MRS. WATTS: Rolly never touched a drop o' spirits in his entire life — 'though some dim-witted fool was forever trying to slip some hard stuff into his gingerale when he wasn't lookin'. Eventually Roland developed a habit of restin' his palm on the top of his glass or cup.

AGNES: *(Remembers something, laughs.)* Bruno was notorious for spiking drinks.

MRS. WATTS: Got so I had to taste all his liquids before he'd take a sip o' anything.

AGNES: When he was in the Army he and two of his buddies poured a gallon of bootleg whiskey into the fresh fruit punch at the Charleston U.S.O.

MRS. WATTS: Even water. Put a terrific strain on my kidneys.

AGNES: The Army placed the U.S.O. off-limits for the rest of the war, and the woman in charge of the entertainment committee was asked to leave Charleston immediately.

MRS. WATTS: He was such a baby ... The only baby I ever had.

AGNES: Bruno *loved* the Army. He often said he spent the best years of his life in defense of his country.

MRS. WATTS: The Army wouldn't accept Roland. Neither would the other branches. Too skinny. When the recruiter told him that none of the services had a uniform that would fit, Roland, being the patriotic soul that he was, offered to sew his own. *(Short pause.)* They made him take his physical alone.

AGNES: Bruno would never have become a policeman if it wasn't for his experience in the Armed Forces. He had his Army fatigues sealed in an air-tight plastic bag so the moths wouldn't eat them.

MRS. WATTS: Roland was a member of the Cub Scouts for two weeks. Should give him credit for that, I suppose.

AGNES: I was positive Bruno was going to be killed in the war, knowing what a maniac he was for taking chances. In one of his letters he told me he was deliberately driving on the right side of the street, which is the wrong side of the street if you're operating a tank in London. He was such a crazy guy. Once, at the Farmer's Market, he stuck his index finger through forty ripe tomatoes.

MRS. WATTS: A lawyer friend of mine advised me to go to the courthouse and check on his people's records. Thought there might be a history of instability in the family. Only his great uncle Morris seemed peculiar. He was arrested seventeen times for poaching.

AGNES: Bruno was arrested once. He killed an antelope with an empty beer bottle. In July.

MRS. WATTS: Other than that, his family looked pretty straight. On paper, anyway.

AGNES: It was a tame one, at Animal Wonderland. He told the owner the antelope tried to bite him. The State

Troopers were called and they made us pay for a new antelope.

MRS. WATTS: We went camping in Canada on our honeymoon. One night Roland claimed that a grizzly bear came into the tent and stared him in the face for thirty-five minutes. I told him it was probably a dream, but he refused to fall asleep until I surrounded the tent with pieces of broken glass. *(Pause)* If he had lived he would have been eighty years old next Tuesday. It's easy to remember 'cause he . . . passed away on his birthday.

AGNES: That's amazing. Bruno died the day before his. Happened at the Police Station during muster. Dropped to the floor just as the sergeant called his name. Everybody laughed because they thought he was clowning around. *(Slight pause.)* I still have his revolver in my jewelry box.

MRS. WATTS: Used to be you could see the cemetery from here if you squinted real hard. Now it's next to impossible ever since they put up that big sign advertising country fried chicken.

AGNES: Some people have no respect for the dead. What a place to stick a billboard.

MRS. WATTS: I wrote a letter of complaint to the mayor, but he never bothered to answer.

AGNES: *(Ironical laugh.)* He prob'bly owns the chicken place.

MRS. WATTS: *(Somberly)* He does. *(Sighs)* Sun's goin' down.

AGNES: *(Deep sigh.)* Yeah.

MRS. WATTS: Air's gettin' cool.

AGNES: Yeah. *(Slaps her arm.)* Darn bugs startin' to bite.

MRS. WATTS: Eat you half alive you give them half a chance.

AGNES: They *sure* would.

MRS. WATTS: *(Proffers bag.)* Have another cookie.

AGNES: Thanks, but I'll pass. How 'bout yourself?

MRS. WATTS: No — I'm afraid that's it, for tonight. *(MRS. WATTS closes the paper bag, brushes a crumb from her lap. AGNES adjusts the beret in her hair. Both women look off into the distance.)*

– 105 –

BUG SWATTER

by
JOEL SELMEIER

Joel Selmeier has been playwright-in-residence at Lake Erie College and at Ohio Northern University. He founded the Playwrights project at the Cincinnati Playhouse in the Park and has critiqued plays at new play festivals. His documentary *La Tirana* was funded by the National Endowment for the Humanities. He wrote *Bug Swatter* in 1984.

Production Suggestions

Business with props forms a counterpoint to the real action in *Bug Swatter*. For purposes of invention and timing, it is important you start using the real props early in your rehearsal period.

Address all inquiries concerning performances, readings, or reprinting of this work *or any portion thereof* to Joel Selmeier, 2446 Turnberry Dr., Cincinnati, OH 45242. For details, see "Part II: Securing Rights for Your Production," pages 223 to 232.

BUG SWATTER

by
JOEL SELMEIER

The action takes place in the backyard of David Hochmuth's suburban home, on a summer evening in the present.

Characters:
DAVID HOCHMUTH — a real estate investor
ROBIN — a career graduate student

Setting: *The backyard is cluttered with the remains of a neighborhood picnic.*

AT RISE: Wearing golf clothes, DAVID enters stage right dragging a charcoal grill. Something on it comes apart — perhaps the handle, or its leg. He stops to examine it, then exits. He returns with a screwdriver as ROBIN enters carrying two full garbage bags.

DAVID: *(Crossing to barbecue and getting under it to work on it.)* **Wonderful out here, isn't it?**

ROBIN: *(Dropping a garbage bag, swatting a mosquito on her neck, and looking at its remains on her hand.)* **Yea. Wonderful. If you like having your blood sucked.** *(She drops the other bag and spends a second following the path of a flying mosquito until she claps her hands together on it. As she looks at and wipes off its remains.)* **Don't any of your friends own blue jeans?**

DAVID: **Come here.** *(Pause)* **Come here.** *(She crosses to him. He grabs her, pulls her down to where he is, and kisses her.)*

ROBIN: **I never saw anyone more in his element than you forking flaming steaks and putting them on your friends plates.**

DAVID: **I'm a damn good barbecuer.**

ROBIN: **You are so at ease with all your friends walking around eating and swatting bugs. That's really you. That's where you belong.**

DAVID: I'm a damn good bug swatter.

ROBIN: Even if you are stuck up about it.

DAVID: *(Going back to work on the grill.)* Did I pay enough attention to you?

ROBIN: No.

DAVID: Sorry. *(He belches.)*

ROBIN: You're so sincere. *(He smiles stupidly and nods in agreement.)* You were too engrossed in talking re-zoning to know I was there.

DAVID: I noticed where you were, but I was busy being happy. I think everyone was happy tonight.

ROBIN: Did you talk about anything other than the re-zoning?

DAVID: Golf.

ROBIN: You're such a *wasp.* You invite the whole neighborhood over, get them half drunk, and talk nothing but business and golf. I don't think there was a single issue oriented person here tonight.

DAVID: Normally I avoid people who debate issues with strangers.

ROBIN: *(Rising)* What am I doing here? Downtown I have everything in such good order. My neighbors talk about music and art and issues. My apartment is in walking distance of the library and the university. The bus went everywhere I ever wanted to go until this. Now you have to come and pick me up to get me way the heck out here.

DAVID: I don't mind coming to get you.

ROBIN: Next you'll be trying to get me to get a car so I can get myself way the heck out here. They'd probably cut off my scholarship if I looked rich enough to own a car.

DAVID: Don't put it in your name and you won't have to worry about it. I'll buy one cheap enough for you to feel comfortable in and we'll call it yours.

ROBIN: What'd I tell you? You're already trying to get me to get a car.

DAVID: As long as you've brought it up, it does seem like it'd be better if you didn't do so much walking for a while.

(She sighs, shakes her head, and looks away.) **What cha' lookin' at?**

ROBIN: Hm? Oh. This. You were right. With the way they laid this out, it does need flowers. I guess we should have planted some.

DAVID: It doesn't look bad now that the stalks are mown down. Boy, that would really have made us look official, wouldn't it have. "Hello, Scott, Julie. Yes. Aren't they nice flowers. Robin planted them."

ROBIN: Official?

DAVID: Well, they're not used to seeing me with a woman. When you and I met, I dropped out of sight. I was always busy weekends. Now all of a sudden I invite them over and here you are serving macaroni salad. Now that's official. Serving macaroni salad is official.

ROBIN: Official what?

DAVID: An official couple. Planting flowers would just have been putting a brass stamp on it. Then there would have been no doubt in anyone's mind. Did you notice how people asked you, "And where do you live?"

ROBIN: I guess they were more polite with you. Pete just came out and asked if we were still doing it under separate roofs.

DAVID: That guy is unbelievable. I suppose I should be surprised that's all he asked. That is all he asked, isn't it?

ROBIN: *(Lying)* Yea. *(He looks at her.)* **Are we going to put all this away tonight?**

DAVID: Of course.

ROBIN: Of course.

DAVID: Otherwise the raccoons would go hungry. They can't find it unless it's in garbage cans. Did you tell anyone?

ROBIN: Who would I have told? I don't know any of them.

DAVID: When women get together, something chemical happens that forces them to all tell each other everything. The impulse is particularly pronounced in pregnant women.

ROBIN: I didn't say anything. Who did you tell? Or should

I ask how many you told?

DAVID: No one. It would have been too much of a shock for them. They all know me. It was enough for them to see me throwing a party with you as hostess without my saying, "We're having a baby shower and you're all invited." I hadn't thought of that. You'll have one of those, won't you?

ROBIN: A baby shower?

DAVID: Even socialist mothers need *something* for a baby, don't they? I mean, socialist babies don't come equipped with all that stuff, do they? Even if they do, his father's a capitalist, so he probably wouldn't come *completely* equipped.

ROBIN: I can't have a baby shower. Then we would talk and they'd figure out this was only temporary

DAVID: No more temporary than half the couples who swear it's forever for better or worse. Probably less temporary. Besides, you don't know. You might grow to like having a child in a house with me.

ROBIN: What have you talked me into?

DAVID: Didn't you have a good time tonight?

ROBIN: Yea. I had a good time.

DAVID: And didn't everyone else have a good time?

ROBIN: Yes.

DAVID: That's what you got yourself into. That's what suburbia is all about. Out here everyone just always has a good time.

ROBIN: All I wanted was to get a Ph.D. in Poli Sci. A month ago I thought just trying to do that and teach a few classes was a lot to think about. I didn't know what complicated was. Now I wake up at night and I get really worried.

DAVID: Next time wake me up.

ROBIN: Did you ever try to wake you up? You don't wake up. You say you're awake, but you're not awake. You don't remember it in the morning.

DAVID: How do you know?

ROBIN: Do you remember if I woke you up last night?

DAVID: You didn't wake me up last night.

ROBIN: That's what I mean. I was awake last night. A million of your neighbors were going to be coming over today and I was going to meet all of them. I felt like a ship about to get christened. And the most I could get out of you was interrupted breathing. What have I let you talk me into?

DAVID: You're going to love it. You'll see.

ROBIN: How do you know?

DAVID: I have observed other mothers.

ROBIN: I'm different.

DAVID: That's for damn sure ... *(She looks at him and he quickly gets out of that inappropriate comment by raising his hands and saying.)* but I wouldn't have loved you if you weren't.

ROBIN: *(She continues to look at him. She turns away shaking her head and, carrying the garbage bags, walks Offstage Left muttering to herself.)* I never asked for this. I never wanted anyone to expect anything from me. I never wanted to get my blood sucked. All I wanted was to work on my degree, have a few friends, see a movie once in a while with some interesting guy I'd never seen before and would never have to see again ... *(She exits. She returns without the garbage bags.)*

DAVID: So tell me the latest version of how Pete's secretary doesn't understand him.

ROBIN: *(Crossing Stage.)* What?

DAVID: His story. His line.

ROBIN: What line?

DAVID: Oh, never mind. This is what I get for buying the cheapest grill. The expensive ones were probably made of steel.

ROBIN: *(Exiting Stage Right.)* Never mind what?

DAVID: Hm?

ROBIN: *(Offstage)* Never mind what?

DAVID: Oh. In a minute. I can't talk and fix this at the same time. It's still hot. Fixing a hot barbecue demands as much concentration as carrying nitroglycerin on a pogo stick. Otherwise you burn your hands. *(She re-enters carrying barbecuing tools, salt and pepper shakers, perhaps an iced tea pitcher, etc., and stands waiting impatiently as he works on the barbecue.)* It doesn't demand as much concentration as golf, of course. *(He finishes working on it and stands up.)*

ROBIN: Never mind what?

DAVID: Huh?

ROBIN: What you were talking about? Never mind what?

DAVID: What was I talking about?

ROBIN: Peter.

DAVID: Peter? Now it's "Peter" is it?

ROBIN: What were you going to say?

DAVID: I don't know. What was I talking about?

ROBIN: *(Shouting angrily.)* That's what I'm asking. You started to say something and then you said, "Oh, never mind," and I've been waiting here to find out oh-never-mind what? What were you going to say?

DAVID: *(Moving to her and putting his arms around her.)* Hey, hey. Calm down. It's been such a good evening. And right now it feels really nice to be in love with you. Let's forget about everything else. We don't get to feel like this often enough.

ROBIN: *(Shouting)* Like what? I'm exasperated again.

DAVID: *(He hugs her lifting her off her feet and kisses her so she can't talk. He puts her feet back on the floor, but does not stop kissing her as he bends her over backwards. He keeps her bent over backwrds when he stops kissing her and talks, all of which causes problems for her since her hands are full.)* Whatever I was talking about isn't as important as the fact that we're together right now holding each other, is it? . . . Is it?

ROBIN: I suppose not.

DAVID: Am I paying attention to you?

ROBIN: Yes.

DAVID: Do you feel loved?

ROBIN: Yea.

DAVID: Am I great at making you feel loved or what?

ROBIN: Yea. You're terrific.

DAVID: So are you. So let's forget about it and clean this up and go to bed. *(He lets go of her and resumes work.)*

ROBIN: That's it? You're not going to tell me?

DAVID: I'd rather avoid it.

ROBIN: What is it?

DAVID: It's something that probably shouldn't have worried me but did and I don't want to spoil this evening but I was jealous and I shouldn't have been. OK?

ROBIN: Of who?

DAVID: Peter, heretofore known merely as Pete. Why? Who else handed you a line tonight? Are there others I should be jealous of too?

ROBIN: He didn't hand me a line.

DAVID: Robin. Don't tell me that. That worries me. I know Pete. I know how he works. I know what he was saying to you when you two were over by the bug light. Don't tell me he didn't hand you a line. It just makes me think you're hiding something. But I'd rather you didn't tell me anything. Let's forget about it. I know it's nothing.

ROBIN: It's not nothing if it bothers you.

DAVID: It is tonight because I want to ask you something.

ROBIN: What?

DAVID: This wasn't such a bad night, was it?

ROBIN: What do you mean?

DAVID: I know it's not like having honking horns and sirens and breaking bottles all around you like you do downtown, but you still have your apartment there and all. So you don't feel like you lost your identity by being here, do you?

ROBIN: Only kind of.

DAVID: So that the last weeks here have been all right?

ROBIN: They've been all right.

DAVID: We're going to have a kid, right? ... I know I've asked for a lot already, but I'm going to ask for one more thing, and it'd only have to be for as long as you wanted so you wouldn't have to give up your apartment and lose your identity and all that. But, when our child is born, do you think maybe his mother could have the same last name as his father just long enough for him to be legal? It can be undone anytime you want. You don't have to feel like you're getting swallowed up or anything.

ROBIN: Same last name?

DAVID: I was speaking figuratively. I wasn't suggesting for you to take my name. Keep your own name. Or make up a new one if you want. I just wondered if we couldn't make this legal. Nothing would be different from what we're doing already. It's just a matter of some paper work. I mean, it seemed that as long as we're already doing all the rest of it, it didn't seem like it'd be too hard to kind of give the baby that one extra thing. It'd only take an hour for us to go downtown and do it sometime. *(Pause)* Well, think about it for a while. I won't badger you about it.

ROBIN: *(Quietly. Defeated.)* I'll do it.

DAVID: *(Pause. Solemnly, not believing it.)* You will?

ROBIN: Since you put it that way.

DAVID: You'll marry me?

ROBIN: This must be what a swatted mosquito feels like.

DAVID: Did you say "yes?"

ROBIN: *(Sigh)* Yes.

DAVID: *(Pause. Still solemn. Slowly, haltingly.)* I don't know ... whether ... to kiss you ... or put away the grill.

ROBIN: Put away the grill. I'll kiss you upstairs in a few minutes. *(He nods and crosses to the grill. She exits. He hauls the grill Offstage.)*

THE END

Scripts for Three Actors

FIREWORKS

by
MEGAN TERRY

Megan Terry, a major playwright for The Open Theatre in the 1960s and 70s, now writes for and works with The Omaha Magic Theatre in Nebraska. She wrote *Fireworks* in 1979 on a commission from Actors' Theatre of Louisville.

Production Suggestions

The players, their personal props, and their costumes are all that is needed for this production. The crowd and the sound and light of the fireworks can all be imagined; if the actors "see" and "hear" these things, so will the audience.

If you are playing the role of Raymie or Joan, you will need to watch some children very carefully in order to portray them believably without either over-acting or stereotypical behavior. The playwright's advice on this problem is: "Direct the actors to look for the child within themselves: to discover this quality and project. I don't believe it is necessary to change voices, or to play 'at' being a child. It may be best to put the children's ages in the program to save audience confusion at the outset."

Address all inquiries concerning performances, readings, or reprinting of this work **or any portion thereof** to the playwright's agent, Elisabeth Marton, 96 Fifth Avenue, New York, NY 10011. For details, see "Part II: Securing Rights for Your Production," pages 223 to 232.

For more information about Megan Terry, read *Women in American Theatre* by Helen Krich Chinoy and Linda Walsh Jenkins (T.C.G. Book, 1987), pages 285 to 292, and Phyllis Jane Rose's article in *The Dictionary of Literary Biography* (Gale Research, 1981), Volume 7, Part 2, pages 277 to 290.

FIREWORKS

by
MEGAN TERRY

The action takes place in July, 1946, in Green Lake, a city park in Seattle, Washington.

Characters:

DAD, 35 — recently returned from military service in the Pacific
RAYMIE, 9 — his son
JOAN, 11 — his daughter

AT RISE: DAD, a muscular man of medium height, picks his way through the crowds at a beach. He is carrying a picnic basket; a beach blanket is thrown over one shoulder. He holds RAYMIE, a boy of nine, by the hand. The boy wears an officer's overseas cap with Captain's bars and he carries a lit sparkler in his free hand. The cap is too big for him and from time to time it falls over his eyes causing him to trip on other people's legs and blankets. (The crowd at the beach may be imagined by the actors.) JOAN, a girl of eleven, follows — hopping over obstructions. She wears a white cowboy hat, red T-shirt and white shorts. Two six-guns in white holsters ride on her hips. Silver bullets line the back of the gun belt. She practices drawing and shooting as she moves. Her guns are loaded with caps. Firecrackers go off at random. There is the occasional whoosh of a small rocket and swirling light from Roman candles. DAD is dressed in a short-sleeved jungle fatigue shirt and officer's tropical slacks from World War II. He has great energy and genuine warmth in his voice. He radiates health and strength.

DAD: *(Putting down basket, he reaches in breast pocket for cigarettes and lighter.)* **I'm having a nicotine fit.**

RAYMIE: **Quack, quack, I'm going to duck out of here.**

JOAN: **Stop it.**

RAYMIE: **Quack, quack, I'm going to duck out of here.**

JOAN: **You make me feel ferocious.**

RAYMIE: **You make me feel ducky!**

DAD: Hey you guys, be nice. *(He spreads out beach blanket.)* I didn't fight the war just to come home to listen to you argue. Joanie, don't point guns at your brother.

JOAN: Sorry Dad. He gets on my nerves. *(Helping to smooth out beach blanket.)*

RAYMIE: I thought you didn't have nerves like "other girls." *(They all sit on blanket and face the audience. They look out toward the lake. In the middle of the lake is a barge from which the fireworks will be set off.)*

JOAN: I don't. Only when you . . .

DAD: Listen, Chicken Little!

JOAN: *(Lowering her guns.)* OK. OK.

DAD: Come here punkin. You hungry? What's this Grandma made for us? *(Unpacking picnic basket.)*

JOAN: Chicken, cooked in butter.

DAD: Real butter?

RAYMIE: Dripping with real butter.

DAD: I haven't had real butter in four years. *(Handing around plates, etc.)*

RAYMIE: Yippie!! I can eat two ducks.

JOAN: That's enough about ducks.

RAYMIE: That's enough out of you, dopey!

JOAN: Daddy!

DAD: *(To RAYMIE.)* You want a backhand?

RAYMIE: No, Dad.

DAD: Be nice.

JOAN: Pass the potato salad.

DAD: I've never seen so many people at Greenlake before.

JOAN: There's almost as many people here as were on the streets V-J Day.

DAD: Were you downtown then?

JOAN: Oh Dad, you should have seen it. Everybody was hugging and kissing.

RAYMIE: And they didn't even know each other.

JOAN: Three soldiers and ten sailors hugged me.

RAYMIE: You're telling stories.

JOAN: They did, too.

RAYMIE: It was Peter Ferris in his Scout uniform.

JOAN: Hey Dad, did you know I helped shoot the Japs in the two-man sub that was captured in Puget Sound?

RAYMIE: Those are just cap guns, you dumb Nazi!

JOAN: They didn't know that. These guns look real! Tojo Toejam!

DAD: Cut that out. I'm not going to tell you kids again.

RAYMIE: Did you see the big bomb drop, Dad?

JOAN: Did you see the mushroom cloud? We saw it on *March of Time* at the movies.

RAYMIE: Did you see the people melted into their own shadows on the sidewalk?

JOAN: Will the fireworks have mushroom shapes?

DAD: They usually look like flowers.

RAYMIE: Did you see it Dad, did you?

DAD: No, I was in Kobe City. It happened long before I landed in Japan.

JOAN: We didn't get to have fireworks for four whole years. We had to paint the headlights on our car black. I love the Fourth of July.

RAYMIE: I love the Fourth of July, too.

JOAN: Do I look different to you, Dad?

DAD: You're taller.

JOAN: Would you know I was your daughter?

DAD: I spotted you on the dock and waved, didn't I?

RAYMIE: Me too, you waved at me too.

DAD: Sure I did.

JOAN: Do I look the same as when you went away — or am I more grown up?

DAD: Well, you have these neat little curves at the corner of your mouth that make you look like you're happy, even when you're not smiling.

JOAN: I do. Where?

DAD: Here, right here, and right here.

RAYMIE: Do I have them too?

DAD: Your ears are smiling. You sure got a lot of hair. *(Massages his head.)* **If we start the massage now maybe you'll keep yours longer than I will.**

JOAN: Benjamin Franklin was bald. Bald men have lots of brains.

DAD: Yes they do, but I'm not bald. Not yet.

JOAN: I think you look real handsome. All the kids at school get jealous when I show them your picture in your captain's uniform.

RAYMIE: How many zeros did you get?

DAD: Ten, maybe twelve.

JOAN: They're going to start the fireworks now. *(She lies back to look at sky.)*

RAYMIE: **Oh, Wow! There it goes.** *(Sound of loud boom as fireworks are lit and shoot up into sky from barge in the lake.)*

DAD: Hey, look at that one. It's like a giant chrysanthemum.

RAYMIE: Yeah.

JOAN: I wish they'd send up a marigold.

DAD: Watch up there. Right up there. Maybe the next one will look like a marigold.

JOAN: Can we have a garden again? We had the best garden before the war. We had an acre of marigolds and glads.

DAD: Two acres.

JOAN: Yeah. Can we do it again?

RAYMIE: I want a greenhouse full of tomatoes.

DAD: You ate all the tomatoes as high as you could reach.

RAYMIE: I did, didn't I? I haven't had any tomatoes since. Can we have a greenhouse again?

DAD: *(To RAYMIE.)* Hey, did you see that redhead?

RAYMIE: What?

DAD: Over there. Look at that redhead. She has a great figure. See there, how she's built.

RAYMIE: Which one?

DAD: She just sat down on that green blanket. I wonder if she's with anyone?

RAYMIE: That woman over there?

DAD: *Yes*. What a figure! She's built like a racehorse.

RAYMIE: She has a funny nose.

DAD: I'm not talking about her nose. I'm showing you how to spot a great figure.

JOAN: Momma has a nice shape.

DAD: She's turning around. I think she saw me.

JOAN: Dad, that woman isn't good looking. Her face is scrambled.

DAD: I'm not looking at her face.

RAYMIE: Momma's beautiful.

JOAN: We can't wait to see Momma when she gets home from work. She's so beautiful.

RAYMIE: Which part of the lady are you looking at, Dad? This part? *(He makes round gestures at his breast.)*

JOAN: I love to watch her get ready in the morning. I love to watch her put on her make-up, and get into her stockings.

DAD: Look at the body on that woman.

JOAN: Why do you want to look at bodies so much?

DAD: If you had a body like that you'd know.

JOAN: I don't want a body like that. It's all lumpy.

DAD: Yeah . . .

JOAN: I'd hate to jiggle when I walk. All the nasty boys make remarks about girls who jiggle when they walk. They say that girls who jiggle will do anything.

DAD: Have you talked to your mother about that?

JOAN: About what?

DAD: You know, about *that*.

JOAN: What about what?

DAD: You're growing up. Wearing a T-shirt three sizes too big doesn't hide everything.

JOAN: Daddy!

DAD: Boys are going to want to sleep with you. Did your mother tell you what to do about it?

JOAN: I don't want to talk about it now. *(She gives a meaningful look at RAYMIE. She chokes and puts down her plate.)*

DAD: Boys are going to ask to sleep with you. Do you know how to protect yourself?

JOAN: I can beat up any boy my age.

DAD: The men down at the fishing dock whistled at you when we walked by.

JOAN: At me? I'm only eleven.

DAD: You're a pretty kid.

JOAN: *(Embarrassed)* Oh Dad! Well, all I can say is, thank God I'm not a redhead.

RAYMIE: Don't swear.

JOAN: I'm not swearing. I'm giving thanks.

RAYMIE: Is that a good figure, Dad?

DAD: Where?

RAYMIE: That blond over there?

DAD: Not bad, but the redhead is still number one.

JOAN: Why don't you bozos look at the sky? That's where real beauty is. You two make me sick.

DAD: We're just healthy, red-blooded American boys.

JOAN: You'd get a bloody nose, if I was bigger.

DAD: Such talk. You're as tall as you're going to be.

JOAN: I'm doing stretching exercises every day. I'm going to join the Marines when I'm eighteen. I know judo. I used that judo you taught me. I dumped a big man on his can. This guy came up to me on the street from behind and put his arms around me. I did that thing you showed me. I reached down like this and grabbed his ankle and pulled. You could hear him bellow all the way to San Francisco when he hit the sidewalk.

RAYMIE: *((Pulling out German luger squirt gun.)* It's true, Dad, she really did it. I shot my squirt gun right in his mouth while he was yelling, then we ran like sixty.

DAD: Where was your mother?

JOAN: At work.

DAD: Things are going to change. You kids aren't going to be on your own anymore.

JOAN: I don't get scared at night. I'm not afraid of anything anymore. **After they captured that Jap submarine in Puget Sound, nothing can scare me, 'cause I'm the fastest draw in Seattle.** *(She whips out both guns and blazes away with her caps.)*

RAYMIE: When you coming back home, Dad?

DAD: I won't be coming back home, Raymie.

RAYMIE: But you *are* home. Why are you living at Gramma's?

DAD: Your mother and I . . . your Mother and I will be getting a divorce.

JOAN: Oh, no. We waited for you to come home from the South Pacific four whole years. You're back in Seattle. You should come home.

DAD: Your mother doesn't want me to.

JOAN: She does, she does. The whole war, all we lived for was you coming back home.

RAYMIE: It's awful to have you home, but not at our house.

JOAN: All the kids in the neighborhood think it's funny. They all love you and they're waiting to see your war souvenirs.

RAYMIE: The flags and swords and the Japanese rifle you captured. All the kids want to see them.

JOAN: We thought when the war was over we could have fun again.

DAD: I did, too. That's all I lived for, too.

RAYMIE: You don't have to be in the Army any more.

DAD: Have to sell the house.

JOAN: But it took us so long to build it . . .

RAYMIE: We all built it together . . .

JOAN: It took us a long time — my whole life, almost. We love our house — why would you want to sell it? I laid lots of the brick for the garage.

DAD: Yes, yes you did.

JOAN: I did. I laid it and I didn't even need plumb line.

DAD: That's right, Joanie — you have a good eye.

JOAN: That brick will stay up forever, won't it, Dad?

DAD: It sure will, punkin.

RAYMIE: Don't you love Mommie anymore?

DAD: She doesn't love me.

RAYMIE: Would you stay married if Mommie was a redhead?

JOAN: All the time you were gone we loved you. She loved you. We couldn't wait to get your letters.

DAD: *She* didn't wait for *me*. She entertained herself with Clint Berry.

RAYMIE: Uncle Clint?

JOAN: *(Kicks RAYMIE.)* When the Japs bombed Pearl Harbor, you remember that day? When it came on the radio, we were all scared, and Mommie was scared and you held Mommie in your arms on the couch right by the radio. And Mommie cried and you told her you'd protect us, and not to be scared.

DAD: I don't remember being on the couch.

JOAN: You held her like this. *(Demonstrating with RAYMIE.)* It made my heart break to see that. *(DAD wipes his eyes.)*

RAYMIE: What's the matter, Dad?

DAD: Nothing. My eyes puddled up, that's all . . .

JOAN: Don't you remember? President Roosevelt came on and said . . .

DAD: Yes . . . I remember . . . I remember . . .

RAYMIE: *(Sotto voce.)* Dad, she's looking at us.

DAD: What?

RAYMIE: You know, Dad, the redhead with that great figure.

DAD: *(Smiles)* I still got it. Sooner or later they give me the eye.

RAYMIE: What is it you do, Dad?

DAD: Watch me.

RAYMIE: But I don't know what to look for.

DAD: It's the way I hold my head and body. And my eyes, my bedroom eyes.

JOAN: Yeah, that's always what Momma said about you.

DAD: She did?

JOAN: She said she married you for your bedroom eyes.

RAYMIE: Do I have bedroom eyes?

DAD: You have refrigerator eyes. *(He pats his stomach.)* **To** develop bedroom eyes you have to stay out of the refrigerator.

JOAN: Hey, look at that one, Dad. That's the best yet. It's still shooting, two, three giant showers of colors. *(Boom)* Oh great — it's making stars. Hey, it's a flag. In the sky, they made a flag!

RAYMIE: See the flag, Dad, see it?

DAD: I see it.

RAYMIE: How do they do it?

DAD: *(Holding them.)* It's good, it's good . . .

JOAN: Oh rats, it's starting to fade.

DAD: It's so good to be home.

JOAN: Dad, won't you come back to our house to live?

DAD: I can't.

RAYMIE: Please.

DAD: No, your mother and I can't make a home together anymore.

JOAN: What good was it then? What good was it your going away to fight?

DAD: I had to. I had to go and fight to protect you.

JOAN: But if you'd stayed home, we'd all still be together. It isn't fair.

DAD: I fought for you and I fought for the flag.

JOAN: But it isn't any fun without Mother.

DAD: I'll get you a new mother.

RAYMIE: We love Mommie.

DAD: I'm sorry. Don't get upset. We'll go phone this great woman I met. You guys can talk to her. She has a really great figure.

RAYMIE: Better than the redhead?

DAD: Better than the redhead. After you get to know her on the phone, I'm going to ask her to marry me. You'll love her.

JOAN: Does she know about us?

DAD: We're going to tell her. Come on. Let's find a phone.

JOAN: I hate to talk on the phone.

RAYMIE: Where did you meet her?

DAD: In the Phillipines.

RAYMIE: Is she a Filipino?

DAD: No, a Bostonian.

RAYMIE: What's that?

DAD: Someone from Boston, Massachusetts. We live on the Pacific Ocean. Boston is on the Atlantic Ocean, clear across the United States.

RAYMIE: How did she get to the Phillipines?

DAD: The Army sent her. She was in the WACs.

JOAN: Weren't you in Boston?

DAD: Cambridge. That's where the Army sent me to Navigation School. Your old man is a Harvard man. *(Uses Boston accent.)*

JOAN: You didn't meet till you were both in the South Pacific?

DAD: We met right after the invasion of Hollandia.

JOAN: Just like the movies?

DAD: I was born lucky.

JOAN: Did you date?

DAD: I took her out on my boat whenever General Kruger was away, which was most of the time.

JOAN: Does Mommie know she was on your boat?

DAD: Hey, look at that. Up to the right. That's triple burst. Look at the colors change. *(They watch a moment. DAD stands.)* Come on, kids, let's pack up and go phone her. You'll love her. Come on, the fireworks are nearly over. We don't want to get stuck in this crowd.

JOAN: I don't want to talk on the phone on the Fourth of July.

DAD: Be a good sport and pack up the picnic things — *(To RAYMIE.)* Come on, pal — *(To JOAN, he strokes her back and she pulls away.)* Hey, Scooter, we'll meet you at the phone booth over there. *(JOAN picks up RAYMIE's squirt gun and empties it at them. She turns and begins to pick up the picnic things and throws them into the picnic basket as the lights fade. There is one last burst of fireworks.)*

JOAN: *(Through clenched teeth.)* **Well, at least the Japs didn't get him!**

THE END

PROPERTY OF THE DALLAS COWBOYS

by

SAM SMILEY

Sam Smiley is the head of the Department of Drama at the University of Arizona. His book, *Playwriting: The Structure of Action* (Prentice-Hall, 1971) is the standard work in its field. And his new book *Theatre: The Human Art* was published this year by Harper & Row. *Property of the Dallas Cowboys* premiered at the Bloomington Playwright's project theatre in February, 1984.

Production Suggestions

Take care with accents in this play. Accurate, slightly underplayed Texas accents would help; generalized, phony Southern accents would not. The rhythms of the dialog as written should carry the actors along, and "thick" dialects would impede the flow. The actors might want to use David Allen Stern's tape *Acting with an Accent: Texas* available from Dialect Accent Specialists, Inc., P.O. Box 44, Lyndonville, VT 05851. If the actress playing Cora is not herself middle-aged, she should study middle-aged women to find specific physical and vocal details for playing this difficult age.

Address all inquiries concerning performances, readings, or reprinting of this work *or any portion thereof* to Dr. Sam Smiley, 5799 N. Via Amable, Tucson, AZ 85750. For details, see "Part II: Securing Rights for Your Production," pages 223 to 232.

PROPERTY OF THE DALLAS COWBOYS

by
SAM SMILEY

The action takes place in a laundromat in Texas, late one Saturday afternoon, in the present day.

Characters:

CORA — middle-aged
EULALEE — her daughter
PURCELL — about 25

Setting: *One one side are three chairs and a stack of worn magazines, on the other a table for folding clothes. There's an entrance from the outside and an archway leading to the interior of the laundromat.*

AT RISE: Late one Saturday afternoon, two women sit in a laundromat. The older one, CORA, is smoking a cigarette and leafing through a magazine.

CORA: Eulalee, cut that out. I hate a snivelin' woman.

EULALEE: *(Crying into a tissue.)* I can't help it, Mama.

CORA: People might come into this laundromat and think I hit you.

EULALEE: You've never been mean to me, Mama. And Daddy never hit me like Billy Joe did. *(EULALEE cries into another tissue.)*

CORA: Wish they'd get some new magazines. I got these memorized. Dog-eared pages ... reminds me of growing up on the ranch. We kept the Sears Roebuck catalog, you see, in the privy. You had to rip out a page, *(She does)* wad it up, and roll it around in your hand. To make it soft, don't ya know? Then you'd spread it across your fingers. *(Her middle finger tears through.)* Damn, they sure need some new magazines. *(Car headlights shine in.)*

EULALEE: *(Rising)* Oh look, Mama, what a nice lookin' van.

CORA: Nice lookin' man?

EULALEE: Van. I said van. It's painted so pretty. Wish I had me one instead of that beat-up Mustang.

CORA: You should've married an oil man 'stead of a football player.

EULALEE: But I like football.

CORA: No, you don't. You like football players.

EULALEE: Wish Billy Joe still played football like in high school. I thought he was going to Texas Tech and be a Red Raider, then maybe one day a Dallas Cowboy.

CORA: He's too dumb for college. I told you that when you married him. He's so dumb he can't find his ass with both hands. *(PURCELL, about twenty-five, enters with a bag full of dirty laundry.)*

PURCELL: Hi. *(They look at him.)* Any empty washin' machines?

EULALEE: Right over there. *(She and PURCELL grin at each other; then he disappears to the washers.)*

CORA: Why were you grinnin' at him that way?

EULALEE: Just bein' friendly. He's the one with the van. *(Beat)* Mama, will you? please, will you?

CORA: Will I what?

EULALEE: Let me and Jingle come live here with you. 'Cause if you don't, I'll be destitute. Positively destitute.

CORA: Should've thought of that before you walked out on Billy Joe.

EULALEE: He hit me. Hard!

CORA: So what? Your daddy smacked me around. You got to expect that from a man. They drink, get mad, and hit you. And so it goes until one day somebody takes off. Right now Billy Joe's got a steady paycheck. So he hit ya, so what?

EULALEE: It's OK he hit *me*, but not Jingle.

CORA: What a dumb name for a little girl. Where'd he hit her?

EULALEE: On her butt.

CORA: Shoot. I was hopin' he slapped her up the side of the

head. Quiet her down. Loudest damned kid I ever met.

EULALEE: Mama, she's your grandchild!

CORA: Huh-uh. But she's so ugly I can't stand it. You're right pretty. But that loud-mouth kid looks like Billy Joe, and she's cockeyed just like your Uncle Carl. And you know what? She stutters to beat the band.

EULALEE: She does not.

CORA: Hell she don't. She calls me G-g-g-g-grandmaw. How'd you like to be called G-g-g-g-grandmaw?

EULALEE: Mama, you just got to take us in! Please. I can't live with Billy Joe no more.

CORA: Well, I'll tell you one thing, Billy Joe bought a mighty nice trailer for you to live in.

EULALEE: I can support myself. I'll get a job.

CORA: Somethin' piddly. And what'll you do with little Miss Ugly?

EULALEE: I got to figure that out. Mama, you have to let us stay. I'm your little girl! Look. *(Opens her purse.)* Eighteen bucks. That's all I got. We'd have to sleep in the car. *(From Offstage comes the sound of someone slapping a coke machine.)*

CORA: What's that?

EULALEE: *(Looking off.)* It's that fella with the van. He must've lost some quarters in the coke machine. *(Calling off.)* You gotta kick it.

PURCELL: Oh. *(He does.)* Still doesn't work. *(He enters.)* That damn machine took my last quarters.

CORA: It's been broke for six months.

PURCELL: Well, I'm just visitin'.

CORA: So what? It's still broke.

EULALEE: Huh-uh. Wait a minute. *(She gets coins.)* Here.

PURCELL: Thanks. Be right back. *(This time he goes outside.)*

CORA: I've seen all I need. You flirtin' with that man. I won't consider takin' you back, Eulalee, unless you get right with Jesus. I wonder if maybe Billy Joe kicked you out. Maybe he come home early from work, and found you shacked up.

EULALEE: That's a lie! Did he call you up?

CORA: Tell the truth! If that's what happened, I ain't takin' you in. You can stay a week, and I'll even feed you and little Miss Ugly. But one week — that's it! *(PURCELL re-enters with a box of tools.)*

EULALEE: Whatcha got them tools for?

PURCELL: You'll see. *(He disappears inside.)*

CORA: Even if I let you stay a week or two, you'll have to pull your own weight. Help out and all, and behave yourself. If I catch you foolin' around like in high school . . . Well, you know what I mean. Now go get them clothes out of the dryer and fold 'em. I got to get ready for my date.

EULALEE: Your what?

CORA: I got me a date. Hell, it's Saturday night.

EULALEE: At your age?

CORA: At my age it's still Saturday night. At my age I deserve some fun. At my age I got enough sense not to get knocked up by some football player. *(As EULALEE starts to cry again, there's a clatter from the other room. CORA goes to look.)* Would you look at that! He took the front off that coke machine.

PURCELL: *(Entering with two sodas.)* Want a can?

EULALEE: Thanks. *(He pops the top for her.)*

CORA: I ought to tell the manager.

PURCELL: Go ahead. He's my uncle. *(He shakes his soda and opens it.)* Kapow! *(Laughs.)*

CORA: Everybody's a rip-off artist. *(Turns to EULALEE.)* Everybody. Well, fold them clothes while I go up to the apartment and get ready. I just hope little Miss Ugly ain't awake. Jesus! *(EULALEE goes off to the dryers.)*

PURCELL: Hey. Mind if I look at one of those magazines?

CORA: Help yourself. *(He gets one.)* You by any chance a football player?

PURCELL: I watch the Cowboys on the tube. Why?

CORA: Nothin'. If you was a football player, I wouldn't trust you here with my girl.

PURCELL: You don't have to worry. My name's Purcell

Roberts. I'm a nephew of the manager. Your daughter's safe with me.

CORA: You been given' her the eye.

PURCELL: Oh no, ma'am.

CORA: I saw you. You looked at her boobs, didn't you?

PURCELL: Yes, ma'am.

CORA: Well listen, just this afternoon my daughter left her husband, and she's got an ugly little girl. So ugly you wouldn't believe it! Anyway, you'd be smart to leave her be.

PURCELL: Sounds like she could use a friend.

CORA: Her husband wants her back. Says anybody lays a hand on her, he'll shoot um right in the ass. Thought you ought to know. *(She goes out. PURCELL reads the magazine until he realizes a page is missing. He finds it on the floor and tries to read it. Then he puts a finger up through it. At the same time, EULALEE re-enters with a basket of dry clothes to fold.)*

EULALEE: Hey, could you ... Could you help me fold this sheet?

PURCELL: Sure. *(He looks around.)*

EULALEE: Expectin' someone?

PURCELL: Me? No.

EULALEE: Are your hands shakin', or what? I can't stand timid men.

PURCELL: I'm not timid. *(She smiles at him.)* Your mother said, uh, that you're married.

EULALEE: Separated. But don't worry, my husband ain't out looking for me or anything.

PURCELL: Oh. Well, that's good. *(He goes to sit down.)*

EULALEE: I guess you don't like women who've been married.

PURCELL: No.

EULALEE: That's what I thought.

PURCELL: No, I mean I like 'em fine. I prefer women who've been married. They've had more practice. What I mean is, it makes 'em easier.

EULALEE: Easier?

PURCELL: Easier to talk to. They've had practice with a man.

EULALEE: Well, I'm easy to talk to, and I'm easy-going. But I'm not *easy*. *(She sniffles.)* You understand?

PURCELL: Sure. I don't think you're easy. I think you're nice.

EULALEE: Even if I just left my husband this afternoon? Even if I got no place to stay? *(She cries into the dry clothes. He touches her shoulder, and she buries her face on his chest.)* I got a little kid, eighteen bucks, and no place to stay.

PURCELL: What about your mother and dad?

EULALEE: Dad took off eleven years ago, and Mom don't want me. She said she'll turn me out after a week, 'cause she's havin' dates. *(She cries.)* I got a husband who hit me, a rusted out car, and a little girl who can't talk plain. My life's such a mess. All I want is a little fun. You like fun?

PURCELL: Sure. I like fun.

EULALEE: What kind of fun do you like?

PURCELL: Oh ... football. You know, the Cowboys and all that.

EULALEE: Football! Are you by any chance ... You got awful big shoulders. Nice big biceps.

PURCELL: That ain't all that's big.

EULALEE: *(Giggles.)* Stop. You're not by any chance on a team?

PURCELL: Sure. I play football.

EULALEE: You do? Which team?

PURCELL: The Cowboys.

EULALEE: *(Squeals with delight.)* The Cowboys? Are you kiddin' me? Now, wait just a cotton pickin' minute. If you play for the Cowboys, where's your Super Bowl ring?

PURCELL: I ain't no showboat. I just wear it to parties.

EULALEE: I still don't believe it. I got programs from games, what's your name?

PURCELL: Roberts, Purcell Roberts, but in the program I'm listed as Isaiah.

EULALEE: I thought Isaiah Roberts was a black man.

PURCELL: Well, from a distance . . . I look pretty dark.

EULALEE: Oh. Well, when you drove up in that van and got out, I had me an intuition — you know, like women have — the neon lights started blinkin' inside my head, sayin' "foot-ball!"

PURCELL: Yeah. I'm a wide receiver.

EULALEE: Oh Lord! And I bet you catch ever'thing they throw your way!

PURCELL: You better believe it. So you're gonna live here in these apartments, huh? *(EULALEE glances outside.)*

EULALEE: Wups. Here comes Mama. *(He disappears as CORA comes in dressed in cowboy boots, skirt, and a fancy blouse. She carries a drink.)*

CORA: Were you talkin' to that man? I saw you.

EULALEE: He asked me what time it was.

CORA: Watch yourself! *(Drinks)* Ah! Whiskey settles me down.

EULALEE: You look nice, Mama. Who's the man?

CORA: The city bowling champion of 1962, but he's kept his touch. Man by the name of Dennis Earwig. *(EULALEE starts to laugh, but CORA stares her down.)* Some people think that name's funny. But it ain't. It's a serious name. Earwig. That man wears one-hundred-and-seventy-five dollar custom-made bowling shoes — that's serious. Anyway, there's something special about a bowler.

EULALEE: Daddy used to bowl.

CORA: Forget about him. When he pushed you and me out of his life, that was it. Outa sight, outa mind.

EULALEE: You always go out with bowlers, don't you, Mama? Daddy and Mr. Dennis Earwig. *(Giggles)*.

CORA: You better get serious, Eulalee.

EULALEE: Oh, I am. Mama. I been thinkin' while you was upstairs. Would you let me and Jingle stay if I turned over a new leaf?

CORA: What do you mean?

EULALEE: First off, I'll go to church regular. Like you, every Sunday.

CORA: That'd be a good start. But, girl, I got my own life to —

EULALEE: And I'll try to quit smokin' them funny cigarettes.

CORA: You ought to! Whenever you puff one of them things, Eulalee, your very soul goes up in smoke.

EULALEE: OK, Mama. I'll quit I swear. Now, will you let us stay till I get my feet on the ground?

CORA: *(Thinking)* You know, when I went back to the apartment, your little Jangle —

EULALEE: Jingle.

CORA: Jingle, Jangle — who the hell cares? Little Miss Ugly woke up and smiled at me. She's crosseyed and she can't talk plain; but she's kin and so are you. Seein' her smile like that and hearin' you promise to clean up your life, it gives me pause. Eulalee, if I take you in, I don't want you in the way, either one of you, when Mr. Earwig shows up.

EULALEE: Cross my heart. And I promise, no more football players! Not ever! I know you don't like 'em.

CORA: Yeah, you been a mattress-back for football players ever since junior high.

EULALEE: I have not.

CORA: You're pretty, Eulalee. But you ain't got sense enough to pound sand in a rat hole. Every time a football player looks at you, you're on your back with your skirt over your head.

EULALEE: Mama! Anyway, I promise to stay away from 'em for good.

CORA: And you'll get right with Jesus? *(Gulps whiskey.)*

EULALEE: Yes, ma'am. I'll get right with Jesus. What do you say?

CORA: All right. You can stay.

EULALEE: Oh, thank you, Mama, thank you. You won't regret it.

CORA: Well . . . Now, I'll be back about midnight, and we'll go to church tomorrow at nine A.M. Here's an apartment key. *(Reads the tag.)* Number two-oh-three. Don't lose it. *(She gives it to EULALEE.)*

EULALEE: Oh, Mama, you make me so happy. *(Stares at it.)*

Two-oh-three. *(Car headlights shine in.)*

CORA: There's Mr. Earwig. *(She waves.)* **You get the laundry, and don't dare think of goin' out.**

EULALEE: Yes, Mama. *(CORA leaves.)* **Have a nice time.** *(EULALEE turns, and there's PURCELL grinning. She finishes folding clothes.)*

PURCELL: **Your old lady's gone, huh? That means you're free tonight?**

EULALEE: **I have to take care of my little girl.**

PURCELL: **Aw, that's too bad.**

EULALEE: **She goes to bed at seven-thirty. But I have to stay in the apartment with her. Bein' a mother is very demandin'.**

PURCELL: **There's a football game on TV. LSU versus Ol' Miss.**

EULALEE: **I'll pop some popcorn, pour me some bourbon, and maybe watch.**

PURCELL: **Starts at eight. When your little kid gets to sleep, I know a nice bar with a big screen TV.**

EULALEE: **Oh, I couldn't go out. I promised Mama not to fool around.**

PURCELL: **We wouldn't fool around.**

EULALEE: **Can't, 'cause I promised. Well, I gotta go feed my girl.** *(A buzzing noice interrupts them.)* **Your machine's off balance.**

PURCELL: **Don't go 'way. All right? Wait right here!** *(He disappears. She goes behind the table, picks up the dry clothes, and leaves. PURCELL returns, looks around, shrugs. He spots something on the table and picks it up.)* **Two-oh-three.** *(He smiles and pockets the key.)*

THE END

DOG EAT DOG

by
TIM KELLY

Tim Kelly is the most published playwright in the United States. He has won innumerable awards including the Nederlander Playwriting Award and grants from the National Endowment for the Arts and the Office of Advanced Drama Research. In 1984, a shorter version of *Dog Eat Dog* was performed as part of a program entitled *An Evening of Grand Guignol,* produced by Theatre Laurel in Hollywood, California. The present form of the play was first performed by the Louisville Experimental Theatre under the direction of Tim Cockrel.

Production Suggestions

Play these characters as realistically as possible; avoid comic and melodramatic stereotypes. For accents, trust the spellings and syntax of the script without trying to force a dialect. If the actor who plays Mr. Starr is younger than middle age, he should carefully observe some older men to catch the physical and vocal nuances of middle or old age.

Address all inquiries concerning performances, readings or reprinting of this work *or any portion thereof* to the author's agent, William Talbot, Samuel French, Inc., 45 West 25th St., New York, NY 10010. For details, see "Part II: Securing Rights for Your Production," pages 223 to 232.

For more information about Tim Kelly, read "Playwright Tim Kelly" by Larry Ketchum in *Drama-Logue,* September, 1982, or "Tim Kelly: a Playwright Who Refuses to Fit in a Box" by Leon Stutzin in *Modesto Arts,* November, 1982.

DOG EAT DOG

by

TIM KELLY

The action takes place in the present in a shack located in a desert area of the Southwest.

Characters:

BILLY — a rural type — fairly young, but mean.

MR. STARR — middle-aged or older. Contemptuous of both Billy and Roy.

ROY — another rural type, none-too-bright. This character may be played as female, in which case her name is OPAL.

Setting: *A table and a couple of chairs; an entrance from the outside.*

AT RISE: BILLY is seated. His hands are tied behind the chair. He's very still. Cautiously, he looks over his shoulder, as if he feared something unpleasant were lurking in the room. Pause.

BILLY: *(Tentatively)* **Mr. Starr . . . ?** *(Louder)* **Mr. Starr.** *(Satisfied that he is quite alone, BILLY struggles to free himself.)* **Tied me up good, he did. I probably got me marks all over my wrists. I think my arms is gone to sleep.** *(He struggles all the harder.)* **World's full of crazy people. I swear I don't know what's happenin' to folks nomore.** *(Struggles, sighs.)* **Hope that ole fool ain't gone off and left me. Gone off and left me to starve. Billy-boy could die hyar. No one be the wiser.** *(Determined)* **Ain't gonna happen.** *(Fights against the restraints all the harder.)* **I can do it. Billy-boy can get loose.** *(His face shows pain as he tries to break free.)* **I can do it . . . do it . . . auuugh.** *(Gives up, sighs in defeat.)* **I can't do it.** *(Angry)* **He'll pay for this, he will. I'm gonna make that a promise, if'n I'm still alive come mornin'.** *(Wiggles in chair.)* **These things hurt. Did he use rope or rawhide?** *(MR. STARR enters from Upstage left. He's a middle-aged man, or older. He's led a hard life in the desert and it shows. Carries a pail and a rifle.)*

– 142 –

MR. STARR: Rope.

BILLY: *(Twists his head trying to see his captor.)* **How's that?**

MR. STARR: That's what I used. Rope. You must have a heap of money saved up, Billy. Only folks with money hid someplace can git away with talkin' to themselves.

BILLY: I ain't got no money hid. I keep my money in the bank. *(A sudden thought.)* Is that why you done this? You want my money? Why, you ole coyote, you're a thief, that's what you are.

MR. STARR: *(Flat)* I don't want your money.

BILLY: *(Desperate)* Then what do you want? Why you done this? *(No answer.)* Tell me. *(Again no answer. BILLY's frustration builds.)* Ole man, you're in a mess of trouble. I wouldn't be in your shoes for nothin'. You can't go around kidnappin' folks and tyin' 'em up like they was stray dogs.

MR. STARR: Why not? *(BILLY doesn't have a ready answer. Thinks a moment. Settles for —)*

BILLY: Ain't legal. *(MR. STARR gives BILLY a long hard look and this makes the captive all the more uncomfortable. BILLY decides on a new tactic, forces himself to smile.)* Ah, it's all a joke, ain't it, Mr. Starr?

MR. STARR: How come you ain't laughin, Billy?

BILLY: *(Trying to be jovial.)* That's what it is. It's a big fat joke. And I fell for it. Ha, ha. Hear that, Mr. Starr? Billy-boy is laughin'. I know how to take a joke. Ha, ha. I can play along. *(His speech betrays his underlying uneasiness. Nonetheless he presses on.)* I knowed who put you up to this. It was them Claggett Brothers, weren't it?

MR. STARR: I don't have nothin' to do with them Claggetts. *(BILLY attempts to keep the mood "light and friendly," but it's a lost battle.)*

BILLY: They's good friends of mine.

MR. STARR: I knowed.

BILLY: Well, now, if'n it weren't them Claggetts who could it be? *(Searches for the answer.)* Hmmm. Only other person I can think of is Roy Sawtelle. *(Could it be Roy?)* Only he's stupid. He ain't got the good sense of a flea. You ain't gonna tell me it was Roy? *(No answer.)* Well, well. What do you know. That's one on Billy-boy. Imagine Roy Sawtelle thinkin' up a funny joke like this. Ha, ha. *(Then)* I'm gonna break his neck.

MR. STARR: Weren't Roy Sawtelle.

BILLY: *(Loses control.)* Then who! *(Stares at MR. STARR.)* You stop lookin' at me like that. You look like a hawk over the henhouse. *(Loses control.)* Stop lookin' at me, I said! *(MR. STARR stares for a second more, steps to somewhere in the cabin, leans the rifle, puts down the pail. BILLY cranes his neck to watch.)* When I git out of hyar I'm gonna report you to the welfare people. They gonna take away your check. They gonna put you in a home for senile people what don't know the time of day, or what year it is, or nothin' like that. You hear me, ole man? *(Again, BILLY fights the ropes. No luck. MR. STARR dips into the pail and comes up with a dog collar. He crosses to the terrified BILLY who continues to spew out his anger.)* World don't make no sense no more. You's probably the victim of some kind of atomic radiation and don't knowed it. It's affected all your brain cells, that's what. Them radiation particles, they jus' hang up there in the air 'til they drop down. And that's what they done. They dropped down into your head and you didn't have nothin' to say about it. That's why I ain't holdin' you responsible. You's a victim of them particles.

MR. STARR: Billy.

BILLY: What?

MR. STARR: Shut up.

BILLY: Don't you go tellin' me to shut up after what you done. I bet you even got a driver's license! Crazy ole coot like you drivin' on the highway endangerin' decent folks. *(Demanding)* You let me out of hyar! Now! I ain't gonna ask again. *(Frantic)* You listen to me, Mr. Starr!

MR. STARR: This ought to fit.

BILLY: *(Leery)* What ought to fit? *(MR. STARR puts the collar*

around BILLY's neck, buckles it. BILLY's fear has momentarily
paralyzed him. He offers no resistance.)

MR. STARR: *(Pleasantly)* **Ain't too tight, is it, Billy? If it's too
tight I can always loosen it.** *(BILLY is bewildered.)*

BILLY: **It's a, uh, dog collar ... ain't it?**

MR. STARR: **Let me look.** *(He steps back and looks at the collar,
rubbing his chin as he pretends to ponder BILLY's dumb question.)*
**'Pears to me to be a dog collar. Looks like a dog collar. Do
it feel like a dog collar?** *(BILLY remains frozen. He doesn't know
what to say or what to do. MR. STARR steps to his captive and
investigates a tag on the collar.)* **Well, what do you know.**

BILLY: **What?**

MR. STARR: **Says here you been rabies vaccinated.**

BILLY: **You having a good time, ole man? I know what you
are. You're one of them sick people you read about in the
newspaper at the supermarket.**

MR. STARR: **Maybe that collar ain't tight enough.** *(BILLY
reacts to the threat in MR. STARR's words.)*

BILLY: *(Contrite)* **No, no. It's tight enough.**

MR. STARR: **Sure?**

BILLY: **Honest. I wouldn't lie about a thing like that.**

ROY: *(From Offstage right.)* **Billy-boy? Hey, Billy, you in there?
Billy!**

BILLY: *(Somewhat relieved.)* **I was right! That's Roy out there.
He did put you up to this.**

MR. STARR: **You keep your mouth shut. If you say one more
word, I might kill you. Understand?** *(BILLY swallows hard,
nods that he understands.)*

ROY: *(Offstage)* **Billy!** *(MR. STARR steps back, out of sight of ROY
who is about to enter. **NOTE:** The role of ROY can be switched
to OPAL. If this is done the actress should wear a man's rough
clothing. There is nothing overtly feminine about OPAL. Pause
for effect. ROY enters.)* **Mr. Starr?** *(Steps in further.)* **Hey, Mr.
Starr, you to home?** *(ROY is somewhat dim-witted. He sees
BILLY.)* **How come you didn't answer me when I called
you? Didn't you hear me?** *(Pause)* **What's the matter with**

you? *(ROY steps to BILLY and notices the dog collar, rope.)* **What kind of game you playin'? You look kinda sick. Or somethin'. What you wearin' a dog collar fer? Better not wear that outside. People 'round hyar will think you're one a them punk rockers. That won't look too good.** *(BILLY can't stand ROY's idiotic chatter for a second more. Despite MR. STARR's warning, he shouts out —)*

BILLY: You simple-minded fool! Can't you see I'm in trouble!

ROY: *(Matter-of-fact.)* **Billy-boy, you knowed I don't like it when you call me simple-minded. You can call me a fool if'n you want. That's OK. Everybody calls me a fool. But I don't like "simple-minded" fool. Don't sound polite.** *(As if the peculiar MR. STARR weren't enough, BILLY must now deal with this illiterate. He breaks down into a few silent sobs.)* **What you cryin' fer? Billy-boy, what is the matter with you?** *(BILLY nods in the direction of MR. STARR. ROY turns as MR. STARR emerges from his hiding place. The rifle is now trained on them both.)* **Howdy, Mr. Starr.** *(Tries to make sense out of the bizarre scene.)* **Billy done somethin' bad?**

BILLY: If'n you had anythin' to do with this, Roy, I'm gonna pull off your ears and feed 'em to the hounds.

ROY: *(Staring at the rifle.)* **I trust that thar rifle ain't loaded, Mr. Starr.**

MR. STARR: *(Quietly)* **It's loaded.**

BILLY: He blew apart some tin cans to show me what that rifle can do. It's loaded, all right.

ROY: *(To MR. STARR.)* **Then you shouldn't be pointin' it at us. Television says more folks get shot in the house than on the outside.**

MR. STARR: Is that a fact?

ROY: Yes, sir. That's a fact.

BILLY: Git some help. *(Choking back another dry sob.)* **Please.**

ROY: Lookee hyar, Mr. Starr, I don't knowed what you got agin' Billy, but this ain't no way to settle no dispute.

MR. STARR: Is that another fact, Roy?

ROY: Yes, sir. That's another fact. You called me and told

me to come hyar. You told me Billy wanted to see me. Well,
I'm hyar. *(To BILLY.)* **What did you want to see me about?**

BILLY: I didn't want to see you.

ROY: Then how come Mr. Starr said you did?

BILLY: Why don't you ask him?

ROY: Mr. Starr, how come —

MR. STARR: *(Cutting him off.)* **Put your knife on the table.**

ROY: Knife? I don't carry no knife.

MR. STARR: *Do it!* (MR. STARR *makes a threatening gesture
with the rifle. Alarmed,* ROY *takes a knife from the inside top
of his boot. He tosses it on the table.)* **Set.**

ROY: *(Feebly)* **I don't mind standin'. I'm used to standin'.
Sometimes I stand all day. Fer hours and hours. Roy likes
standin'.**

MR. STARR: *(Another threatening gesture with the rifle.)* **Guess
you didn't hear me the first time. I said —** *set.*

BILLY: Do like he says. He's been radiated and don't know
it. *(Dutiful, aware that things are very strange,* ROY *sits in the
other chair at the table.)*

ROY: What does that mean — he's been radiated? Is it
somethin' catchin'–

MR. STARR: Hands up.

ROY: What fer?

MR. STARR: *Up!* *(The rifle again.* ROY *holds up his hands.)*

ROY: *(To BILLY.)* **Somethin' don't seem right, Billy-boy.**

BILLY: *(Snaps)* **Now you're catchin' on.** *(Aside)* **Fool.**

ROY: *(Worried)* **Uh, Mr. Starr, sir. Mind if'n I ask a question?**

MR. STARR: Ask.

ROY: Why you doin' this?

MR. STARR: Maybe it's like Billy said. I ain't responsible for
what I do. I'm radiated and don't knowed it.

ROY: *(To BILLY)* **I figured you was settin' up a fight. I figured
you'd have it goin' by the time I got hyar.**

BILLY: You moron . . .

ROY: *(Flashes)* **Don't you all me a moron. I ain't no moron.
You can call me a fool, but don't you call me a moron. I**

don't like the way you talk to me, Billy. Ain't right. Not when we's supposed to be friends. *(To MR. STARR.)* No fight, eh, Mr. Starr?

MR. STARR: Not today, Roy. No dogfight, anyhow. You came runnin' figurin' you could make some money bettin' on what hound will kill first.

ROY: What if'n I did? Lookee, Mr. Starr, I knowed you don't like dogfights, but there's plenty what does.

MR. STARR: That give you the right to edge 'em on 'til they tear each other apart?

ROY: It's my business. I breed dogs.

MR. STARR: You breed 'em. *(To BILLY.)* And you stage the fights.

BILLY: What if'n I do? Man's got a right to make a livin'. It's in the Constitution of these United States of America. It's writ down. *(Pause)* I think.

MR. STARR: What about them dogs? They got any rights?

ROY: They's fightin' dogs. Fightin' and killin' each other is all they's good fer.

MR. STARR: You know what I am, Billy?

BILLY: A psycho person.

ROY: *(Anxious to calm MR. STARR.)* No, he ain't. You hadn't ought to say somethin' like that, Billy. Mr. Starr ain't no psycho person. He's a nice man. *(Smiles)* You're a nice man, Mr. Starr. Ain't you?

MR. STARR: Am I? *(ROY looks glum.)* I'll tell you what I am. *(Pause)* I'm a dog lover. Always have been.

ROY: I love dogs, too.

MR. STARR: You love what they can do fer you! Ain't the same thing. Yup, I love all kinds of dogs. The big mutts and them l'il fellas. *(Icy)* I seen what you do to dogs.

BILLY: What we do ain't none of your business.

MR. STARR: I'm making it my *business*. When you're done with them dogs you toss 'em away to fend fer themselves. Don't even have the decency to put 'em to sleep. People can't have no pit dogs fer no pet. Ain't the dogs' fault.

ROY: *(Lowers his arms.)* **You save some of the dogs, don't you? That's what folks say.**

MR. STARR: **I save the ones that find their way to this cabin. Half-dead, half-starved, paws all cut and bleedin' from the desert. 'Course you never figured a dog would last on the desert, did you?** *(Notices the lowered arms.)* **Keep them arms up!** *(He motions with the rifle. Up goes ROY's arms.)*

BILLY: **Accordin' to the law you ain't got no right to keep them dogs. They don't belong to you.**

MR. STARR: **Don't you talk to me about the law. Dogfights ain't legal.**

ROY: **Sheriff don't mind.**

MR. STARR: **That's 'cause Billy lets the sheriff win. Sheriff don't care about them dogs no more than you do.**

BILLY: **You got us hyar to complain about how we earn our livin'? You could've done that with a postcard.**

MR. STARR: **You call what you do a livin'!**

BILLY: **What would you call it?**

MR. STARR: **I call it a great sadness. A great crime against a creature that only wants to be a friend.**

ROY: **My arms are gettin awful tired.**

MR. STARR: **Put 'em behind your head.** *(ROY obeys.)* **First dog I ever had me was named Buddy, half-collie and half-who-knows. Fourteen years he was with me. Never was mean to me, never was unkind. Give him a pat on the head, call him a good dog and he was happy. Too bad people can't be like that.**

BILLY: **You let me go and I'll git you another dog jus' like that.**

MR. STARR: **There was only one Buddy jus' like there's only one me. One you, one Roy.**

ROY: *(Innocently)* **I gotta be goin'.** *(He gets up, takes a step toward the door.)*

MR. STARR: **You sit down or I'll blast you into the wall!** *(ROY quickly sits again.)* **Behind your head, like before.** *(ROY puts his hands behind his head.)* **I reckon I lost track of all** the dogs what been friends with me. Friends, good friends. Dogs ain't killers. Man has to larn 'em. You two larned 'em good. They's out there in their cages, their kennels. *(BILLY and ROY exchange a frightened look.)* **They's waitin'.**

BILLY: Who . . . who's waitin'?

MR. STARR: Them dogs. Told you already — they can't run free no more. They's dangerous. You make 'em that way.

BILLY: *(A terrifying thought.)* **Them dogs . . . wait a minute . . . hold on. I think I knowed what you're plannin', ole man.**

ROY: What?

BILLY: *(To MR. STARR.)* **You ain't gonna do it?**

ROY: *(Scared)* **Do what, Billy?**

BILLY: *(To MR. STARR.)* **You ain't gonna *feed* us to them dogs?**

ROY: Oh, no. Don't do that, Mr. Starr. I won't breed no more dogs if'n you let me go.

BILLY: Shut up, stupid.

ROY: Don't you call me stupid!

MR. STARR: Nothin' to be afeard about. I ain't gonna let them dogs have you. *(BILLY and ROY breathe an audible sigh of relief.)* **I 'spect they'd like to get at you, though.**

BILLY: *(Wary)* **What you plannin', then?**

ROY: You ain't gonna . . . kill us . . . nothin' like that?

MR. STARR: *(To ROY.)* **There's gonna be a fight after all.**

BILLY: But you don't like dogfights.

MR. STARR: I'll like this one. This fight is gonna be a li'l different. 'Cause you two is gonna be the dogs. Put your hands down, Roy. *(ROY lowers his hands.)*

BILLY: *(Glum)* **You want me and Roy to fight?**

MR. STARR: Uh-huh. In front of them cages. All the dogs is gonna watch. I told 'em you's comin'. *(An order. To ROY.)* **Untie him.** *(ROY is afraid to move.)* ***I said untie him!*** *(ROY quickly goes behind BILLY's chair and proceeds to untie him.)* **It won't be a crowd of bums jeerin' you on — it'll be them dogs.**

BILLY: What makes you think we'll fight?

MR. STARR: You'll fight.

BILLY: No, we won't. No way you can make us.

ROY: *(Stalling)* How long we got to fight?

MR. STARR: 'Til the end.

BILLY: End? End of what?

MR. STARR: It's gonna be jus' like the real thing — you'll fight 'til *one* of you is dead. *(BILLY springs from the chair, goes for the knife but MR. STARR slams the rifle barrel over the blade.)* No, you don't. *(He prods BILLY with the barrel and BILLY steps away. To ROY, indicating.)* Dig your paw in that pail.

ROY: Huh?

MR. STARR: Do it!

ROY: Yes, sir! *(Terrified that MR. STARR will discharge the rifle, ROY crosses to pail, sticks in his hand and comes up with a dog collar.)*

MR. STARR: Put it on.

ROY: It's a dog collar. I ain't no dog.

MR. STARR: You ain't fit to be a dog. I said — put — it — on. *(He pumps the rifle for ready. Instantly ROY buckles on the collar.)*

BILLY: *(Nervously)* Rules say dog don't have to be dead. He only has to stop fighting to lose.

MR. STARR: Them's your rules, not mine.

ROY: You won't git away with it!

MR. STARR: I ain't gonna worry about it. If you fight, one of you will walk away — alive. I give that promise. If you don't fight you *both* is gittin' buried on the desert. Food for gophers. Whereabouts unknown.

ROY: No! *(Whimpers)* Please let me go. I got things to do.

BILLY: We won't do it.

MR. STARR: It's up to you. You know my rules. If you fight you got a fifty-fifty chance. If you don't — goodbye, adios and farewell. *(Growls)* Move!

BILLY: We ain't gonna do it.

ROY: Billy's right. We ain't gonna fight. *(BILLY and ROY begin to back Upstage left.)*

MR. STARR: You'll fight. You'll fight for that one chance to hang on. You'd fight your own mother to stay alive. You're *both* stupid. I can forgive people for bein' stupid. But not for bein' mean. Bark.

BILLY: Huh?

MR. STARR: I said *bark.* Bark like you're angry, bark like you're mad about somethin', bark cause you're scared. *(The rifle.)* I want to hear you. I want them dogs to hear you. *Bark!* *(On the edge of hysteria, BILLY and ROY begin to bark.)* Good, good. That ought to get the blood rushin'. *(He pokes at them with the rifle.)*

BILLY: Stop it, Mr. Starr.

MR. STARR: Too late for that.

ROY: Them dogfights was all Billy's idea! Kill him, not me.

BILLY: Shut up, you simple fool! *(MR. STARR is nudging them Offstage, out of sight.)*

MR. STARR: Keep movin'. *(Yells)* Place your bets . . . place your bets . . . the fight is on . . . *The fight is on!*

THE END

POTATO GIRL

by
CHRISTINE RUSCH

Christine Rusch is artistic director of The Playwrights Fund of North Carolina, Inc. Her plays have been performed at the Ensemble Studio Theatre, Smith College, Charlotte's Mint Museum, the North Carolina Black Repertory Company, and other theatres supporting new work. *Potato Girl* was performed in workshop at the Ensemble Studio Theatre in 1981 and at the Best Lunch Theatre Ever in Greenville, North Carolina, in 1982.

Production Suggestions

Potato Girl contains a wealth of details about each of the three characters; use every analytical skill you have to dig out this information in order to give your characters full life beneath the lines. This script presents its actors a real challenge in dealing with dialog. On the technical level, do not push for a dialect but rather trust the spelling, the syntax, and the rhythms of the lines as written; the result will be believable, regional speech. On a deeper level, make absolutely certain you know exactly what each character means by every line and every word; if you know what the lines mean, your audience will understand the dialog; if you don't, the audience will go away confused. Finally, start early using the props; the handling of the potatoes is almost as important as the handling of the speech forms in this script.

Address all inquiries concerning performances, readings, or reprinting of this work *or any portion thereof* to Christine Rusch at 101 Middleton Place, Greenville, NC 27858. For details, see "Part II: Securing Rights for Your Production" on pages 223 to 232.

POTATO GIRL

by
CHRISTINE RUSCH

The action of the play takes place in a farm warehouse, in the time of plastics and breakfast cereals.

Characters:

DOROTHY WHITELY — a potato sorter in her mid-twenties
NARCILLA JONES — a potato sorter in her late teens
HANK LACEY — their boss and Dorothy's boyfriend.

Setting: *The sorting area of the warehouse has a window and at least two crates. One of the crates has a seat pad on it; the other is situated near a window.*

AT RISE: The play opens with DOROTHY and NARCILLA dragging bushels of potatoes into the warehouse. They take seats on crates: DOROTHY's has a mat; NARCILLA's faces a window.

DOROTHY: Don't it matter, you always getting the hard one?

NARCILLA: Uh uh. *(No)*

DOROTHY: I always figger one time I'll come in here late and you'll have this here mat, with me havin to set on the hard one.

NARCILLA: Uh uh. *(Yes)*

DOROTHY: Are you listenin?

NARCILLA: Uh uh. *(Yes)*

DOROTHY: Well, why ain't you never beat me to my place?

NARCILLA: I like this one just fine. *(Pause)*

DOROTHY: Oh ... Well, wait'll you been knocked around some, girl. Had you some kids. See if you don't look out for them soft places like a hound looks to suck eggs.

NARCILLA: Ain't on the way again?

DOROTHY: Does a polecat stink?

NARCILLA: How far?

DOROTHY: Dunno. Usta could tell. Been doin' so poorly after Clyde, haven't kept my time straight since . . . Get yourself fixed up, and you might could turn a boy.

NARCILLA: I ain't tryin.

DOROTHY: You tellin me! . . . Girl, one thing is stuffins. First place they look, and ain't no way you gonna draw any with a front like that.

NARCILLA: I said I ain't tryin.

DOROTHY: Order off for em. I seen em in that there wish book outen the two-holer. Reasonable, for stuffins . . . *(She stops suddenly in her work.)* Damn if it ain't a stone.

NARCILLA: Can I hold it?

DOROTHY: What you want with a rock? . . . Oh yeah, you ain't had any. I forgot. *(She laughs.)*

NARCILLA: Looks just like a real potato, don't it? Just like it. If you wasn't fixin to eat it.

DOROTHY: Be like eatin them rubber pork chops down't the Seven Day Advertisers. Gracion Smithers, she's doin service there and she says they eat pork chops what's made of rubber. Or plastic. Ain't proper meat, leastways.

NARCILLA: I'd take one a these here rock taters. Pretty, and they wouldn't get all squishy.

DOROTHY: Get on, girl. They'll be pickin all mornin, 'fore the rain.

NARCILLA: *(Returns to sorting.)* I seen flowers a plastic.

DOROTHY: I got me some. Red and blue. Done up the yard with em. Stuck em right there along the walk. Right pretty. Every time the snow'd melt, there they was, red and blue as ever.

NARCILLA: *(Looking out window.)* Cloudin up.

DOROTHY: They ain't gonna get done 'fore the rain. Short now, bein as Jake's got hisself busted.

NARCILLA: Jake? . . . Why?

DOROTHY: Don't you know nothin, girl? They broke in,

caught em all workin, took his plates and all. He's settin
in Columbus waitin for his trial. And Sarah don't know
how she's gonna feed all them kids.

NARCILLA: Jake don't pick good anyhow.

DOROTHY: Yep. Don't know why they call it counterfeit
when it'll get you milk and beans. Now me, I feed my kids
good . . . You seen them Sugar Frosted Fruities? Finished
up two boxes just yesterday. You seen em?

NARCILLA: Went for a walk on lunch break yesterday. Seen
three of em settin on the wall. Figured Clyde was home
sleepin.

DOROTHY: Sugar Frosted Fruities, girl. You ever seen em?

NARCILLA: I ain't much for noticin names of stuff.

DOROTHY: Purty as you could think after. Red, green, blue,
yeller . . . they don't fade out. Clyde, he gits down there't
the floor, so's he kin grab them stragglers.

NARCILLA: What are they? The Frosties. Do you know what
they are?

DOROTHY: Fruities, girl. Sugar Frosted Fruities. That's all.

NARCILLA: What'd they taste like? *(Pause)*

DOROTHY: Clyde ain't but a knee baby, and he's wild for
em . . . I feed em good . . . Got me a new table set.

NARCILLA: *(Looking out window.)* Uh huh.

DOROTHY: My hind foot. Why ain't you listenin to me, girl?
I'm talkin to ya.

NARCILLA: I was just . . .

DOROTHY: Starin out that window, that's what you're doin.
Lookit you. Ain't got no chest on ya, ain't got no man,
and ain't even got your taters half sorted out . . . and there
ya go starin outa the window. *(NARCILLA works to catch
up.)* I can't even tell which is your bakin and stuffin, your
middle size, and your whole boilin pile . . . What the hell
you doin, tryin to get me in trouble with Hank? Now you
just tell me what in the hell you are doin with that there
basket of taters.

NARCILLA: I . . . I have to go awhile before I know which is which.

DOROTHY: Oh, Lord, all the jimmy-jawed girls in Paw Paw, and I gotta work with a bitch what's got a head what's empty as a dry moon.

NARCILLA: Sometimes I seen one and thought it was big, til I seen the next . . .

DOROTHY: Crack-brain. Empty as a dry . . .

NARCILLA: This . . . This here's for bakin, this one's middle, this here's whole boilin . . . and the rocks go here. *(Pause)*

DOROTHY: Well, that's better . . . My new table, now . . . If it was here, you could fit alla your piles, and alla mine on it.

NARCILLA: Must be right good size.

DOROTHY: Course it is. Alluv us kin set down't it t'gether. When Hank's there, we even got place fer him.

NARCILLA: What's it look like?

DOROTHY: Well, if you was to look at it, you swears it's wood. But if you was to rub yer hand across the top, it don't leave no splinters. Yep, one a the girls was changin Clyde on it just last night, and he ain't got no butt fulla wood slivers now, no sir.

NARCILLA: Sounds right pretty. I'm glad for ya.

DOROTHY: My hind foot . . . Gold. Got a strip a gold around it, too. All the way around it. Don't you be tellin me you don't want it fer yourself.

NARCILLA: *(Glancing out window.)* I ain't got but myself.

DOROTHY: There. All done. Looky here, you ain't but half done, and I'm all done. *(NARCILLA continues to stare out window. Enter HANK, dragging another bushel of potatoes.)*

HANK: Here's some more . . . *(To DOROTHY.)* Well, ain't we feelin good this mornin.

DOROTHY: Hank . . .

HANK: Damn if you coulda put out last night.

DOROTHY: Hank, I . . .

HANK: Blowin off, loudin off, mouthin off. Giver a little and she figgers she kin talk er way outa workin . . . What'd 'ya see out there, bug eyes? *(He puts his hand on*

NARCILLA's shoulder. To DOROTHY.) **Willie Joe seen her
out walkin, starin, walkin some more.**

NARCILLA: Almost done, Hank.

HANK: Lookin? What 'ya lookin for, bug eyes? Huh, baby?

**DOROTHY: New table works good, Hank. Havin stew fer
supper.**

NARCILLA: There. Bakin ... Middle ...

**HANK: No use lookin out there, baby. It's here. It's right
here. And all you gotta do is ...**

DOROTHY: I says the damn table works good, Hank.

HANK: Don't mind her, Narcilla. She gets that way.

**DOROTHY: My apron's ridin high, but I didn't tie it by
myself.**

NARCILLA: Is there another basket out back?

HANK: Another basket? *(Laughs)* **Is that what you been
lookin for? Why didn't you say so? Let old Hank get it for
you ...**

**DOROTHY: I ... I need somethin, Hank. For my back. Hurts
somethin awful ...**

**HANK: Followin the shade around the barn. You know what I
bet? I bet you wouldn't bitch like that. Would you,
Narcilla, baby?**

NARCILLA: I'll get them taters myself.

HANK: *(Laughs)* Spunky little ... *(NARCILLA exits.)*

DOROTHY: You stay away from her, Hank Lacey.

HANK: Since when I gotta listen to you?

DOROTHY: What's she got? *(He laughs.)* **I had you kids.**

HANK: You got money. Everybody knows I put you up.

DOROTHY: I been grateful. I have. But ... I was tired ...

**HANK: Well they ain't gonna laugh at me, woman. Old Hank
doin favors for his girl and she ain't givin im none. I ain't
bein nobody's joker. Nobody's.**

DOROTHY: In a little bit, I'll be feelin ...

HANK: Yeah. *(Pause)*

DOROTHY: She ain't got no shape.

HANK: Well, looky who's talkin bout shape.

DOROTHY: You know what you make me? Sick.

HANK: You know what you can do? You kin go to hell.

DOROTHY: I shoulda never let your hindparts near my door.

HANK: Ain't nobody forced you.

DOROTHY: What'd you know about that? Ain't no other way for a man to do it.

HANK: You tryin to say . . .

DOROTHY: Ain't tryin. Just am.

HANK: Bitch. Practically begged me. You begged me. You did. Ain't been for me, you'd be a dried up old thornback.

DOROTHY: Think there ain't been nobody else?

HANK: Hah. Knew it. Clyde ain't got my bones.

DOROTHY: He's the spittin image if you count temper.

HANK: Probably Jake or crazy Willie Joe.

DOROTHY: You sayin I been with Jake? I ain't that desperate. Willie Joe? How am I gonna get him out't the window? Crap. I ain't that desperate.

HANK: What do you mean, not *that* desperate?

DOROTHY: I give *you* some, didn't I?

HANK: I'm gonna cut your water off and take the meter out.

DOROTHY: You think I ain't seen you over't Sarah's after they come and got Jake? You didn't even wait til er bed cooled off, you dirty . . .

HANK: She's gotta feed them kids, don't she? *(NARCILLA enters with another bushel.)* Narcilla, honey. Let me help you with that there basket.

NARCILLA: I kin get it.

DOROTHY: *(Getting up.)* Let er git usta it, Hank.

HANK: *(To DOROTHY.)* Where you goin on my time, woman?

DOROTHY: Take a leak. *(She exits.)*

NARCILLA: *(Working quickly.)* Funny, all them shapes.

HANK: *(Amused)* What?

NARCILLA: Taters. Some got one shape, some got another. Lookit this one here.

HANK: Like me and you, baby.

NARCILLA: Mr. Lacey, I . . .

HANK: The good Lord, my child, made you shaped special, just to fit the way the good Lord made me. Did you know that?

NARCILLA: Dorothy, she don't take long. She's comin back any time now ...

HANK: He made me so's I fit you; he made you so's you fit me. Now what could be nicer than that? You just tell me what could be nicer than that?

NARCILLA: I ... I got me a man. *(Pause)*

HANK: Oh, he ain't gonna mind ... Who is it?

NARCILLA: I ... I see him bout every day.

HANK: *(Laughing)* Why, you sly little thing. Here we was all figgerin you was crazy ... Who is he?

NARCILLA: I ... I ain't tellin.

HANK: Come on, Narcilla. You kin tell old Hank ...

NARCILLA: No. You leave me alone, Mr. Lacey. I ...

DOROTHY: *(Entering)* What d'ya think you're doing? Get away from her before I ...

HANK: Ain't nothin to worry for, Dotty. Narcilla here says she got a man. *(Pause)*

DOROTHY: What? And you believed her, I guess? Her? She ain't got no shape.

HANK: You ain't foolin old Hank?

DOROTHY: Who is it, girl? Ain't none, is there? Who is it? Quit your playin.

HANK: Old Hank don't like his girls tellin stories ... *(Pause)*

NARCILLA: I pass his window every day ... Sometimes he's there, watchin out beyond ... Standin, leanin against the window frame ... Like a picture. I've smiled fer him, I've cried fer him ... I watch how he moves, when he moves ... And figger his story. *(Pause)*

HANK: They was right.

DOROTHY: What'd I tellya, Hank. Crack-brain.

NARCILLA: From my safe place this side of the glass, his story is fer me: His empty bed, the new jacket hangin on a nail by the toilet, the rusty sink, the potroast of oatmeal . . . The question to hisself as he watches out beyond for the answer . . . He knows what mornin and night smell like . . . He's got his own safe place that side of the glass . . .

DOROTHY: Narcilla, you got to keep your mind on your work, girl. You think Hank wants a crazy girl on his payroll?

HANK: I ain't gonna have them laughin at me havin no crazy girl on my payroll . . . She's makin it all up.

DOROTHY: Hank, I believe she's talkin bout crazy Willie Joe up there . . . Always starin out't the window.

HANK: Damn waste a money feedin im. Empty headed jerk like . . . that's where our taxes go, Dotty. Oughta line em all up and blow em to bits. What's the use keepin a buncha empty faces fed up? You tell me, what's the use? *(Pause)* . . . C'mon, baby. Let's get you some lunch. You always did get powerful hungry when you was carryin . . . Narcilla, lover, listen to Dot here and get your shittin taters sorted. *(Exit HANK and DOROTHY. Pause.)*

NARCILLA: *(To stone potato.)* He got no use. No reason. He got no story? . . . I gotta tell you. It don't matter . . . Lookin for them . . . that's how I live.

THE END

POTATO GIRL
by Christine Rusch

PHONECALL FROM SUNKIST

by

NORMAN A. BERT

Besides editing this book, Norman Bert teaches playwriting and chairs the Department of Theatre & Dance at Texas Tech University. His other books, also published by Meriwether Publishing, Ltd., include *Play It Again: More One-Act Plays for Acting Students, Theatre Alive! — An Introductory Anthology of World Drama,* and *The Scenebook for Actors. Phonecall from Sunkist* previously appeared in *Quarry 4,* published by Indiana University's Department of English in 1974.

Production Suggestions

The vocal and physical differences between young and middle-aged men are subtle but significant; if you are cast as Keller or Hanson and you are traditional college age, you will need to observe some middle-aged men very carefully in order to speak and move believably in your role.

"Bowles" are the underwater portion of deep-well water pumps; made of cast iron, they contain the impellers that drive the water up, and they are very heavy. Keller would be driving home the sleeves that hold the impellers on the shaft. To do this, a heavy metal tube is thrust along the shaft and slammed into the impeller sleeve. A satisfactory sound effect can be created by sliding a loose weight along the shaft of a set of barbells so that it slams into another weight.

Address all inquiries concerning performances, readings, or reprinting of this work *or any portion thereof* to Norman A. Bert, 5704 Nashville Avenue, Lubbock, TX 79413-4601. For details, see "Part II: Securing Rights for Your Production," on pages 223 to 232.

PHONECALL FROM SUNKIST

by

NORMAN A. BERT

The action takes place during the summer in the present in Southern California, at the machine shop of Pump Sales and Service, a business that installs and repairs deep-well water pumps.

Characters:

BILL HANSON, 19 — son of Raymond Hanson and part-time worker in his father's business

HENRY "GUNNER" KELLER, late 30s — foreman in the shop

RAYMOND HANSON, late 40s — owner of Pump Sales and Service

Setting: *A corner of the shop. It contains a dirty, cluttered desk with a telephone, an old desk chair, and perhaps one other chair or high stool.*

AT RISE: BILL, 19, wearing old clothes heavily stained with oil, dirt and rust, is sweeping the area. Just Offstage, from KELLER's workbench, there is a continuous, loud noise of metal slamming into metal. The telephone begins to ring. Five rings. The banging stops. KELLER enters and answers the phone. In his late 30s, he wears a grey shirt and pants, a shop uniform. His clothes are stained with rust from leaning against the set of bowles he has been repairing.

KELLER: Yeah, shop ... Yeah, we got spiders ... Yeah we got *eight-inch* spiders ... Yeah, eight-inch *O D* spiders ... Look at what? I can see 'em from here — I'm looking at 'em! *(He pantomimes to BILL to go check for the item in stock. BILL puts down the broom and exits to the stock room.)* Don't know ... I said, I don't know. Prices ain't my area. You'll have to ask 'em up front ... No, I can't transfer you. Phones don't work that way. You'll have to call back ... Yeah. *(He hangs up. BILL returns.)*

BILL: Couldn't find 'em.

KELLER: They're right there. Second bin from bottom, middle of the aisle.

BILL: I looked there. The bin's empty.

KELLER: It's labeled, damn it.

BILL: I looked in the labeled bin.

KELLER: None there?

BILL: Right.

KELLER: *(Starting off.)* Must be out.

BILL: But what if the customer comes in for 'em?

KELLER: Then we tell 'em we just sold the last ones. Just before he came in. To the guy in the pick-up just leaving. *(He gestures to the imaginary pick-up in the yard, and BILL, taken in, turns to look.)* Don't bother me. These bowles don't get done by noon, the old man'll have my butt in a sling. *(He exits. The noise starts again. BILL exits to the stockroom. He returns and yells.)*

BILL: Eight-inch O D?

KELLER: *(The noise stops. Yells from Offstage.)* What?

BILL: Eight-inch O D?

KELLER: *(Offstage)* What eight-inch O D?

BILL: The spiders — eight-inch O D?

KELLER: *(Offstage)* Yeah.

BILL: None there. I looked again.

KELLER: *(Offstage)* Hell's bells! For that I gotta stop work? *(The slamming recommences. The phone rings. Seven rings. BILL considers answering, but doesn't. The banging noise stops. From Offstage:)* Damn! Damn! Damn! *(He enters and grabs up the receiver.)* Shop! . . . What? . . . No, Nacho not here. *(Looking at BILL.)* No one's here. All out on jobs . . . Working — y'know, *obrar?* . . . Look, lady, he'll be in at five, *comprende?* *(He hangs up.)* Christ! "Tell Nacho bring home *leche*." I gotta take milk orders for the tacos? How the hell am I supposed to get any work done around here?

BILL: You want some help with the bowles?

KELLER: No, I don't want any help. Just answer the phone.

BILL: I'm not supposed to. Dad says they all have to talk to you sooner or later anyway.

KELLER: What, about the milk orders?

BILL: I know. I know I could handle some of the calls. But Dad's boss, so I guess he knows best. He says, "Don't answer the phone — it's Gunner's job."

KELLER: Gunner's job is to finish the bowles.

BILL: I could help with the bowles.

KELLER: No, you couldn't. Ain't nothing for you to do. Just sweep.

BILL: I think I could help.

KELLER: Your old man says, "Have Bill get this mess cleaned up," so that's what you'll do. Gonna be able to damn-well eat off the floor in here. *(He exits. The banging begins again. The phone begins to ring. BILL wants to answer it but can't. Nine rings. KELLER yells from Offstage.)* **William, will you answer the damned phone?!**

BILL: *(Jumping to obey.)* **Pump Sales and Service, shop ... Yes, sir. Just a moment.** *(He shouts over the din.)* **It's for you, Gunner! Sunkist Growers.**

KELLER: *(Offstage)* **Oh, hell.** *(The banging stops. KELLER enters talking.)* **That'll be the wet-back crew. Either Nacho dropped the pump down the hole or Big Stupe tried to set up over somebody's wife. Damned tacos.** *(He takes the phone.)* **Yeah. Keller ... What kind of an accident? ... What? ... Oh, my God ... What were they doing? ... Yeah. I'll tell him.** *(He hangs up the phone, but remains seated on the desk.)* **Damn, stupid wet-backs.**

BILL: What's the matter, Gunner? What'd they do this time? *(Pause)* Gunner? Were they horsing around again?

KELLER: Shut up. Just shut up a minute, will ya? *(To himself.)* Think, man, think. Just take it easy. Be calm. Gotta think about it. Just to stay. Gotta stay with it. Damn, damn, damn, damn, damn.

BILL: Maybe you should talk about it?

KELLER: Talk about what? No. Never could talk about

nothing. Just, maybe, I dunno, *feel* for a minute. Or think. Better to think. Go on, sweep.

HANSON: *(He enters from the left. In his mid 40s, he wears suit pants and a sport shirt open at the collar.)* **I figured I'd catch you sitting on your bum. And on my time. Don't know why the union doesn't just come right out and ask for bum-sitting breaks. Cigarette?**

KELLER: **Yeah.** *(He does not see HANSON's offered cigarette and lights one of his own instead.)* **Hell on wheels. Why? All those damned times on jobs. Then this.**

HANSON: **Hank? Not sore are you? Shoot, I was just kidding around. Look, I just came out to see how you're doing on the bowles for Quality Farms. You going to finish them today? Old Becker'll wet his pants if we don't get his pump back in tomorrow.**

KELLER: **Let him wet 'em. At least he still can.**

HANSON: **I guess he can. Hey, you know what he did the other day? It's no wonder Jonesy calls him "Bag-it Becker." We were out there behind the last house where their well is, and right there that crazy goof reached right down and . . .**

KELLER: **Oh, hell, Ray. I don't give a damn about Becker. 'Specially not now. Not now. Not with something like this. If I could just think of . . .** *(His voice trails off.)*

HANSON: **Think? Be glad you don't have to think. Wish I didn't. Hey, you hear about the old boy who wanted to spend all night thinking? Well, she says to the old boy . . .**

KELLER: **Not now, Ray. Damn it, not now.**

BILL: **Dad, he just got a phone call.**

HANSON: **Oh, a phone call. I'll bet it was a woman. His old lady probably isn't getting enough. Been getting behind in your home work, Gunner?**

KELLER: **Oh, hell, Ray.**

BILL: **It wasn't a woman. Dad, I think something really bad happened. What happened, Gunner?**

KELLER: **Would you both get the hell outta my shop? Just**

scram please?

HANSON: Aw look, Hank. I didn't mean anything about your wife. Damn good woman you have there. I was just telling Billy the other day. Your mother or Mrs. Keller, I said. Look for a woman like your mother or Mrs. Keller.

KELLER: I can't. I just can't. Hell. Those stupid wet-backs. You tell them and tell them. Sure, they understand. Sure, they'll be careful.

HANSON: Gunner?

KELLER: You go to church, Ray. Not me. Never did. Maybe should've. Times like now come. What the hell's it all about, Ray?

HANSON: What? Church? Well, I, uh . . . Heck, guess you sort of caught me off guard. It's sort of what we owe the Old Boy upstairs. You ought to go sometime. Might even like it.

KELLER: Not church, damn it. Us. The preacher there ever tell you about us? I mean, if we're so important, why do we break so easy, and why are we so damned stupid?

BILL: What happened, Gunner?

HANSON: Speaking of stupid, did you see the Bums last night? Like the ladies' aide trying to catch grunion without their glasses. They couldn't do anything right.

KELLER: Stop, Ray, stop. Quit your screwing around, will you? What the hell's a ballgame got do with anything?

BILL: What happened, Gunner? Dad, let him say what happened out at Sunkist.

KELLER: No, don't think you want to hear what happened out at Sunkist, Ray. Don't think so at all. Wish to hell I hadn't.

HANSON: Sunkist. Who's out there? Nacho and Manuel, isn't it? Real good crew. I've been meaning to talk to you about them, Hank. You better let up a little. Take it easy on them. You ride them too much, and it makes them nervous. Keep on, and someday they're going to ruin something.

KELLER: Yeah. I make them nervous. *(A terrible possibility occurs to him.)* Hell. God, no. I hope not. But yeah, you're right about them ruining something. Ray, I'd sort of like a little time off. Won't be worth a damn anymore today anyhow.

HANSON: Time off? Becker'll give me time off if those bowles aren't ready for tomorrow. Thinking. Time off. Church. What's the matter, Keller? They drop the pump out there? Let's hear it.

KELLER: Don't think I can tell you, Ray. Think I'd — think I'd — dunno — go off — bawl or some damn thing. Then it'd be the funny farm for good ol' Gunner. *(He heads off to change clothes, mumbling.)* Call Sunkist. Sunkist won't bawl. They'll tell ya. *(He's gone.)*

HANSON: *(Simultaneously with Bill's line.)* What the . . .?

BILL: *(As KELLER heads Offstage, simultaneously with KELLER's exit lines.)* Gunner, wait. You have to talk. Dad just wants to help. You gotta talk — get it out so you can deal with it. Repress it, and it'll just eat at you.

HANSON: Billy, just be quiet, and watch how problems are solved in the real world. "Repress it!" Too much school, Billy. You got too much school. *(Starting off, calling to KELLER.)* Hank? Are you gonna tell me or do I have to call . . .

BILL: *(Stopping him.)* Wait, Dad. Let me do it. Let me talk to him.

HANSON: Let go of me, Billy. Settle down. How come everyone's so tense around here?

BILL: Dad, Gunner's got a problem. I think a *real* problem. I *can help* with that. I've *learned* how to talk to people — how to listen.

HANSON: Gunner's problem is that he's in *there* instead of on those bowles.

BILL: No, Dad. It's some kind of personal thing — the phone call and all. You know. You've had problems that just tore you apart. Haven't you?

HANSON: Not enough to make me walk off the job. You gotta keep going, Billy. Learn that, and you'll be OK. Now get outta my way. *(Calling off.)* Gunner?

BILL: *(Hanging on.)* No. This I can do. For you and for Gunner.

HANSON: *(Trying to shake him off.)* Billy, damn it . . .

KELLER: *(He enters buttoning up a light-colored sport shirt. He has forgotten to change his pants or to wash, and his grimy fingers soil the shirt as he works at the buttons.)* Only a couple days, Ray. Gotta get past this. Maybe the beach. I dunno. A little booze. Shouldn't but probably will. Maybe a ballgame.

HANSON: Beach my butt! Where the hell are you going? What about Quality . . .

BILL: Dad, Quality Farms isn't the point right now. *(He's going to leave with KELLER.)* Come on, Gunner, let's . . .

HANSON: *(Over BILL's last line.)* Quality Farms is exactly the point. Ask Gunner — he knows.

KELLER: All I know is, there's two dead Mexicans out at Sunkist, and I gotta go tie one on.

HANSON: Dead? What are you talking about?

KELLER: You listening now, Ray? I got your attention? OK. Here it is. Nacho and Big Stupe got it. This time they really got it. They raised the boom into some high lines. Nacho was burned in half at the waist. Big Stupe must have had his hand against the rig. His arm evaporated and his boots burned. Dammit, Nacho's got three kids. Nacho's not going home again. Nacho and Big Stupe are in pieces. Why, Ray? That's all I want to know. Why? I gotta get out of here. *(He exits left.)*

BILL: No, dammit, no. Oh no.

HANSON: Watch your language, Billy. You mother wouldn't like that at all. Nacho and Manuel. What got into those guys? How many times have I told them to watch for high lines? Damn it, they were my best crew. Now I'll have to send Elmer and Sol to Quality Farms tomorrow — that is, if I can get the bowles assembled.

BILL: Quality Farms?! Quality Farms?! You really don't care, do you?

HANSON: Of course, I care. I gotta call the wives. We'll attend the funeral. We'll send flowers, but . . .

BILL: Flowers! What good are flowers? All this time you've been the granddaddy around here. Big hearted Mr. Hanson. The old man. Always the jokes and poking in the ribs. Always the church and the Ol' Boy upstairs and all. And you never even cared. I can't hear you any more. Never, never any more. *(He exits left.)*

HANSON: Billy, come back here. Sure, I care. But caring isn't going to bring them back, is it? Caring isn't going to get Becker's pump running. You have to keep going, Billy. You can't stop the world every time someone dies. *(BILL does not return. HANSON sits on the desk.)* Damn schools are ruining the kids. Why don't they teach them about the real world anymore? Why don't they teach them you have to keep going?

THE END

VALLEY FORGERY

by

PATRICIA MONTLEY

Patricia Montley, chair of the Theatre Department at Chatham College in Pittsburgh and director of the Chatham Players Touring Company has had nine plays produced, five plays published, and has won several playwriting awards. *Valley Forgery* is one of four segments which comprise *Founding Mothers*, a feminist satire of American history, which premiered at Goucher College in 1976 and is published by the Eldridge Publishing Company.

Production Suggestions

Carefully developed and rehearsed Virginian, Irish and French accents will add texture to this play. To avoid inaccuracies and generalized stereotypes, the actors might want to use David Allen Stern's tapes *Acting with an Accent: American Southern, Acting with an Accent: Irish,* and *Acting with an Accent: French* available from Dialect Accent Specialists, Inc., P.O. Box 44, Lyndonville, VT 05851.

The playwright suggests using standard rehearsal "black boxes" to represent the logs, rock, and boat in the set. She suggests the actors wear the following costumes: Martha: A long, full, blue skirt, an off-white blouse, a full-length dark red cape, and a tri-cornered hat; Fanny: A long, full, green and white checked skirt or apron with bib, a full-length dark green cape, and boots; Marie Antoinette: a long, full, purple skirt of rich-looking material, a lacy revealing blouse, and a long black cape with hood and contrasting trim.

The playwright says, "It is not realistic writing, nor should the acting style be realistic. The satiric style calls for a broad style of acting, suitable for farce. For instance, the audience doesn't have to believe the actors are 'doing' middle age."

Address all inquiries concerning performances, readings, or reprinting of this work *or any portion thereof* to Eldridge Publishing Company, Franklin, OH 45005. For details, see "Part II: Securing Rights for Your Production" on pages 223 to 232.

VALLEY FORGERY

by

PATRICIA MONTLEY

The action takes place on the banks of the Delaware River in 1776.

Characters:

MARTHA WASHINGTON, 40 to 45 — a born leader without pretentions; shrewd, warm, natural

FANNY HOWE, 55 to 65 — lively, clever, rhetorical

MARIE ANTOINETTE, 20 to 30 — short, dark, plump, passionate, outlandishly romantic, fiery

Setting: *Martha's boat, Down Right. Fanny's boat, with Fanny asleep in it, Down Left. At Center a hibachi with seat-logs Left and Right of it and a higher seat-log Up of it. At Up Left Center, a tall rock.*

AT RISE: Lights up on MARTHA, Down Right, posing in boat like Washington in "Washington Crossing the Delaware." FANNY, unseen by MARTHA, is asleep in boat Down Left. MARTHA holds pose, surveying the river until she spots land. She "paddles" Up, gets out of boat, takes duffle bag out, drags boat to shore and turns it upside down.

MARTHA: 'Deed I don't know what's got into that man. He's mad as an walrus to be holing up in this Pennsylvania ice rink when he could be home in Virginny roasting chestnuts and singing carols. For a man who calls himself the Father of His Country, he sure is lacking in family spirit. Well, that's men for you — full of inconsistencies. Take this joker of a ferryman who didn't want me to make this dangerous trip up the Delaware and then rented me a boat with a leak. *(Takes long underwear from duffle bag.)* Now these long johns are soaked. I'll hang them on that

– 174 –

rock over there. *(Crosses Up Left to rock and spreads out underwear with bottoms draped down front of rock.)* **Drat it all! They'll be stiff as an icicle shortly. Oh well — nothing like stiff drawers to keep a soldier in shape.** *(Spots campfire.)* **What's this? The remains of a campfire.** *(Sees knapsack on Up log-seat.)* **Look here — a knapsack — with the initials "M.A."** *(Searches knapsack.)* **Hmm . . . cheese . . . French cheese. And a bottle of wine . . . Chateau Versailles, 1769 . . . empty.** *(Drops knapsack. Letter falls out, unnoticed. MARTHA crosses Down of fire and stoops to get warm, her back to audience. FANNY wakes up and stretches. Her first speech is not heard by MARTHA.)*

FANNY: **Sure and it's damp as a baby's diaper out here and me poor ailing back is breaking with the stiffness. Christmas in Killarney was never at all like this. Faith — would you look here now! I've drifted all the way into shore.** *(Gets out at Down Left of boat.)* **O, Blessed St. Patrick, let it be the shores of Philadelphia, for I've no desire to be rowing any farther this night.** *(Spots MARTHA.)* **But what's this I'm seeing? Why it's another traveler. I've a mind to be getting directions from that one.** *(Crosses Right.)* **Ah — begging your pardon, Miss, but would you be —**

MARTHA: *(Jumping up.)* **Who are you?!**

FANNY: **Me name is Fanny Howe and I'm looking for Philadelphia.**

MARTHA: **Well, you're not far off. It's a few miles that way. But come and get warmed up a bit.**

FANNY: *(Crosses Right.)* **Thanks then. I'm near to freezing.**

MARTHA: **Have you got family in Philly, Fanny?**

FANNY: **I have, indeed. And I'm just coming to remind him of it.**

MARTHA: **Remind who?**

FANNY: **Me family: Major General William Howe of His Majesty's fiftieth regiment. I'm the general's long-**

suffering wife.

MARTHA: How do you do. I'm Martha Washington of Mount Vernon, Virginia. *(They shake hands.)*

FANNY: *(Sits on Left log-seat.)* Is your husband also in Philadelphia then?

MARTHA: *(Crosses Right to duffle bag.)* No, I'm afraid the town's not big enough for both our husbands. And since yours won the last battle, he's got the city for the winter. *(Takes bag of marshmallows from duffle bag and starts back Left with them.)* My George is up the road a piece at Valley Forge, freezing and starving himself like a sadistic little Spartan — *(She pops a marshmallow in her mouth.)* — just because he's too embarrassed about losing to come home for Christmas. *(Sits on Right log-seat.)*

FANNY: Well, I'm sure he could go to California for all Sir William cares. I know me husband, and I'm telling you, Martha, once himself is cozied into some posh winter quarters, he's not about to go out in the snow to be fighting any battles. It's a summer soldier, he is.

MARTHA: *(Roasting a marshmallow.)* Tell me, Fanny, how did a decent Irish woman like you ever get tied up with a limey soldier like Howe?

FANNY: *(Stands)* Well, the British is a bad lot — and I don't blame you for wanting to be rid of the whole crowd of them. *(Crosses Down Left.)* But Sir William cut a fine figure in his bright red coat and flashing saber when he come to be stationed in Ireland in '63. Oh, the man was a picture. He'd a slew of medals on his chest and a string of stories on his tongue that'd charm the sense out of any innocent Irish lass — *(Reaches into her boat for tea kettle and two mugs.)* — especially one as had nothing more exciting to look forward to than minding bar in her father's public house for the rest of her life. *(Crosses back Right to fire.)* Anyways to cut it short — for to tell the truth, I'm bored talking about it — Sir William got to thinking there'd be no end to his stay in Ireland. So himself decided to get married. Little did the bride suspect that after the honeymoon, she's still be tending bar while her soldier-husband went gallivanting around the colonial countryside courting trouble.

MARTHA: Yes, and trouble's not all he's courting, so I hear.

FANNY: Don't I know it! Rumor has a way of traveling, you know. And now it's after making trans-Atlantic flights.

MARTHA: You know, Fanny, you've got a natural way with words. Did you ever think of submitting this story to *Redbook Magazine?*

FANNY: Oh, to be sure. I've already got a whole pile of rejection slips — from *Ladies Home Journal* and *Good Housekeeping* and all the rest of them. *(She takes out rejection slips from pocket.)* They're all telling me the story won't sell on account of its being too common.

MARTHA: Yes, I guess there's truth in that. Ah — I think you dropped one there.

FANNY: Where?

MARTHA: There by the knapsack.

FANNY: *(Picking up a piece of paper that had earlier fallen from the knapsack.)* This bit of paper? No, this one's not mine. It seems to be a page from some sort of military manual. *(Reads)* "Regulations for the Order and Discipline of the Troops of the United States." *(Marie Antoinette enters Up Left, unnoticed by others.)*

MARIE: Mon Dieu! I am discovered! *(Crosses Right to rock and hides behind it.)*

MARTHA: Let me see. *(Takes paper from FANNY and crosses Down Right.)* Hmm ... look here, there's something handwritten on the back. It's a letter ... from the looks of it, a love letter. Some of it's in French.

FANNY: And is it signed then?

MARTHA: Yes. "Yours till Niagara falls. Joseph L." And it's addressed to "M.A."

FANNY: M.A.? Do you know anyone with those initals?

MARTHA: No. And I don't think I'd want to. This turkey sounds really freaky.

MARIE: Freaky! *(Reveals herself, crosses Center.)* **You Anglo-Saxons are all bumpkins!** *(FANNY jumps up and she and MARTHA look at each other.)*

MARTHA: Who's that? *(Together)*

FANNY: Who's that?

MARIA: C'est moi, of course!

MARTHA: Mademoiselle, this must be your campsite. My name is Martha Washington and this is Fanny Howe.

FANNY: Fanny Conolly Howe.

MARIE: I am pleased to make your acquaintances, Mesdames. My name is Marie . . . eh . . . Marie Adrienne Lafayette.

MARTHA: *(Putting letter in pocket.)* Ah — Madame Lafayette! How happy I am to meet you at last. I'm very fond of your husband, you know.

MARIE: Is that right?

MARTHA: *(Crossing Up.)* Oh, yes. He's been to dinner at Mount Vernon many times. A charming young man, your Joseph.

MARIE: Oui — tres charmant! Do you by any chance know where he is?

MARTHA: Why of course — he's at Valley Forge with George.

MARIE: Yes, of course, but —

MARTHA: Ah, I see — you don't know the way there. Well, my dear, I'm going that way myself — to take George some thermal undies for Christmas. We can go together.

MARIE: Magnifique! *(To FANNY.)* And you also, Madame?

FANNY: *(Cool. Giving MARIE the once-over.)* No, not I. *My* marital obligations take me to more comfortable quarters.

MARTHA: My husband will be so pleased to see you again.

MARIE: *(Nervous)* Again?

MARTHA: *(Crossing Center towards MARIE.)* Why yes. The last time he returned from Paris, he spoke of nothing but the lovely time he had with you and Monsieur Lafayette at your country chateau.

MARIE: He did?

MARTHA: *(Stalking Left behind MARIE.)* Yes, he went on and on about your grand stature.

MARIE: Well, the journey has taken a lot out of me.

MARTHA: *(Crossing back to Right of MARIE.)* And your gorgeous blonde hair —

MARIE: I am afraid it is a little dirty now.

MARTHA: And your sparkling blue eyes.

MARIE: They change the color with the light.

MARTHA: Yes, I am sure General Washington will be delighted to see you — whoever you are, my mysterious Madame Imposter! *(Takes MARIE's arm threateningly.)*

MARIE: You are making a big mistake.

MARTHA: It's you who have made the mistake. Now perhaps you will tell us who you really are!

FANNY: *(Finally recognizing her.)* Faith and begorra! She don't have to!

MARTHA: What? *(Together)*

MARIE: Quoi?

FANNY: Sure and there's not a living soul in the whole of Europe that don't know the flippant face of the vixen of Versailles. *(Grabs MARIE's other arm.)* This is the sovereign strumpet herself — Marie Antoinette!

MARIE: *(Breaks away and jumps up on Up log.)* Qui! Marie Antoinette! The grand and glorious Queen of France! Vive la reine! And now, Mesdames, if you value your impudent little lives, you will grovel at the feet of the mighty monarch of France, and she may — because of her noble and generous nature — deign to spare your insignificant selves.

FANNY: *(Crosses Down Left and sits on edge of boat.)* Would you listen to the airs of this one!

MARTHA: Madame, this is the United States of America! There'll be no groveling here!

MARIE: No groveling? Very well then — just kiss my hand. Go ahead — baisez la main de la reine. *(Steps down to level with MARTHA.)* **Well? Baisez — baisez!**

MARTHA: There'll be no baisaying of hands either. How can you indulge in such undemocratic deportment while less than twenty miles off, our American boys are starving — with not even horsemeat to eat?

MARIE: Then . . . let them eat steak! What do I care for starving Yankees?

MARTHA: You shall see, Madame — your audacity will not go unpunished. In America, even queens must come to justice!

MARIE: The justice for the queens! What a ridiculous idea! What are you going to do, hein?

MARTHA: Well, since you're so hot to join Monsieur Lafayette, we will go to Valley Forge, where you will be forced to acknowledge your scandalous behavior.

MARIE: Scandalous behavior! Ha! You Americans are such naive idealists.

FANNY: Do you mean to be suggesting that it's a decent sort of queenly behavior to be making cuckolds of kings?

MARIE: My Louis, a cuckold? That is a good one! *(Pushes MARTHA aside and crosses Down Right.)* **Mesdames, you are both from backward, underdeveloped nations and so your innocence must be excused. But in France we live in an age of sexual freedom called The Enlightenment. My Louis and I — we are a totally liberated couple. In the French court, we are the leaders of the Let Set — I let him do what he wants; he lets me do what I want. Versailles is a veritable palace of sexual delights: mate-swapping, group orgies, the latest crazes in S and M, touchy-feely, and sundry other kinky perversions. Our policy there is: among two or more consenting adults of any sex or species, nothing is a no-no.** *(Sits on boat Down Right.)*

MARTHA: Be that as it may, our policy here is that there are many no-no's — among them impersonation and adultery.

MARIE: "Adultery!" How medieval!

FANNY: *(Crosses Right to MARIE.)* **Medieval, is it? Well then, it must be deserving of a medieval punishment. What do you say to that, you Loose Lassie, you!?** *(Shakes her by the ear.)*

MARIE: **I say there will be no punishment at all. You have no proof that your accusations are true.**

MARTHA: *(Takes out letter and waves it.)* **No proof, eh? What about this?**

MARIE: **Mon Dieu! I forgot about the letter!**

MARTHA: *(Crossing Down to MARIE.)* **The letter found on the ground beside your knapsack.**

FANNY: **Aye — and in the presence of a witness.**

MARIE: **How incriminating!**

MARTHA: **How indecent!**

FANNY: **What does it say?**

MARTHA: **You asked for it.** *(Reads with heavy American accent.)* **"Ma chere petite bonne aimee Marie Antoinette, how I —"**

MARIE: *(Stands and snatches letter from MARTHA.)* **Give it to me! Such passionate words must be read avec une grande sensibilite! Americans have no sense of these things.** *(Reads, crossing to Center.)* **"Ma chere petite bonne aimee Marie Antoinette. How I miss the sight of your little poodle face, with its dreamy doe eyes, its tiny wet-kitten nose, its pouting little monkey mouth —"**

FANNY: **By the sound of it so far, the lad's a frustrated veterinarian.**

MARIE: *(Crossing Left.)* **"I am desperate for the taste of your bon-bon kisses. I am mad with lust to touch the tips of your fingers, the tips of your toes, the tips of your ear lobes, and ... other assorted tips."**

FANNY: **Thank God for generalizations!**

MARIE: **"But to get to the heart of the matter —"**

FANNY: **Oh, no!**

MARIE: **"We are to be garrisoned here at Valley Forge for the winter."**

FANNY: **Whew!**

MARIE: **"This nincompoop Washington is afraid to march**

on Hairy Howe, the Don Juan of the Delaware —"

FANNY: *(Collapses onto boat at Down Right.)* Oh, me poor heart!

MARIE: "And even more afraid to march home to his wife, the Termagant of the Potomac."

MARTHA: Think of the dinners I wasted on that one!

MARIE: *(Crossing to Up of fire.)* "So here we are. The nights are cold. Unless I have the passionate pants of my hot-blooded little poodle to keep me warm, I shall perish. You must save me from this fate. You must come to me, my Little Cream Puff, or my game with life is lost. I adore you, I love you, I long for you, I live for you, etcetera, etcetera." Signed: "Yours till Niagara falls — Joseph L." So! Now you have seen the flame of the true passion — and will never see it again. *(Tosses letter into fire.)*

MARTHA: *(Crosses Left, retrieves letter.)* Oh, no you don't, my Little Cream Puff! You won't get off the hook that easily!

MARIE: *(Crosses to Right log-seat and kneels on it.)* Oh, Madame, you must not show this letter to your nincompoop husband. He will take the stripes off my Joseph's shoulder and put them on his back. Please — I beg of you! I will do anything — anything!

FANNY: Would you be up for signing a peace treaty?

MARIE: *(Standing)* **Quoi?** *(Together)*

MARTHA: What?

FANNY: Would you be willing to forge King Louis' name on a treaty of peace with Britain?

MARTHA: What are you up to, Fanny?

FANNY: *(Stands)* Are you after thinking this Lafayette is the only lad who's writing such blarney to his mistress? Why, they'll all be wooing their wenches if this war's to be dragging on forever, I'm telling you, it's got to be stopped — war means the breaking down of the nuclear family!

MARTHA: *(Sits on Left log-seat.)* And do you really think we can get away with forging a peace treaty?

FANNY: Why not I ask you? It's your two countries fighting against mine, ain't it? Well now, if we all three sign our husbands' names on a treaty of peace, what's to keep the fighting going on?

MARTHA: Well, I'm game. *(To MARIE.)* How about you, Toots?

MARIE: *(Sits on Right log-seat.)* I will do anything to get the letter back.

FANNY: All right, then. *(Sits on Down Right boat and takes out pencil and rejection slip. Writes on the back of this.)* Let's be getting on with the terms of agreement. So now . . . All that the limeys care about is trade and waterways and the like. So you give us the right to be cruising up and down the Mississippi River as much as we please.

MARTHA: Fine, fine.

FANNY: What do you want?

MARTHA: *(Crosses Left to boat and picks up map hanging over side of it.)* Well, the only thing Yankee men give a hoot about is land. They're all real-estate crazy. So you give us . . . Oh, I don't know . . . how about all the land as far west as the Missouri?

MARIE: No, no, you may not have the French Quarter. We must keep the Louisiana.

MARTHA: No sweat. Make it as far west as the Mississippi.

FANNY: Just as you say then. *(Writes)*

MARTHA: And as far south as the thirtieth parallel.

FANNY: *(Writing)* Thir . . . ti . . . eth parall —

MARTHA: No, wait. A round number will sound too logical. It might give us away. Should be something the men would come up with — something arbitrary. Make it the thirty-first parallel.

FANNY: *(Erases and writes.)* Thirty-first parallel.

MARTHA: And to the north, make the border . . . the Hudson Bay. *(Tosses map into boat.)*

MARIE: *(Stands)* No. No. You must not give Canada to the Americans. It would mean the corruption of their language.

MARTHA: *(Crosses to Left log-seat and sits.)* Oh, very well then.

Keep Canada.

FANNY: *(Crosses to Right Log-seat and sits.)* **I've got it all down now** — **a fine settlement. So then** — *(Offers it to Martha.)* — **here it is for the signing.**

MARTHA: *(Takes paper and pencil, starts to sign, hesitates.)* **You know, there's something . . . incomplete about this.**

FANNY: **Well, sure and it's understood that the fourth boundary be the great ocean itself.**

MARTHA: **I don't mean that.**

MARIE: **Mais qu'est-ce que c'est?**

MARTHA: *(Stands, crosses Left.)* **I mean here we are — for the first time in history** — **three women drawing up an important document that will have a great effect on the future of our world . . .**

FANNY: **Aye — so?**

MARTHA: **So I think we should take advantage of the opportunity and give ourselves a few rights.**

FANNY: **Rights for women?**

MARIE: **It is tres radical!**

MARTHA: *(Crosses Up to rock.)* **Yes, I have it now! We'll draw up an act giving ourselves rights the same as the men! The Equal Rights Act we'll call it.** *(Writes on treaty, using top of rock to rest on.)* **E-qual . . . Rights . . . Act. We'll make this ERA a part of the treaty.**

FANNY: **What sort of rights are you thinking of?**

MARTHA: *(Crossing Down.)* **Oh, you know — property rights, suffrage, educational opportunites, equal pay for equal work — the whole bit.**

MARIE: **Ha! What a joke! I assure you, Mesdames, it will never happen in France. Equality means the end of romance. And France will never abandon the romance for the reason!**

MARTHA: **What about the British Empire?**

FANNY: **Not a chance will it have there. The British Empire is built on the principle of Divine Right: the men think they're divine, even though the women know we're right.**

MARTHA: Well, this is the United States of America! Land of opportunity for all! Cradle of Democracy! Fount of Freedom! Lover of Liberty —

MARIE: Oui, oui, so what?

MARTHA: So I think the ERA will have a chance here. I tell you in this country it will happen!

MARIE: When?

MARTHA: When?

FANNY: Aye — when?

MARTHA: Well, maybe not tomorrow.

MARIE: Ha!

MARTHA: But someday.

FANNY: Someday?

MARTHA: Someday soon.

MARIE: How soon?

MARTHA: Well, maybe a hundred years. Two hundred at the outside.

MARIE: Deux cents ans! Mon Dieu!

FANNY: Blessed St. Patrick! You won't be around in another two hundred years, woman! Who's to see to this ERA business?

MARTHA: *(Crosses Down.)* I am not the Mother of my Country for nothing. My daughters will see to it. Or my daughters' daughters. Or my daughters' daughters' daughters. Or my —

MARIE: C'est bon, c'est bon. But how will they find out about it?

MARTHA: I'll pass this document on to them.

FANNY: That'll be a bit dangerous, won't it though? I mean supposing it falls into the "wrong hands?" Why then it'll be woe to the lass as was harboring it.

MARIE: She has a point there, no?

MARTHA: Yes, I guess you're right. But I refuse to just let it go to the winds.

MARIE: Ah — then let it go to the waters.

MARTHA: What?

FANNY: I know what the lass means. You want to be putting

that paper into some sort of bottle and tossing it into the Delaware — to be discovered by posterity.

MARTHA: Well, the idea's got possibilities.

MARIE: Un moment! *(Crosses Up Center.)* I have an empty wine bottle in my knapsack.

MARTHA: *(Crossing Down Center.)* That way it won't have far to go to reach some enterprising American Congresswoman.

MARIE: Congresswoman! Ha! *(Crosses to Down Left of MARTHA.)*

FANNY: *(Crosses to Down Right of MARTHA.)* Let her be, lass. In a country of dreamers, the crazy woman is queen.

MARIE: Voila la bottle, Madame Washington.

MARTHA: *(Holding document.)* And voila the hope of America! *(MARTHA rolls up paper and stuffs it into bottle, while reciting. MARIE and FANNY strike appropriate poses at the end of each phrase, as music fades in.)* We the Founding Mothers of these United States, in order to form a perfect union, establish justice, provide for the common defense against domestic tragedy, promote the general welfare of both sexes, and secure the blessings of liberty to our daughters, do ordain and establish that — *(FANNY and MARIE go down on one knee.)* — equality of rights under the law shall not be denied or abridged on account of sex. *(She tosses bottle into audience.)*

MARIE: Liberte!

FANNY: Equality!

ALL: Sorority!

THE END

THE AMERICAN WAY

by
LAVONNE MUELLER

Lavonne Mueller is a vital part of the Women's Project at The American Place Theatre in New York. She won the 1986 Drama League Award and has participated in Robert Redford's Sundance Institute. *The American Way* was first produced at The American Place Theatre in 1984.

Production Suggestions

One of the challenges in performing a successful production of *The American Way* is finding the appropriate style. Do try to define the style as you discuss the play with your partners, but refrain from trying to "stylize" your performance. Let the style grow naturally out of your rehearsals.

This script calls for a plethora of props. Don't despair; think of a way to solve the problem. Here are two suggestions from the playwright: "Davenport can wheel in a large bin in which actors can look — rummaging within. I think it's even better if we don't *see* — only "hear" these artifacts. The furniture in the room should be cardboard — items should be overly easy to remove. That is the thing: One can denude the White House with ease. Or: Mimed props are possible. After all, these objects are things that we the people hear about and rarely see. Their historical reality is defined by the perceptions of others. And, like everything else in Washington, they, too, can have assassins."

Finally, refrain from trying to smooth out the play. The rough edges of this political satire are part of its fabric.

Address all inquiries concerning performances, readings, or reprinting of this work *or any portion thereof* to Lavonne Mueller at The American Place Theatre, 111 West 46th Street, New York, NY 10036. For details, see "Part II: Securing Rights for Your Production" on pages 223 to 232.

Read about Lavonne Mueller in *Breaking In* (Doubleday, 1982) edited by James Tinen, pages 36 to 39.

THE AMERICAN WAY
by
LAVONNE MUELLER

The action takes place at the present time in the master bedroom of the White House.

Characters:
THE PRESIDENT
THE FIRST LADY
DAVENPORT

Setting: *Furniture used in the play, including the bed and dresser, should be made of cardboard. See the playwright's comments in the Production Suggestions, page 187.*

AT RISE: The PRESIDENT and his WIFE are sitting at the breakfast table near opened portico doors. They are drinking coffee.

WIFE: Darling ... I've been thinking ...

PRESIDENT: Yes.

WIFE: I want to have a yard sale.

PRESIDENT: A what?

WIFE: A yard sale.

PRESIDENT: Honey, you can't do that. I mean ... we're not in the position to do things like that.

WIFE: I have some stuff we brought with us from California. And now that the children are married ...

PRESIDENT: I really don't think we're in a position to ...

WIFE: I have no intention of ... well, selling anything historic. Just old bedding, furniture, clutter from the attic.

PRESIDENT: We're living in a national archive, honey. My God ... Washington slept here ... Grant slept here ...

WIFE: *I* slept here!

PRESIDENT: I'll tell you what. I'll bring it up at the staff meeting this morning.

WIFE: Why do those buffaloes have to know about our personal business?

PRESIDENT: Our business is everybody's business. I'm in the public's eye.

WIFE: I've got the right to sell my own property. That's in the Constitution.

PRESIDENT: My job, honey, makes me vulnerable. We don't want to do anything ... well ... indiscreet.

WIFE: What's indiscreet about selling some old furniture and books?

PRESIDENT: I'm not an ordinary person. I have a job that ...

WIFE: You and your job. Do I have to give up my body and soul for your lousy job!

PRESIDENT: I told you when we started ... when we came to Washington. I said it wasn't going to be easy. I said we had to make a few sacrifices.

WIFE: I don't mind making sacrifices that mean something.

PRESIDENT: If it were up to me ... hell, what do I care. You could sell off the whole damn place.

WIFE: Then let me do this, honey ... just let me have a little bitty yard sale so I can make a few dollars of my own. (*A knock is heard at the door. Then DAVENPORT comes in wheeling a breakfast tray. She is dressed in her Class-A WAC uniform. She is nearing sixty and limps from an old war wound. She sets a tray cart of toast, juice and coffee before the PRESIDENT.*)

PRESIDENT: (*To DAVENPORT.*) Any coups last night?

DAVENPORT: None of importance, sir.

WIFE: You can start having the stuff brought down from the attic, Davenport.

DAVENPORT: Oh, good. Then it's on.

PRESIDENT: Just a minute, honey. I said I'd bring the matter up at the cabinet meeting this morning.

WIFE: Davenport and I are setting up.

PRESIDENT: (*To DAVENPORT.*) Davenport!

WIFE: (*To DAVENPORT.*) Davenport!

DAVENPORT: *(Looking at WIFE.)* **Which yard?**

WIFE: **Just ... pick one.** *(DAVENPORT shakes her head in agreement. She exits. The PRESIDENT stands to read.)*

PRESIDENT: *(Hitting paper angrily with his hand.)* **Look at that. They're calling us Imperialists!** *(Pause)* **That's all I hear. Imperialists! We gave the Philippines back! What about the Marshall Plan? We'd fork over to Malaysia ... but hell, they manage their own affairs too well.**

WIFE: **Eat your breakfast.**

PRESIDENT: *(Still standing with the paper.)* **Insurgencies everywhere.** *(Pause)* **So we give the world handouts. Pave their pockets even as we blast their damn pants off. Are we just pawns to be led inna cul-de-sac which has no leeway?**

WIFE: **Sit down and eat a decent breakfast like you're supposed to.** *(They sit before the breakfast tray. PRESIDENT reaches for the cream.)*

WIFE: **Don't you dare touch that cream.** *(Pause)* **You're not going to run your blood pressure up on me. You're not going to do that to me on top of everything else.** *(Silent pause as they drink their coffee. Then, a knock at the door.)*

WIFE: **Davenport?**

DAVENPORT: **Yes.**

WIFE: **Come in.**

PRESIDENT: **You enjoy your second cup, honey. I'll go shave.** *(Exits to the bathroom.)*

DAVENPORT: **I got us a yard.**

WIFE: **Good.**

DAVENPORT: **Real nice one. Off the West Wing Office.**

WIFE: **We'll have the bulk of it carried downstairs this afternoon. We can do the price tags after dinner.**

DAVENPORT: **I'll see to it.**

WIFE: **Go over the inventory. If you find a little end table ... odd stool ... something not listed. You know what I'm talking about, Davenport.**

DAVENPORT: **Certainly.**

WIFE: And advertise in the *Embassy Newsletter*. Those little independent African countries love to buy cheap junk.

DAVENPORT: Of course.

WIFE: Small ad. Nothing gaudy. Small and tasteful.

DAVENPORT: Yes.

WIFE: I know "He" doesn't altogether approve. But I have the right to sell things. Just like other women. Isn't that right, Davenport?

DAVENPORT: Most certainly.

WIFE: We'll do everything tastefully. So there's no criticism.

DAVENPORT: I'll supervise everything myself.

WIFE: Good. *(Pause)*

DAVENPORT: ... I ... I

WIFE: What is it, Davenport?

DAVENPORT: I have a few odd belongings of my own that ... that I'd like to get rid of ... couple frag grenades ... OD blanket ... sampan ... little portable howitzer ...

WIFE: Just toss them in.

DAVENPORT: I'm saving for a fondue set.

WIFE: Bring your things on down with the others. *(DAVENPORT exits. PRESIDENT comes out of the bathroom after shaving.)*

WIFE: Did you use the razor I gave you for Christmas?

PRESIDENT: Yes.

WIFE: It's not the closest shave in the world. *(She looks at him closely.)* Why is it ... that you're getting to look more and more like your passport picture?

PRESIDENT: I'm under pressure. Everybody's on my back. I got a cabinet meeting this morning that'd make your hair stand up on end.

WIFE: That again.

PRESIDENT: I tell you ... time's on *their* side.

WIFE: Who?

PRESIDENT: The insurgents. They keep creeping out of the jungles ... three by three. Nothin stops them. You don't wipe out guerrillas with artillery. Guns ... bombs ... they keep coming back. It's the one-hundred years war. What the hell. It's all right with me. Just tell the damn taxpayers that. *(The PRESIDENT and his WIFE drink their coffee silently. A pause, a thud is heard at the door.)*

WIFE: Davenport?

DAVENPORT: Yes.

WIFE: Come in. *(DAVENPORT comes in carrying two long house roof-gutters which she struggles with.)*

PRESIDENT: What the hell?

WIFE: *(Happily)* Davenport, I certainly hope that's what I think it is.

DAVENPORT: I thought you'd be pleased. *(Pause)* Where can I put them?

PRESIDENT: Make sure the war-head's removed. One of those MACE-A things misfired at ...

DAVENPORT: House gutters, sir.

WIFE: Put them on the Portico. *(DAVENPORT dumps the gutters on the Portico as the PRESIDENT watches curiously and WIFE watches happily.)*

DAVENPORT: Doesn't rain on the West Porch. I see no reason why we need gutters on the West Porch.

WIFE: Marvelous. You're a genius, Davenport.

DAVENPORT: They're not on the inventory.

WIFE: Marvelous.

DAVENPORT: I thought you'd approve.

PRESIDENT: Approve what?

WIFE: It's for our yard sale.

PRESIDENT: Now look here, honey. I never said you could go through with this.

WIFE: *(Ignores the PRESIDENT. To DAVENPORT.)* You can be thinking about how much to ask. We want to offer bargains ... but let's not give things away.

DAVENPORT: Exactly what I think.

PRESIDENT: I specifically said I'd have to think it over.

WIFE: *(Looking at PRESIDENT as she muses.)* I don't suppose you know how much they cost originally?

PRESIDENT: What?

WIFE: The gutters.

PRESIDENT: How would I know that?

WIFE: Naturally. I can't count on you to know anything.

DAVENPORT: I could ask around.

WIFE: Would you?

PRESIDENT: I said I'd bring it up at the staff meeting this morning. That's all I said.

DAVENPORT: *(Looking at the PRESIDENT.)* How old would you say?

PRESIDENT: A fat 70 . . . to hear everybody talk.

WIFE: Not you. The gutters.

PRESIDENT: I don't know how old they are.

DAVENPORT: It makes a difference, sir. On the price. I try to be fair.

WIFE: *(To DAVENPORT.)* I hate to ask you to make decisions like this . . . but . . . I do want you to know how much I appreciate what you're doing. *(DAVENPORT shakes her head knowingly.)*

PRESIDENT: Don't make this yard sale definite till I've thrashed out the particulars with my cabinet.

DAVENPORT: *(To WIFE.)* I'll ask around in the kitchen.

PRESIDENT: *(To DAVENPORT.)* While you're out there, find out what's for dinner.

WIFE: *(To PRESIDENT.)* I don't want you even thinking about dinner. We haven't finished breakfast yet.

DAVENPORT: And . . . sir . . .

PRESIDENT: What is it, Davenport?

DAVENPORT: About my promotion . . . *(Pause)* . . . you were going to look in to it, sir. *(Pause)* If I might remind you, I haven't been promoted since . . . since Korea, sir.

PRESIDENT: *(Suddenly bathed in a pleasant memory.)* Ahhhhh. Korea.

WIFE: Don't get him started on that, Davenport.

DAVENPORT: Sorry, ma'am.

PRESIDENT: *(Fondly)* Korea.

DAVENPORT: I was a PFC on Chinaman's Hat.

PRESIDENT: *(Dreamily)* Yes ... yes ...

DAVENPORT: The Orderly Room was hit. My typewriter got it by a mortar shell. A grenade went off next to my leg. I got me "Capital C and R" fragments in my left ankle.

PRESIDENT: Those Democrats really screwed up Korea. Not even a War. Police Action. *(The PRESIDENT laughs.)*

DAVENPORT: Then ... a machine gun tracer set fire to the filter I was putting in the Command Post coffee pot. I was all in silhouette ... holding a dictation pad against my ribs.

PRESIDENT: I'm aware of your record, Davenport.

DAVENPORT: That was 1951, sir.

PRESIDENT: We're rank heavy. My hands are tied. I'm only following orders.

DAVENPORT: But ... you give the orders, sir.

PRESIDENT: I have to follow the orders I give! *(Pause)* That will be all, Davenport.

DAVENPORT: Yes, sir. *(DAVENPORT exits. The PRESIDENT and his WIFE silently drink coffee. After a pause:)*

PRESIDENT: I've gone over some budget matters, honey, and I find you've wiped out National-Park-Service-Petty-Cash. *(Pause)* If you're going shopping, fill out Reimbursement Voucher R-V101. You just can't walk into Petty Cash and grab a wad of bills.

WIFE: I don't have time to fill out a crummy voucher in triplicate.

PRESIDENT: I can't balance the budget around here without some kind of vouchers.

WIFE: Are you cutting me off?

PRESIDENT: Petty cash is down to zero. I had to take a gold bar from the basement of the Federal Reserve Bank of New York. You know what it's like trying to carry a gold brick around in a budget envelope?

WIFE: What's it worth? The gold bar?

PRESIDENT: The troy weight is multiplied by the assay

number and multiplied by the price per fine ounce.

WIFE: What does that mean?

PRESIDENT: Average gold bullion is worth $14,000.

WIFE: Then give me a bar.

PRESIDENT: That bar's only an index.

WIFE: You trying to say gold's not worth anything?

PRESIDENT: I'm trying to tell you, honey, you can't cash it. You can't cash a *standard.*

WIFE: You give me one of those bars, and I'll cash it so fast you'll wonder what hit you. *(A knock is heard at the door. After a pause, DAVENPORT comes in. DAVENPORT wheels in a supermarket cart filled with items.)*

DAVENPORT: *(To WIFE.)* A few items...pending your approval. For the yard sale.

WIFE: Good.

DAVENPORT: An old pig-in-the-poke, Poke poker.

PRESIDENT: That's from the State Dining Room.

WIFE: *(To PRESIDENT.)* It's worthless.

PRESIDENT: Poke used that poker!

WIFE: Oh...give it to him. *(DAVENPORT gives the poker to the PRESIDENT. Pause as they all look in the cart.)*

DAVENPORT: Some chintz...valance...Monroe candlestick.

WIFE: Marilyn?

DAVENPORT: James.

WIFE: He can keep it. *(DAVENPORT gives the candlestick to the PRESIDENT.)*

DAVENPORT: Flocked   paper...old   treaty...Chester Arthur chesterdrawer...front door swag from the Cross Hall...spare firescreens from the Diplomatic Reception Room...Rosemary Wood's Underwood...Adam's bathrobe...

WIFE: Sherman Adams?

DAVENPORT: John Quincy. No belt. *(She gives the bathrobe to the PRESIDENT.)* Hamilton velvet suit.

WIFE: Alexander?

DAVENPORT: George Hamilton.

WIFE: *(Grabs it.)* I'll keep that myself.

DAVENPORT: Fifteen-amp fusetron ... whiffle ball ... old letter ... cholera belt.

WIFE: Nobody gets cholera any more. *(Gives cholera belt to PRESIDENT.)*

DAVENPORT: Brass doorknob ... inside shutter from the solarium.

WIFE: Quite right. Outside shutters are sufficient in the solarium.

DAVENPORT: Waffle-iron. Excellent condition.

PRESIDENT: Why don't we have waffles anymore?

WIFE: Cholesterol! *(To DAVENPORT.)* There he goes again ... trying to kill himself.

DAVENPORT: You do a good job with him.

WIFE: I appreciate that, Davenport.

DAVENPORT: Turkey platter ... andiron ... walking stick ... bronzed inkstand ... cake basket ... brass-pull ... niche from the North Rotunda.

WIFE: Excellent.

DAVENPORT: On the Portico?

WIFE: Yes. *(DAVENPORT wheels out the supermarket basket full of things to the Portico and then exits.)*

PRESIDENT: *(Looking at newspaper.)* I'm responsible for everything. Everything. Even time. I gotta fight time zones. Maldovia is twelve hours in the future. That means tonight, Maldovia is tomorrow. That means if I drop a ICBM on Maldovia, I have to give orders now to what already happened tomorrow but whose retaliation is received here today.

WIFE: If it isn't Maldovia ... it's El Salvador. I'm tired of all that mish-mash.

PRESIDENT: It's important, honey.

WIFE: You're gonna sit there and tell me El Salvador's important!

PRESIDENT: You ever see a napalm canister fall down from

the bomb shelf of a plane? *(Pause)* **Well, I have. In El Salvador.**

WIFE: **So.**

PRESIDENT: **So ... you see scarlet-orange napalm spin and ripple up from the ground, you've seen something. And white phosphorous grenades. The dead glow in the dark.**

WIFE: **I don't care about some old dead people glowing. I care about the *living*. I care about my yard sale.** *(The phone rings. WIFE answers it. Into phone.)* **Yes. He's here.** *(Pause. To PRESIDENT:)* **The Pentagon.**

PRESIDENT: *(Takes phone. Into phone:)* **President.** *(Pause)* **I don't want you Pentagon people parking on residential lawns behind the Capitol Building.** *(Pause)* **I don't care about your Diplomatic License Plate.** *(Pause)* **I'm asking all of you ... keep off private lawns. Park somewhere else. On traffic islands. In front of fire hydrants. I'm tired of all the complaints from townspeople. I want 'em off my back ... yes ... that's right ... yes ...** *(A knock. Then DAVENPORT comes in pushing a large bin on rollers filled with objects including two file cabinets. WIFE looks eagerly into the bin.)*

DAVENPORT: **Urn shaft ... music stand ... fringe ... slipper chair ... festoon ... splat ... lantern ... sconces ... tureen ... green ewer.**

WIFE: *(Makes face.)* **Federal green.** *(Hands ewer to PRESIDENT.)*

DAVENPORT: **Pilaster ... buckram ... sideboard — French Empire. Bracket from the Colonnade ... terra cotta ... fresco ... one parquet from the North Pavillion ... old hickory stick ... washstand ... pendant from the Grand Staircase ... Eagle top cornice ... settee — Continental Congress design. Left over gilt ... stucco from the gatehouse ... vulcanized rubber ... Stanford White chair — from the Levee Room.**

WIFE: *(Takes chair.)* **Quite right to sell this. Prez doesn't need the NAACP on his back.** *(She throws the chair back into the bin.)*

DAVENPORT: Nosedrops ... molding — egg and dart pattern. Stuffed animal head.

WIFE: *(Takes animal head.)* Endangered species?

DAVENPORT: Just an everyday African Dic-Dic.

WIFE: *(Throwing the animal head into the bin.)* Good. We don't need the Wild-Life People on our back.

DAVENPORT: Saber leg ... flute ... veneer ... plume ... footed glass ... cup of rococo ... Pluribus ... billiard ball ... gravy boat ... punch bowl ... dog dish.

WIFE: *(Takes dog dish and reads name on it.)* "Him."

DAVENPORT: *(Takes dog dish from WIFE and throws it in bin.)* He doesn't need Women's Lib on his back. *(Pause)* ... Chipped Chippendale ... chimney breast ... cornice ... wainscot ... mantle shelf ... green cambric — Federal Green. *(WIFE makes face at federal green cambric. She hands cambric to PRESIDENT.)*

DAVENPORT: Frieze from the Grand Staircase ... wood filigree ... pre-Civil War dimity ... bridge truss ... entablature ... metope ... dado ... burl panel ... call-bell ... balustrade ... Martha's diary.

WIFE: *(Takes diary.)* Martha Mitchell?

DAVENPORT: Martha Washington. *(WIFE makes a face and hands the diary to PRESIDENT.)* And ... two file cabinets.

WIFE: You're a genius, Davenport.

DAVENPORT: *(Pulls out a drawer in file cabinet.)* ... with files!

WIFE: I wouldn't want to sell anything ... "priority."

DAVENPORT: Just old contracts from some East River dikes.

WIFE: Good to get rid of this. President doesn't need "gays" in his files.

DAVENPORT: *(Shakes her head in agreement.)* That's it ... None of it "inventoried." *(Pause as DAVENPORT and WIFE look around the room. They both look at a picture on the wall.)*

DAVENPORT: *(Goes to painting and touches it.)* John Singer Sargeant.

WIFE: Are paintings in this place inventoried?

DAVENPORT: **Nothing below . . . lieutenant.** *(WIFE takes the painting off the wall and tosses it in the bin.)*

WIFE: *(Pushes bin to DAVENPORT.)* **Put all this with the others.** *(DAVENPORT pushes the bin out to the Portico. WIFE stares at the dresser . . . then rolls it toward the Portico.)*

DAVENPORT: *(Says about dresser as she returns from the Portico.)* **That's "inventory."**

WIFE: **Adjust the books, Davenport.** *(Pause)* **Help me with the bed.** *(WIFE and DAVENPORT roll the bed out on the Portico. As they come back in, DAVENPORT fingers the drapes.)*

WIFE: *(About drapes.)* **Federal green.** *(DAVENPORT exits, rolling out the breakfast tray-cart as she goes. The room is now empty. Lights go down as WIFE looks around proudly at the empty room. PRESIDENT is intently mumbling on the phone holding discarded objects.)*

THE END

Monologs

DROWNED OUT

by

ROBERT PATRICK

Robert Patrick was born in Kilgore, Texas in 1937, and educated himself via radio, movies, magazines, and paperback books. He started writing plays in 1964 for the legendary Caffe Cino in New York, the first Off-Off Broadway theatre. His over fifty published plays include *Kennedy's Children*. He lectures widely for the International Thespian Society and received their Founders Award "for services to theatre and to youth."

Production Suggestions

Drowned Out permits a wide variety of performance possibilities; in fact, it almost demands that its actors create innovative approaches to the script. Since the focus is on the female character's response to the music rather than the music itself, the play *must* be performed without actual music. If the play is done as a monolog, the actress should be sure to work with a partner some of the time so that she can base her acting on responses to a real person. She should also realize that doing a monolog demands a special kind of discipline; she will need to give as much actual rehearsal time to this play as she would to a two-character play of the same length. If the play is done as a duet, the non-speaking actor will need to invent almost his entire role, including his intentions, his relationship to her, his business and blocking, and the words he speaks (which she and the audience never hear); all of this invention, however, will need to fit precisely with the clues and cues given in the speaking character's dialog. Notice that regardless of whether the play is done as monolog or dialog, the task of the actor in *Drowned Out* is essentially the same as that of an actor in any other play — turning words on a page into believable, human action.

Address all inquiries concerning performances, readings, or reprinting of this work *or any portion thereof* to Robert Patrick, 1837 North Alexandria Avenue #211, Los Angeles, CA 90027. For details, see "Part II: Securing Rights to Your Production," pages 223 to 232.

For more information about Robert Patrick, read Leah D. Frank's article on pages 623 to 627 in the third edition of *Contemporary Dramatists,* edited by James Vinson and published in 1982 by St. Martin's Press of New York.

DROWNED OUT
(for Carol Nelson)

by
ROBERT PATRICK

The action takes place in a night spot in the present.

Characters:
SHE
HE — her escort

Setting: *A table with two chairs.*

AT RISE: SHE and HE enter. Throughout, SHE is shouting to be heard over very loud music. Asterisks (***) indicate that HE speaks, but we, like SHE, cannot hear a word HE says.

SHE: **What? Oh, yes, this table will be fine. If that's what you asked.** *(They sit.)* **I think that's what you asked. You may have asked me to marry you or to join you in assassinating several politicians. My God, why do they play the music so loud in these places? Why do they play the music so loud every place? Is it because jukeboxes cost a quarter now? Is it to give you your money's worth? No, they can't possibly care about that.**

***

SHE: **Yes, I liked the play. I'm assuming you asked me if I liked the play. I mean, I didn't actively dislike it. I mean, I didn't throw up or run screaming out of the theatre. It was the sort of pleasant little play that makes for interesting conversation afterwards. Ha-ha-ha-ha-ha.**

***

SHE: **You smiled when you said that. You must have been pleased with my response. Oh, I'm beginning to be able to read your expressions. When I get to where I can read your lips, I'll be getting somewhere. In the meantime, I can read the table. We're obviously never going to get a menu. Have you read the table yet? Have you read *any***

interesting tables lately? Lookie here, somebody carved "Life is meaningless" and their phone number.

***

SHE: Why, yes, sometimes I think that life is meaningless. Other times I don't think at all. And sometimes I think I ought to cut my bangs. Do you think I ought to cut my bangs?

***

SHE: That was a definite smile. We're getting someplace. Now, let's see. Did you say, "Yes, I think you ought to cut your bangs; at the moment you look like a Sealyham lapdog," or could you have possibly have said, "Please never cut your bangs; I love your bangs; I dream of your bangs." No, that's too many syllables. Well, I think I'll bob my head back and forth and laugh and tap my fingers on the table in time to the music. La-la-la-la-Boomp-boomp-BOOMPH!!! I'll bet I looked adorable doing *that!* You're looking down at the table. I've embarrassed you. *(Looks around.)*

Oh, I see. Nobody else in the place is bobbing their head or tapping their fingers. They're all engaged in meaningful conversation. How do they do that? Are there scripts you can memorize? Am I just not subscribing to the proper magazines? Oh, no I see. You're not ashamed of me at all. You're reading the table. Hmmmmm. Now, here is a problem. From your side, the caption beside that obscene drawing says, "Wow," and from my side it says, "Mom." Gee, I'd like to share that amusing tidbit with you. Maybe I should rotate the table. If I look up from that filthy picture and smile, will I give the wrong impression? Maybe I should just look around and bob my head and tap my fingers again.

***

SHE: What? Now *that's* the silliest thing I ever said. "What?" Perhaps I'll just nod enthusiastically. Maybe you asked me if I am having a good time. You're nodding, too! We're agreeing on something! I'm nodding harder and so are you. Hey, we're laughing together. I probably just agreed to help you hold up the place. My God, I did. You're reaching in your pocket for a gun! No, it's a dollar! *(Still smiling and laughing merrily.)* I wonder what I just agreed to do for a dollar? *(HE stands up and looks about.)* I know! You're going to offer any man in this place a dollar to take me away! La-la-la-la-diddle-dee-bunk-OOMPH! You're hailing a waitress! *(HE smiles at HER and walks Offstage.)*

Oh, no, you're going to offer the waitress a dollar to bring us menus. Is it any wonder that I love you? Or would it be any wonder if I did? Well, yes, considering that we've never said fifteen consecutive words to each other. "Hi, I've got a cab waiting!" "I think these are our seats!" "I think the show's starting!" "Let's have a drink across the street!" Sweet God in Heaven, the waitress is giving him four quarters. He's calling paramedics to take me to the looney bin. No, there's no escape. He's walking to the jukebox and shoveling quarters in. He's wrinkling his brow and punching buttons. And I know that jukebox. I've read it. You get five selections for a dollar. *(SHE lowers her voice.)* I don't believe it. The music has actually stopped. I can hear plates rattling and the cash register pa-ching!-ing and the pinball machine muttering, "You have defeated Kogar!" And here he comes back. It's true! I have defeated Kogar! I'm going to be able to tell him I want out of this place! *(HE re-enters, waves at her, and approaches the table. SHE opens her mouth and is about to speak again, when music starts again.)*

Oh, boy, he found one that turned on several extra speakers. He's nodding at me with a questioning look on his face. Maybe he's asking me if I'd like to set fire to the place. I'll nod passionately. He's not sitting down. In fact, no one is sitting down. All around me, people are standing up. Maybe everybody has had enough and we're going to tear the timbers down and beat the jukebox into little plastic pieces? No, the couples are all embracing. Are the men going off to war? Are the women going off to the powder room? Are we all about to split up and play football? No, they're all walking out into the middle of the floor. They're all smashing cockroaches under their feet and grinding them into the concrete. Oh, no, could it be . . .? It is. It is. They're dancing! They've surrendered to the music! My hero's choice has conquered their reserve! And there he is, standing there, holding his arms out to me. He's not threatening to strangle me, his hands are too far apart. He couldn't be telling me how big his fish is. He probably wants me to get up and dance. I could get up and dance. Or I could turn him around and offer him for a coatrack. No, that's not all I could do. I could bang my face on the table until he gets the idea. Only then I'd go around with the word "Mom" engraved on my forehead.

***

SHE: Oh, he's committed himself. He said, "I thought we might dance," or else "I'm off to fight in France." Either way, the polite thing is to throw myself into his arms. I can't just sit here clutching the table edge; I'm getting chewing-gum under my fingernails. All right, I'll get up and let him lead me to the dance floor. He'll let go of me when we get there, and I can fall on my hands and knees and crawl to safety. Wherever that may be. And I do mean wherever. *(SHE rises, takes HIS hands and allows herself to be led Offstage to the dance floor. If we couldn't hear her, we'd think SHE was the happiest girl in the world.)*

All right, lead me to it. That's the spirit! That's the drive and energy that made us win in Viet Nam. We didn't? Well, this is a fine time to tell me! *(They are gone.)*

THE END

ONE BEER TOO MANY

by
BILLY HOUCK

Billy Houck teaches at Arroyo Grande High School in Arroyo Grande, California. His plays have been produced in California, Virginia, New York, Oregon, New Mexico, Bangkok, Manila, and London. *Other Stages* magazine and *Dramatics* magazine have published his scripts. *One Beer Too Many* was first produced at the Arroyo Grande Eagle Theatre.

Production Suggestions

Become Skip. Don't push. Enjoy.

Address all inquiries concerning performances, readings, or reprinting of this work *or any portion thereof* to Billy Houck, 1240 Sage Street, Arroyo Grande, CA 93420. For details, see "Part II: Securing Rights for Your Production," on pages 223 to 232.

ONE BEER TOO MANY

By
BILLY HOUCK

The action takes place in a time and place to be determined by the actor.

Character:
SKIP — a seventeen-year-old boy

Setting: *A sad spot of light on an empty stage.*

SKIP: I used to enjoy English. I used to enjoy creative writing. My sophomore teacher, Ms. Lipschitz, told me I was *good.* Said I had *promise.* A *real* original. It was *so* nice to see student writing with such style. Real *quality* work. Ms. Lipschitz. I told my Mom I was gonna be a writer. She said: "That's nice, Honey." I told my Dad. He just looked at me and sat in his black naugahyde La-z-boy recliner and drank a beer.

I hate beer.

Ms. Lipschitz said there was a contest for the best student-written play. The Drama Club wanted to do an original work and the winner would get fifty bucks and the play would be done by the kids in the Drama Club. Ms. Lipschitz said this was my *perfect* chance to show the *world* that I could write. I didn't know what to write about.

Ms. Lipschitz said: "Write what you know."

Write what you know? Write what y'know. Wriwachano.

I thought, what do I know? I don't know what I know. So I told my Mom and she said: "That's nice, Honey." And I was gonna ask my Dad, but he was just sitting there, looking at me, drinking a beer, so I didn't even bother. So I went to my room and got out a sheet of paper and wrote: "Write What You Know." And I looked at the paper.

And I looked and I looked and I looked at that white white sheet of paper. And no words appeared on it.

I looked at that paper a long time.

I didn't see anything.

I could hear the TV in the living room and Dad's La-z-boy recliner creaking and Dad opening another beer.

And then I wrote a play! It was all about a man who was so self-centered that all he ever did was drink beer all day long in his La-z-boy recliner and he stacked up his empty cans in a pyramid and the pyramid got too high and it tipped over and the man was crushed under it and he died. Nobody could believe it was an accidental death so the man's son was charged with murder and he said he didn't do it but nobody would believe him so he went to prison and when he got out he was *old* and all *he* wanted to do was sit in a La-z-boy recliner and drink beer all day. I didn't have a chance to show my play to Ms. Lipschitz because the deadline was the next day, so I took it straight to the theatre and left it on the drama teacher, Mr. Larker's, desk. I called my play "One Beer Too Many." I was pretty proud of myself. Ms. Lipschitz said so, too. "Just for trying." I guess that meant she thought I didn't have much of a chance of being picked. I thought it was a sure thing, though, cause nobody else at that school, at least nobody I knew, was gonna write a play. Except one girl. Her name was Melody. Melody Golden. Really. She told me she was going to write a play about young people's dreams of stardom, and about how every young heart dreams of treading the boards and being in the spotlight. *(Snorts)* I mean, Melody was cute and I liked her and all that, but who would want to see a play about young hearts on boards? Not me. So when I got called out of class to go to the counseling office and I saw Ms. Lipschitz and Mr. Larker in there with my counselor, Mr. Sanchez, I *knew* I was in.

They were going to do my play and they called me to

the counselor's office to congratulate me.

I was so proud.

Then I saw their faces.

Ms. Lipschitz looked embarrassed. And Mr. Larker looked mad. And my counselor looked like he had some real bad news to tell me. Then I remembered that Mr. Larker was the drama teacher, and I figured that they were just . . . being dramatic . . . in . . . there.

So I pasted on a smile and swung in there and waited for the *good news*. And Mr. Sanchez shut the door. And Ms. Lipschitz wouldn't even look at me.

And I waited for a minute.

And nobody said anything.

And I remembered that blank page that didn't have any words on it except "Write What You Know." And all of a sudden Larker is shouting: *"Who* do you think you're dealing with here? I'm a professional!" And Ms. Lipschitz told him to calm down and Sanchez tells them both to remember what they're here for. And he looks at me like a sad puppy and says: "How long have you had fantasies of killing your father?"

I said: "Does this mean you guys aren't going to do my play?"

And Lipschitz starts to cry and Larker is shouting again about how this contest is for plays *by* students *about* students, and how "This Drama Department has standards that will never allow this kind of drivel to see the light of day."

And I realized that this guy Larker probably *loved* Melody's play. Then all three of them started yelling and Sanchez suggested I wait outside so I sat on a hard plastic chair in the hall and listened to them yell. Larker was blaming Lipschitz for "spawning a monster" and Lipschitz said she had no idea that I would write *"that* kind of play." And Larker yells *"by* students *for* students" so loud my plastic chair vibrates. And I stood up and yelled at the door: *"I'm* a student *too!* I was never in one of your stupid high-standard plays, but I'm a student *too!"*

And I left.

I thought I'd get in trouble, but *nobody* ever mentioned it again.

Just like I thought, they did Melody's play.

And the next summer, Ms. Lipschitz and Mr. Larker got married. I don't even know what happened to the one and only copy of *One Beer Too Many.* I guess they threw it away.

But nobody ever mentioned it again.

It was just like I never even wrote a play.

So I don't write any more.

Not plays.

Not nothin'.

And my life works out just fine.

Y'know?

THE END

ADVICE TO A NEW ACTOR

by
LAVONNE MUELLER

Lavonne Mueller is a vital part of the Women's Project at The American Place Theatre in New York. She wrote *Advice to a New Actor* for a benefit performance by Colleen Dewhurst in April, 1984, at The American Place Theatre.

Production Suggestions

The actor who prepares *Advice to a New Actor* needs to guard against abusing the freedom from relating to an acting partner; you need to exercise considerable self-discipline and go through all the steps of a normal rehearsal schedule in order to succeed with the play. If you find you do not have the necessary self-discipline for this task, or if you mistrust your self-perceptions, find a friend who will meet with you regularly to assist in rehearsals.

The lyric diction of this play requires special work from the performer. As in any play, the words of this monolog must be performed as believable dialog, not just a collection of weird or beautiful sounds and images. To solve this problem, you need to create a character who would actually use this kind of language, and you must know why the character uses these precise words to communicate with the imaginary new actor who has come seeking advice.

Address all inquiries concerning performances, readings, or reprinting of this work *or any portion thereof* to the playwright's agent, Julia Miles, at The American Place Theatre, 111 West 46th Street, New York, NY 10036. For details, see "Part II: Securing Rights for Your Production," pages 223 to 232.

ADVICE TO A NEW ACTOR

by
LAVONNE MUELLER

The action takes place in a time and place to be determined by the actor.

Character:
An experienced actor, age to be decided by the actor.

Setting: *To be determined by the actor.*

So
you want to act!
You come to me now
eager
dropping spangled spoors at my door
like a mindless child
smiling up at me
in your trapeze suit
all eager of summersaults
tambourine begging
for advice
>   *(Pause)*

Go! Run for your life!
>   *(Pause)*

Can't you understand
even grains of sand war for their tiny illusions
displaying passions of stone.
>   *(Pause)*

Everything you see
has a double life —
>   the cutlass, scimitar, blade,
>   messages on wall capillaries.
>   *(Pause)*

Go!
Don't let printed pages

make a pulpit of your eyes.
Don't let strange words
pull you to their confetti.
Acting is singing to yourself
in captivity.
   (Pause)
Leave the theatre.
Break the wishbone by yourself.
   (Pause)
Go!
Acting is dancing
without a father.
   (Pause)
The stage is always empty;
even the curtain feels how little it hides.
Would you be suited to the obedience of painted floors?
Is wood your prologue?
   (Pause)
Go!
Anywhere.
Where the flowers make fists
by the water.
The eye is a stronger mouth.
   (Pause)
What?
So you're still here.
Is there nothing I can say
to stop you?
   (Pause)
Ahhhhhh . . .
I see . . .
you find . . . majestic
   the light behind my ears
   and on my wrist
   like perfume.
   (Pause)

Let me tell you, my friend,
I have learned to carry the inscrutable lie
like a bride.
Dark is the main thing;
it is there
I am tender
and undying.
    (Pause)
You want advice —
    take these truths, damn you.
    (Pause)
Gorge
the forbidden word
translucent line
sweet spiced monolog.
Chew
slapstick
coarse oath
witticism.
Swallow whole
irony
homage
flat chalky prayer . . .
    then
    tie a string around you neck
    to keep it all down
    like a German farmer's goose.
    (Pause)
Be
a word ingress,
a Bach suite of rusty birds.
Mann's Mahler.
Eat with bone-spoons,
bad wine in the wind.
And in the end
fall

as gulls fall
slanting
to the water.
   (Pause)
I tell you
acting
is singing to yourself
in captivity.
Acting
is dancing without a father.
   (Pause)
You have chosen
a dangerous job, my friend.
   (Pause)
When people call you a God
love for them.
   (Pause)
You could walk with tarantulas.
You could live forever.

THE END

Part II

Securing Rights for Your Production

SECURING RIGHTS FOR YOUR PRODUCTION

Why Secure Rights?

A play producer's first responsibility is to secure performance rights for the "property," the script. If you do not have a designated producer, *you* should take care of this legal detail. Three reasons make it important for performers to be scrupulous about securing performing rights to the plays they do:

Artistic Reasons: New plays are the life blood of the theatre, and playwrights are your fellow artists. Knowing you are performing their plays and (when appropriate) receiving money for your use of their property encourages playwrights to turn out more and better scripts. You owe it to your art and your fellow artists to secure rights.

Ethical Reasons: Using a script without permission is theft. It does not suddenly become theft when you join a semi-professional acting company. As a person of integrity you owe it to yourself to secure rights.

Legal Reasons: It's the law. Neglecting to secure performance rights lays you open to fines, lawsuits, and other sanctions.

How to secure Rights for Scripts in This Anthology

In order to make it easier for you to secure performance rights, the playwrights of scripts in this book have agreed to special arrangements. These arrangements apply to scripts in this anthology only.

To secure rights for your production:

1. Using the following descriptions, decide which kind of production you are doing.

2. Fill out the Performance Agreement form or Performance Report which corresponds to your type of production. You may either tear out the form included in this book or else photocopy it.

3. In the case of Competition, Studio, or Full-Scale Amateur Productions, send the P.A.F. and royalty payment to the address at the end of the introduction to your script. Do this *at least* two weeks prior to your performance.

4. In the case of Class Projects and Departmental Juries, you may complete and send the Performance Report after the production.

Types of Productions

Class Projects and Departmental Juries. These performances are open only to students and instructors of your institution. There is no advertising outside your institution and no admission is charged. For **Class Projects and Departmental Juries,** no royalties are charged; however, since many playwrights like to know when their property is being used by students, you are encouraged to fill out the Optional Performance Report and send it to the author as a courtesy.

Competition Performances. This category covers performances done for contests sponsored by recognized state, regional, or national organizations; these performances have no production budget, and no admission is charged the spectators. **Competition Performances** must pay a nominal $5.00 royalty and secure permission by filing the appropriate Performance Agreement Form.

Studio Productions. These are workshop productions performed in spaces with an audience capacity of fifty or less, at which admission charges are $1.00 or less, and for which the production budget is $50.00 or less. **Studio Productions** must pay a low royalty of $8.00 *per performance* and must secure permission by filing the appropriate Performance Agreement Form.

Full-Scale, Amateur Productions. These productions have no restrictions in terms of production budget, size of audience, admission charges, or publicity, but the performers are not members of Actors Equity. **Full Productions** must pay royalties ($15.00 for the first performance and $10.00 for each subsequent performance), and they must secure rights by filing the appropriate Performance Agreement Form.

Other Productions. All other productions, including performances by Equity companies and productions to be broadcast or produced as movies, must negotiate rights and royalties with the playwrights or their agents.

OPTIONAL
PERFORMANCE REPORT
FOR A
CLASS PROJECT/DEPARTMENTAL
JURY PRODUCTION

OF THE PLAY _____

BY _____ , PLAYWRIGHT,

AS THE SCRIPT IS PRINTED IN *ONE-ACT PLAYS FOR ACTING STUDENTS.*

This is to inform you that we of the _____

department of _____ *(institution),*

at _____

_____ *(address),*

performed the above-named script as a Class Project or Departmental

Jury on _____ *(dates).*

This performance had no audience other than students and instructors of our institution. We did not advertise the performance outside our institution, nor did we charge admission to the performance.

We included the playwright's name in all printed announcements or programs.

If we perform this production of this script under circumstances other than those listed above, we will first negotiate performance rights for those performances in a separate document.

We think the playwright would be interested to know the

following details about our production and/or responses to the script:

_____

_____

_____

_____

_____

_____

_____

_____

_____

_____

Signed: _____

Title or Position: _____

Date: _____

At your option, send this completed form, or a photocopy thereof, to the playwright or playwright's agent as indicated in the script's introduction. No royalty payments are required for Class Project or Departmental Jury performances of the scripts in this anthology.

PERFORMANCE AGREEMENT FORM
FOR A
COMPETITION PERFORMANCE

OF THE PLAY_____

BY _____, PLAYWRIGHT,

AS THE SCRIPT IS PRINTED IN *ONE-ACT PLAYS FOR ACTING STUDENTS.*

We hereby request permission to perform the above-named script

in competition under the auspices of_____

_____*(sponsoring organization),* a recognized

LOCAL, STATE, REGIONAL, NATIONAL *(circle one)* organization, on

_____ *(dates)* at _____

_____

(name and address of performance place).

We hereby certify that this performance has no production budget and that no admission will be charged to attend the performances.

If we perform this production of this script under circumstances other than those listed above, we will first negotiate performance rights for those performances in a separate document.

In consideration of the right to perform the script under the above specified circumstances only, we enclose herewith the sum of $5.00.

We further agree to include the playwright's name in all printed announcements of the performances and to include in all programs the playwright's name and the following statement: *"(Title of play)* is performed by special arrangements with the playwright."

Signed: _____

Title or Position: _____

Producing
Organization: _____

Address: _____

Telephone Number: (   ) _____

At least two weeks prior to the performance dates indicated above, send this completed form, or a photocopy thereof, along with a check for $5.00, to the playwright or playwright's agent as indicated in the script's introduction.

Receipt of this form and royalty payment by the playwright or agent automatically secures performance rights to this play under the Competition circumstances and limitations specified above.

PERFORMANCE AGREEMENT FORM
FOR AN
AMATEUR STUDIO PRODUCTION

OF THE PLAY _____

BY _____ , PLAYWRIGHT,

AS THE SCRIPT IS PRINTED IN *ONE-ACT PLAYS FOR ACTING STUDENTS.*

We hereby request permission to present _____*(number)*

performances of a Studio Production of the above-named script on

_____ *(dates)* at _____

_____ *(name of performance space)* at _____

_____*(address).*

We hereby certify that the production budget for these performances is $50.00 or less, that the audience capacity of the performance space is 50 or less, and that the admission prices are $1.00 or less.

If we perform this script under circumstances other than those listed above, we will first negotiate performance rights for those performances in a separate document.

In consideration of the right to perform the script under the above specified circumstances only, we enclose herewith $8.00 for each performance, being a total of $ _____.

We further agree to include the playwright's name in all printed announcements of the performances and to include in all programs the playwright's name and the following statement: "*(Title of play)* is presented by special arrangements with the playwright."

Signed: _____

Title or Position: _____

Producing
Organization: _____

Address: _____

Telephone Number: (   ) _____

At least two weeks prior to the performance dates indicated above, send this completed form, or a photocopy thereof, along with a check for the royalties, to the playwright or playwright's agent as indicated in the script's introduction.

Receipt of this form and royalty payment by the playwright or agent automatically secures performance rights to this play under Amateur Production circumstances and limitations as specified above.

PERFORMANCE AGREEMENT FORM
FOR A
FULL-SCALE, AMATEUR PRODUCTION

OF THE PLAY _____

BY _____, PLAYWRIGHT,

AS THE SCRIPT IS PRINTED IN *ONE-ACT PLAYS FOR ACTING STUDENTS.*

We hereby request permission to present _____ *(number)*

performances of a Full-Scale Amateur Production of the above-named

script on _____ *(dates)* at _____

_____ *(name of performance space)* at _____

_____ *(address).*

We hereby certify that this is a non-Equity production.

If we perform this script under circumstances other than those listed above, we will first negotiate performance rights for those performances in a separate document.

In consideration of the right to perform the script under the above specified circumstances only, we enclose herewith $15.00 for the first performance and $10.00 for each subsequent performance, being a total of $_____.

We further agree to include the playwright's name in all printed announcements of the performances and to include in all programs the playwright's name and the following statement: *"(Title of play)* is presented by special arrangements with the playwright."

Signed: _____

Title or Position:_____

Producing
Organization: _____

Address:_____

Telephone Number: (   ) _____

At least two weeks prior to the performance dates indicated above, send this completed form, or a photocopy thereof, along with a check for the royalties, to the playwright or playwright's agent as indicated in the script's introduction.

Receipt of this form and royalty payment by the playwright or agent automatically secures performance rights to this play under Amateur Production circumstances and limitations as specified above.

Part III

Rehearsing
the Play

The third part of this book provides assistance for actors who are preparing a play without a director. Depending on your experience, you may want to use this section in different ways. Relatively inexperienced actors may want to read and use most of the materials as they work at developing their own rehearsal methods. Actors with considerable experience and training may find much of the material unnecessary; even these actors, however, are likely to encounter rehearsal problems for which they have no immediate solutions, and in cases like these, they may find some of the suggestions helpful as trouble-shooting tools.

SCHEDULING THE REHEARSALS
Sample Rehearsal Schedules

Here are samples of three approaches to preparing a play. If none of them suit your needs exactly, borrow some ideas from them and construct your own schedule. The "Rehearsal Calendar" which follows the third sample schedule provides a convenient place for you to record your plans.

Sample Schedule A: This loosely organized schedule demands considerable self-discipline and inventiveness from actors.

Learning about the characters and the play through read-throughs, discussion, improvisations, and research. Approximate number of rehearsals:_____.

Session with a coach to check progress and get suggestions.

Dealing with technical details such as blocking and memorization. Approximate number of rehearsals:_____.

Session with a coach to get feed-back and suggestions.

Polishing the play for performance. Approximate number of rehearsals: _____.

Performing.

Sample Schedule B: This schedule forms the basis for the rehearsal session guides *(Pages 245 to 258)*.

Analyzing the script.
Reading the script together.
Improvising.
Playing the given circumstances.
Investigating character identity.
Playing the intentions.
Rehearsing with a coach to get feed-back and suggestions.
Incorporating technical elements.
Repeating earlier concentration points (optional, as needed).
Getting off book.
Bringing it all together.
Rehearsing with a coach to get feed-back and suggestions.
Repeat of synthesizing rehearsal (optional, as needed).
Final dress rehearsal.
Performing.

Sample Schedule C: This schedule will work best if you have a coach who will give a lot of time and guidance to your project.

Individual script analysis.
Read-through: group script analysis.
Improvisations.
First blocking rehearsal.
Second blocking rehearsal.
Monitored blocking rehearsal.
Revising your blocking.
Characterization: given circumstances.
Characterization: character analysis.
Characterization: objectives.
Memorization: putting down the book.
Memorization: confirming your memory.
Monitored characterization rehearsal.
Characterization: bringing it all together.
First technical rehearsal.
Second technical rehearsal.
Pacing rehearsal (with a coach's assistance).
Final dress rehearsal.
Performance.

REHEARSAL CALENDAR

Play title:_____

Actor's name: _____ Telephone: _____

Actor's name: _____ Telephone: _____

Actor's name: _____ Telephone: _____

First rehearsal. Date:_____ Place: _____ Time: _____

    Concentration point_____

    Warm-up leader_____

Second rehearsal. Date:_____ Place: _____ Time: _____

    Concentration point_____

    Warm-up leader_____

Third rehearsal. Date: _____ Place: _____ Time: _____

    Concentration point_____

    Warm-up leader_____

Fourth rehearsal. Date:_____ Place: _____ Time: _____

    Concentration point_____

    Warm-up leader_____

Fifth rehearsal. Date:_____ Place: _____ Time: _____

    Concentration point_____

    Warm-up leader_____

Sixth rehearsal. Date:_____ Place: _____ Time: _____

    Concentration point_____

    Warm-up leader_____

Seventh rehearsal. Date:_____ Place: _____ Time: _____

    Concentration point_____

    Warm-up leader_____

Eighth rehearsal. Date:_____ Place: _____ Time: _____

    Concentration point_____

    Warm-up leader_____

Ninth rehearsal. Date: _____ Place: _____ Time: _____

    Concentration point_____

    Warm-up leader_____

Tenth rehearsal. Date: _____ Place: _____ Time: _____

    Concentration point_____

    Warm-up leader_____

Eleventh rehearsal. Date: _____ Place: _____ Time: _____

    Concentration point_____

    Warm-up leader_____

Twelfth rehearsal. Date:_____ Place: _____ Time: _____

    Concentration point_____

Warm-up leader_____

Thirteenth rehearsal. Date:_____ Place: _____Time: _____

    Concentration point_____

    Warm-up leader_____

Fourteenth rehearsal. Date: _____ Place: _____ Time: _____

    Concentration point_____

    Warm-up leader_____

Fifteenth rehearsal. Date: _____ Place: _____ Time: _____

    Concentration point_____

    Warm-up leader_____

Sixteenth rehearsal. Date:_____ Place: _____ Time: _____

    Concentration point_____

    Warm-up leader_____

Seventeenth rehearsal. Date: _____ Place: _____ Time: _____

    Concentration point_____

    Warm-up leader_____

Eighteenth rehearsal. Date: _____ Place: _____Time: _____

    Concentration point_____

    Warm-up leader_____

Performance. Date:_____ Place: _____Time: _____

    Warm-up leader_____

APPROACHING REHEARSALS

Productive Rehearsal Attitudes

Forming good mental attitudes toward time, performance level work, and characterization will help make your rehearsals efficient and productive.

First, determine to use **time** well. Remember that, in contrast to space arts like painting, theatre is a time art. The clock, therefore, is one of your most important tools. Never call off a scheduled rehearsal. Even if you don't feel like rehearsing, do it anyway. Nothing can hurt your performance more than skipping rehearsals. Then, once you start to rehearse, rehearse; don't let yourselves wander off on some conversational by-way. And give it a full shot. If you decide on a 1½-hour rehearsal, rehearse for 90 minutes, not 75; if you can't maintain concentration for 90 minutes, try two 50-minute sessions instead.

Second, commit yourselves to concentrating on performance-level work. As Stanislavski said, every rehearsal should be a performance and every performance just another rehearsal. Never permit yourself to "just walk through the scene" — **act** it. Every time. You will progress farther and faster. And never comment when you make a mistake. Breaking character during rehearsals builds bad habits that may haunt you in performance. Furthermore, once you crack, it takes extra time and energy to get back into character.

Finally, work on **characterization** in every rehearsal. Even if you don't think a particular rehearsal has much to do with characterization (for instance blocking or tech rehearsals), use the time to create your character. Aim to learn something new about your character in each session, and write down these discoveries to help solidify your gains. If you start getting bored, experiment with giving your character a different voice, posture, or personality. And **never** tell yourself or your partner that you need to wait for costumes (or props, or the "real stage," or the Second Coming) before you can really get into character. This game, called Waiting for Santa Claus, is a device poor actors use to deceive themselves. If a costume or prop item is that important, bring it to rehearsal yourself.

Rehearsal Session Procedures

Begin your rehearsal with about five minutes of vocal and physical warm-ups. Warming up will make your rehearsal more successful. Not only will warm-ups help you prepare your body and voice for the different demands you are about to make on them, but they also will prepare you psychologically. If you notice, for instance, that the second or third runs through your play are better than the first, there's a good chance you're using your first run-through as a warm-up; this is a bad habit for actors to form. And equally important, warm-ups provide a clear transition from everyday life to the time you will spend in rehearsal; if you don't do warm-ups, you will find it more difficult to stop visiting and start concentrating on rehearsal. Divide the responsibility for warm-ups between you and your partner so that neither one of you have to find and lead them all the time. If you don't know any warm-up exercises, several books in the bibliography will give you ideas. A good warm-up session includes activities to do four things: warm up the body, warm up the voice, loosen up the actors' sense of play, and get the actors into character.

Once you start through a scene, work straight through it without stopping for anything. Most of the scripts in this book are short enough to go straight through the entire play without a break. Your rehearsal will be far more productive if you don't stop to discuss each problem that occurs. Many of these problems ("Should I hold the broom in my right hand or my left?") solve themselves in successive repetitions simply through the magic of doing; stopping to talk about them wastes your time and breaks your concentration on character.

After you finish a run-through, briefly discuss the major things you want to change. Briefly. Spend your time rehearsing, not talking about rehearsing. If you are spending more than one-third of your rehearsal time talking, you're talking too much. And don't try to solve all the problems in any one of these discussion periods; focus on two or three major changes. The other problems will wait or, more likely, solve themselves.

Conclude your rehearsal by summarizing your progress. Talk briefly and specifically about what you have accomplished and what you need to do next time you rehearse. And before leaving, be sure you've agreed on the next rehearsal time and that you've cleaned up the space.

REHEARSING FOR SPECIFIC OBJECTIVES

Analyzing the Script Individually

Objective:

To discover as much about your play as you can on first acquaintance.

Techniques:

Begin by reading straight through the script. Aim during this first reading to discover the life of the script. You may find that reading the play aloud helps you feel its rhythms and get immediately in touch with its characters. Reading a script demands a different approach from reading an essay, short story, or poem. If, like most people, you have not read a lot of scripts, you might want to look over "How to Read a Playscript" *(Page 259)* before approaching the play itself.

Immediately after your first reading, without taking a break, jot down your first impressions of the play. Aim at description, not evaluation. If you must evalute, focus more on the positive than the negative; the point is to accept and understand the play on its own terms. Some sample descriptive statements might be: "The play moves fast/slowly." "It is funny/sad/like a soap opera." "It is realistic/a mood-piece/weird."

Next analyze the play in detail. The "Study Questions for Individual Script Analysis" on pages 260 to 262 can help you avoid overlooking important aspects of the play. In order to keep your analysis specific and precise, write down your observations.

When you think you've learned everything about the play that you can in one session, give yourself a short break, and then read straight through the script again; aim to see the play as a whole.

Progress assessment:

Take a few moments to register what you have accomplished: What did you know about the script before your first reading, or even immediately **after** the first reading? How much do you know about it now? Congratulate yourself on the difference.

Two further suggestions:

First, don't start memorizing yet; you've got plenty of time, and memorizing too soon may make it harder for you to experiment freely with the script and your role. Second, you may want to highlight your lines, but you're better off not underlining them; underlining fills spaces you may later want for writing notes, and it makes lines harder to read.

Read-Through: Analyzing the Script Together

Objective:

To agree with your fellow actors(s) about the nature of your script.

Techniques:

Begin by reading through the script together. Don't interrupt your reading in order to correct mistakes or try different interpretations; work for flow and worry about improvements later. During this rehearsal, concentrate on your character but don't push; characterization needs to develop naturally throughout the rehearsal schedule. For instance, if you settle on a particular "voice" for your character at this early rehearsal, you may not feel free to experiment with other, potentially better voices later.

After the read-through, briefly tell each other how you understand the play. One way to do this is to share your responses to the "Study Questions for Individual Script Analysis" *(Pages 260 to 262)*. You may want to discuss your differing ideas briefly, but don't let this discussion become heated or lengthy; if you simply register your opinions and then move ahead, you'll save time and your disagreements will begin to solve themselves.

Next, read straight through the script again.

Now, using the "Discussion Guide for Group Script Analysis" *(Page 262)*, talk about the play. If you agree, you might write down your responses to the questions. If you don't readily agree, discuss your opinions **briefly,** and then read through the script again. After re-reading the play, see if you can reach agreement. If so, write it down; if not, write down your differing responses and let it go at that.

Improvising

Objective:

To trigger your imagination for creative play interpretation.

Techniques:

Starting with a lively set of warm-ups will help this rehearsal immensely. You need to approach improvisation with a sense of adventure and playfulness, with the intention of taking risks and making mistakes. Warm-ups will help you tune in to your play impulses. You might conclude your warm-up session by playing Leap-Frog all around the rehearsal area. This game will thoroughly activate your body and will help you get past the fear of looking silly — a fear that can destroy improvisations.

After warm-ups, read through the first one-third of your play. Now put down the scripts, and without speaking, pantomime your way through the section. Talk about what happens in this segment: Who is doing what to whom? What is different at the end than at the beginning? Try to decide this without looking at the script. Now pantomime your way through the section again. Still without looking at the script, decide what physical activity is similar to the human event in this part of the play: Boxing? Seduction? Hide and seek? Rape? Ping pong? A cat with a mouse? Forget the play for a moment and pantomime that activity, complete with appropriate non-verbal noises such as grunts, screams, or laughter. Now re-read the segment you're working with, and then put down the scripts and pantomime it again, this time incorporating some of the behavior of the physical activity you experimented with. Conclude your work on this segment by reading through the scene while doing the pantomime. Don't worry if it doesn't look "realistic"; right now you're after the primitive, underlying lives and conflicts of the characters, not a realistic performance of the scene.

Before going on to the next part of the script, you may want to do a transitional improv to provide variety and help you move from one section to the next. Some suggestions:

Fight-Dance-Fight. Start a slow-motion, no-contact fight with your partner. Do this in character, and be sure to involve your whole body. Gradually let the fight shift into a slow-motion dance, and then change it back into a fight again. For an interesting and productive variation, try switching characters for Fight-Dance-Fight.

Jungle/Barnyard. Pick an animal that your character reminds you of. Imitate the animal, complete with sound, walk (crawl?), and gesture. Once you've "got it," encounter your partner in his/her "animal state." What happens?

Wake-up. Lie on the floor, and completely relax. Imagine yourself to be your character asleep in the early morning of the day on which the events in your play take place. What is your character dreaming about? Morning comes, and your character wakes up, gets out of bed, yawns and stretches hugely. Suddenly, an idea or image or memory pops into your character's mind and you freeze in mid-stretch. Tell your partner what stopped your stretching.

After the transitional improvisation, approach the second segment of the script using the sequence for the first one. Continue to alternate between script-based improvs and transitional improvs until you are through the play.

Progress assessment:

Tell each other one thing you learned about your own character, one thing you learned about each others' character, and one thing you learned about the play.

Problems? If the improvs seem to fall flat and you're learning nothing about your roles, you probably are not committing yourselves fully enough or going far enough with the exercises. In such a case, you might want to ask someone else to help you by directing your improvisations. The assistant's job would be to tell you what to do next, suggest new moves, and push you to experiment further.

Playing the Given Circumstances

Objective:

To **real**-ize your character's situation in terms of time and place.

Techniques:

Prepare your mind for this rehearsal by scouring your script for every scrap of evidence it can give about the location and time of your play. **Where** the play occurs includes not only the country, city, and immediate surroundings (represented by the set), but also what the location and every part of it **means** to your character. **When** the play occurs includes not only the calendar and clock time, but also the psychological moment in your character's life. Writing down all the information you discover about the place and time will help you be specific and is a good device to help you internalize what you have learned. Prepare physically for the rehearsal by collecting any hand props you will need. From now on, use your props in every rehearsal.

Begin by arranging the rehearsal furniture you think you will need, and then do your warm-ups.

After warm-ups, get in "places" to begin your play, and pause. In your mind, go over all the details you discovered about the time and place of your play. Visualize your set as that place; let yourself, as your character, enter into that time. When you sense that both you and your partner are ready, begin the play. Don't worry if you misjudge each other's readiness to start; you can iron out the details later. Go straight through the play, and concentrate **at every moment** on your character living in the time and place of the play.

After your run-through, talk about the beginning of the play. Which one of you gets the scene under way? How will this initiator know when the passive partner is ready? Once you've settled this detail, share your individual lists of time-and-place data. Don't waste time debating your differences — just listen to each other.

Run through the play again. If your perceptions of time and place had significant differences, you might follow this run-through with a brief discussion of any major contrasts in your ideas.

Once you are in places for the next run-through, pause a little longer before starting the action, and imagine where your character has been and what s/he has been doing immediately prior to the play's beginning. If you can visualize this "moment-before" in considerable detail, and if you make a habit of going through it like a mental play-before-the-play prior to each entrance, you'll never suffer the embarrassment of coming on stage out of character. Perform the play, and then briefly discuss anything you'd like to change about your scene. If you have time, it would probably be a good idea to go through the play a fourth time before quitting; remember to concentrate on making real the time and place of the action.

Progress assessment:

Conclude your rehearsal by each telling the other one thing you learned about your character or play during the session.

A note on set arrangement and blocking: You will be wise to postpone blocking until you are more familiar with your characters and the play. Many directors pre-block plays before characterization work, but before blocking, they have invested **days** of study in understanding the script; in contrast, as actors without a director, you will be developing your basic understanding of the script through the rehearsal process itself. At this point, then, simply arrange the furniture you need, and let your characters move around the set as the action and their relationships demand. Gradually, you will discover natural, meaningful blocking patterns.

If, however, you do decide to block before this rehearsal, begin by arranging your set. The "Blocking Checklist" on pages 266 to 268 has some suggestions for set arrangement. Once the set is arranged, act your way straight through the script, and then discuss one or two changes you need to make in your blocking; again, the

"Blocking Checklist" may be of help. Avoid getting picky, at this early stage, about specific gestures or body positions; such fine-tuning this soon will waste your time and may inhibit development of your character. Repeat the sequence of acting and discussing until you are satisfied with the blocking. You'll save a lot of time erasing if you wait until the end of the rehearsal before making blocking notes in the script's margins.

Investigating Character Identity

Objective:

To deepen your acquaintance with your character.

Techniques:

Prepare mentally for this rehearsal by combing your script for every scrap of evidence about **who** your character is. Using the "Character Analysis Questions" on page 262 or the "Character Profiles" on pages 263 to 265 may help you avoid overlooking important pieces of data. Making written notes will help your memory and attention to details. Prepare for the rehearsal physically by assembling a costume. Resist the temptation to postpone using your costume — especially if the costume is different from what you usually wear in public (for instance, a bathrobe) or less than you usually wear (for instance, a swimsuit).

Begin your rehearsal by arranging your set and doing your warm-ups. Then, aiming for concentration and performance quality, act your way straight through the play.

After the first run-through, take about ten minutes to introduce your characters to each other. Each pretend that your character is an old acquaintance of yours but that your character and partner have never met. Tell your partner the things that are really important for understanding who your character is. You may want to ask each other some questions about each other's character, using the same premise of never having met the person before. Have fun with this; the more you can enter into the game, the more you are likely to learn from it.

Now, act your way through the play again. Follow this run-through with a gossip session about your characters. Pretend your characters are mutual acquaintances of you and your partner. Give each other the **real** scoop about your characters. Let the gossip get a little catty; after all, it's for your characters' own good.

Follow the gossip session with another run-through. During the moments of concentration before the beginning of your play, visualize yourself as your character.

After this run-through, you might tell each other how you and your character are similar and different. What can you draw on from your life to apply to this character? How do you have to change yourself to become this character? If you have time, follow this talk session with a fourth run-through.

Progress assessment:

Conclude your session by telling each other how you feel about your progress. This might be a good time to check your schedule to be sure you are rehearsing frequently enough to be ready by the performance date.

Other techniques:

If the introduction or gossip exercises don't work for you, or if they work so well that you want more of the same, invent your own games. For instance, you might compose obituary notices for your characters (imagine they died immediately after the end of the play). Or you might play the role of an FBI agent doing a security check on your partner's character who has applied for a position with the Bureau; grill your partner for details about the applicant.

Playing the Intentions

Objective:

To focus on the chain of intentions which make up your role.

Orientation:

If Character A tries to force her will on Character B, and Character B not only resists but also tries to force his will on Character A, the result is conflict and drama. Most plays consist of a lively chain of shifting conflict. The moment one character has no intention at all, drama ceases to exist, the play gets boring, and the actors begin to fall out of character. The following suggestions will help you investigate the intentions of your characters.

Techniques:

The best preparation for this rehearsal is writing out your character's "through line of action." You may want to refer to the "Guidelines for Constructing a Through Line of Action" on page 265.

Although writing out a through line of action takes time and hard work, it pays huge dividends.

Start your rehearsal by arranging your set and doing warm-ups. Then act the play, focusing with complete concentration at every moment on what your character is trying to accomplish during that moment, and on the transitions from intention to intention.

After the first run-through, compare your character's super-objective with that of your partner's: What is the overall objective of each of your characters? How do their different objectives bring them into conflict? When and how is the major conflict resolved?

Next, play through the script again. Concentrate on living out your character's through line of action.

After this run-through, you might see if you can help each other with one or two moments when one or the other is not sure about his/her characters' intentions. For instance, your partner might say, "I don't really know why I make that first exit." Or you might say, "I get lost during your long speech on page fifteen. I don't know what I'm supposed to be doing, and my mind starts to wander. What do **you** think my character is trying to do during your speech?" Remember while you talk, that it is each actor's own business to determine his/her character's intentions; the point of this discussion is not to take away that responsibility and privilege but only to get assistance in problem solving.

Don't let this discussion drag on and on; rehearsing is doing, not talking about doing. If you find you are talking more than rehearsing, you may even want to use the clock to limit your discussion times. Continue your rehearsal by repeating the sequence of acting and discussing, focusing at every moment on your character's intentions.

Progress assessment:

You might conclude this rehearsal by telling each other what moments in the play you each feel especially good about. Celebrate these bright spots and determine to let them spread through the rest of the play.

Incorporating Technical Elements

Objectives:

To check the play's set, props, and blocking.

Techniques:

Prepare for this rehearsal by collecting any props and costume items which you haven't already been using. If you've postponed attending to these technical elements, procrastinate no longer: Handling actual props will help you invent characteristic business with them; wearing the actual costume will help you develop characteristic mannerisms.

Begin the rehearsal by arranging your set and props and getting into costume. Using the questions about set arrangement in the "Blocking Checklist" on pages 266 to 268, look at your set from the audience's perspective, and make any necessary adjustments.

When you're satisfied with the set, do your warm-ups, and then perform the play. If the presence of new props and costume items or a different set arrangement causes some awkward moments, avoid breaking character; dealing with the problems **after** the run-through will be far more efficient.

After the run-through, critique your blocking using the "Blocking Checklist" *(Pages 266 to 268)*. If you begin to find quite a few problems, limit yourself to talking about one or two, and then correct them while acting the play. After the second run, deal with a couple more improvements and put them into effect. Continue by repeating the acting/critiquing sequence.

Progress assessment:

At the end of the session, if you discovered your play is still missing props, decide which one of you will bring them. Take stock of what remains to be done on your play. Do you need another session on blocking and tech? Or do you need to return to the concentration point of an earlier rehearsal? If you are still dependent on the book and you're having a real problem keeping your place in the script while handling the props, maybe you should devote a rehearsal to getting off book. In the midst of considering what you still have to do, remember to notice and celebrate all the progress you've made so far.

Getting Off Book

Objective:

To free your mind and hands from dependence on the script.

Orientation:

If you've rehearsed frequently and with concentration, and if you've made a practice of going over your lines by yourself outside of rehearsal, you may already by very nearly lines-perfect. If so, you might well eliminate this rehearsal or combine it with another one. If you do a memorization rehearsal, be sure to concentrate on acting and characterization along with the memorization. So called "lines rehearsals" in which actors sit and read lines back and forth without movement and characterization are wrong in theory and inefficient in practice. Such practices reinforce the erroneous idea that the bare words have an importance of their own separate from the characters' lives. Furthermore, by eliminating character and movement, "running lines" cuts the actors off from major aids to remembering the lines.

Techniques:

After warm-ups, begin by putting the scripts down and acting your way straight through the play. Don't stop if you or your partner forget lines. Don't check the script. Don't break character, apologize, or curse yourself, your memory, or the play. If you go up on a line, focus on what your character is trying to accomplish at that moment and ad-lib your way through the spot. If your partner gets lost, don't feed him/her the line; instead either jump ahead to your next speech or ad-lib to call your partner back to his/her character's intention. If both you and your partner get lost, don't stop; muddle through to the conclusion, and stay in character. The goal, of course, is a word-perfect performance exactly as the lines are written. But stopping now in the middle may just train your mind to block up at the same place each time. An ad-lib is better than breaking character.

After the run-through, pick up your scripts and each choose one spot where you lost a line. Go over these two places together several times. Then act through the play without the script again. Continue to alternate between runs-through and work on specific lines until your time is gone or until you've done a performance without memory lapse.

Once you are confident of your lines, check to see that the lines you are speaking correspond to those in the script — that comfortable but inaccurate ad-libs have not crept in. You can do this either by running the play once, script in hand, or else by asking your partner if s/he is aware of any inaccuracies in your lines.

Progress assessment:

If you are word-perfect, congratulate each other and celebrate. If one or both of you still have memory problems, pinpoint them and determine to have those spots learned before next rehearsal.

Rx:

Persistent memory problems are indicative of concentration

problems. Probably the forgetful actors are not concentrating, or else they are concentrating on the wrong things (for instance, their memory problems instead of their characters). If you repeatedly stumble over a particular spot, check your through line of action; chances are you are not clear about your character's intention at the trouble point.

Bringing It All Together

Objective:

To pull the elements of the play together into a satisfying performance.

Techniques:

After arranging the set, do your warm-ups; commit yourself to them so your first run-through will be the best you are capable of.

With full concentration, act the play. Focus on making it performance quality — the best you can do. Remember that when you perform it for your audience, you probably won't have a chance to go through it once "dry" in order to get in the mood.

After the run-through, evaluate your play. Since you are within your own performance, you may find it difficult to view your show objectively; you may realize later (probably after the rehearsal is over, or even after the final performance) that you've given a few aspects of your performance more attention than they deserved while ignoring other important elements. One way to minimize this danger is to have a director watch you and give feed-back, but even directors can have blind spots. Another solution is to use some kind of a check-list; you might construct your own check-list by including the concentration points from your previous rehearsals, or you could use the "Final Performance Feedback Sheet" on page 271.

Remember that rehearsing is doing. Don't talk it to death. Limit yourselves to dealing with one or two points, and then do another run-through.

Progress assessment:

If, by the end of your rehearsal, you still have work to do, return to this concentration point in the next session.

Dress Rehearsal

Objective:

To try out your play under performance conditions.

Techniques:

Prepare for dress rehearsal by scheduling the performance space for your use; if possible, schedule your dress rehearsal at the same time of day as final performance. The reason for this timing is to prepare for events that happen at the same time each day (such as a freight train which thunders past your building daily at an hour which coincides with your performance). In order to provide a "test audience," you might want to invite several friends to watch, and if the performance program will consist of several plays done in succession, you may want to arrange for a couple of other shows to join you.

Meet long enough before the announced time of your rehearsal to do warm-ups and get into costume. If, at performance, you will have to arrange your set and props in full view of the audience or under some kind of time constraints, simulate those set up and strike circumstances during dress rehearsal.

Prior to your show, stay backstage or sit in the audience as you will at final performance. Refrain from burning off useful energy by fussing around stage or bantering with your audience.

At the announced time, set your stage, announce your play, and perform it. When you're done, take your bows, strike your set, and exit.

When you see your friends afterward, remember that if you ask them how they liked your play you are trapping them into flattering you. Just thank them for their presence and for being a good audience. If they want to tell you how they felt about the show, they will do it without your prompting.

Progress assessment:

When the audience is gone, evaluate yourselves. How efficient was your set-up and strike? Do you need to run through those procedures once or twice to correct problems? Did you get together soon enough to get your warm-ups and costuming done? Or did you get together too soon and end up with too much waiting time? How did the presence of the audience affect you? Did you crack? Rush? Make inappropriate eye contact with the audience members? Did you fail to hold for laughs or other audience reactions? What might you do to improve the experience for yourselves or your audience?

Assisted Rehearsals

Objective:

To get feed-back and advice from a knowledgeable theatre person.

Orientation and preparation:

Since you can't step off stage to watch yourselves perform, you may profit from the criticisms of an experienced observer. If your instructor doesn't include monitored rehearsals as a regular part of the course, look for a helper who has had some experience acting or directing. Decide when you want your "coach" to attend rehearsals; probably two visits will be sufficient. Depending on you and your coach, you may want to specify what you want feed-back on. You could use the "Feed-Back Sheets" on pages 269 to 271 or make up your own. Even if you just want general, non-directed feed-back, there may be one or two specific details you want comments on; if so, you'll be wise to tell the critic before performance rather than expecting him/her to pick out small details from a plethora of impressions after the fact.

Get together soon enough to do warm-ups, get into costume, and set the stage before the scheduled arrival of your observer. If you are ready before s/he arrives, don't just sit around and get nervous. Some suggestions of what to do until your coach arrives:

Do a full run-through of your play, and follow it with a normal self-criticism session; you may discover a few last minute improvements you can make.

Do some of the transition improvs from the rehearsal session titled "Improvising" *(Page 246),* or play around with some of the characterization exercises from the session on "Investigating Character Identity" *(Page 250).* These activites will give you a fresh look at your characters which will enliven your performance.

As soon as the observer arrives and gives you the go-ahead, perform the play. Resist any impulses to visit with the coach before performing. Excuses, questions, explanations, and introductions at this point are a waste of everyone's time. They are probably a device you use unconsciously to postpone performance.

After the performance, learn all you can from the observer. Realize that learning to deal profitably with criticism is a valuable part of your training as an actor. Some suggestions:

Write down notes of the coach's observations to help your memory.

Do not argue or offer excuses or explanations; you can evaluate the criticisms later.

Do not respond to criticisms with, "Oh yes, I know;" if you knew, you should have corrected the problem.

Make sure that you understand the suggestions; if you're not sure what a particular comment really means, ask.

Progress assessment:

After the coach leaves, discuss the criticism with your partner. Be sure you both agree on what the observer said. You may want to decide which comments are useful and which you don't agree with, but don't waste time or energy indulging in self-pity, self-recrimination, or arguments with the absent critic. Instead, decide what you need to do to incorporate the useful observations, and either get to work right away or set up your next rehearsal time. Be sure to end on a positive note; **especially** if the criticism was brutal, tell each other at least one aspect of your performance each of you was happy about.

Performing

Objective:

To share your finished art-work for the mutual enjoyment of yourselves and your audience.

Techniques:

Prepare for performance by taking care of yourself. Save partying until afterward, and get to bed on time the night before. Watch what you eat prior to performance; do eat, but refrain from heavy, hard-to-digest foods. Avoid alcohol, uppers, and downers; no matter how these drugs make you feel, their effect is to diminish your rational control. Don't buy a little phony self-confidence at the cost of your ability to concentrate.

Before performance, take care of warm-ups, costuming, and props, and then do what you can to maintain concentration. This doesn't mean going into a trance, but it does mean refraining from loud or physical interaction with others which will burn off energy you need.

When your time comes, perform with all the concentration, energy, awareness, and commitment you can muster.

If your instructor gives oral feedback after your scene, take notes just as you did during monitored rehearsals. The note-writing will help reinforce the learning process, and the activity will help you deal with any negative, post-performance emotions you may experience.

Finally, thank your partner for his/her work, return all borrowed props and costume items, and begin looking for the next show to try out for.

REHEARSAL TOOLS

How To Read a Playscript

A script is a technical document intended for the use of performers and technicians in staging a play. Because of this, playscripts should be read differently than essays, short stories, or poems. The following suggestions will help you be more efficient in reading a script.

1. In your first encounter with a script, read it **straight through.** The novelist expects the reader to read the novel in several sittings with sizable time gaps between; the playwright expects the audience — including you, the reader — to absorb the play in a single, sustained encounter.

2. Read at a rate slightly faster than the spoken word. Don't underline; it slows you down.

3. As you read, imagine the events happening on a stage, not "in real life."

4. Do not focus on word play or symbols. Although these may be present and can add to the enjoyment, they are not what the play is about.

5. Do not focus on philosophical meanings. The ideas in a play add to its power, but they usually are not why the play was written or what the play is about.

6. Focus on character identities and relationships between characters. Changes within and between characters are particularly important, because human change is **action,** and action is what plays are all about.

7. Focus on situations and events. "Situations" are periods of static human relationships; they may contain tension and conflict, but they are unchanging. "Events" are changes in human relationships; they are transitions from situation to situation. Most plays consist of an alternating sequence of situation — event — situation — event — situation.

8. Watch for physical actions and behaviors ("business") which are implied in the dialog. Not all actions are spelled out in the stage directions. (For instance, in *Streetcar Named Desire,* Blanche says to Stella, "Are you deliberately shaking that broom in my face?" To motivate that line, the actress playing Stella must, immediately before the line, have the broom somewhere in the direction of Blanche's face, even though the stage directions say nothing about the gesture.)

9. If you want to take notes on the play (a wise activity), do so

after reading the script, not during the reading.

> *NOTE: These suggestions will work not only for the*
> *short scripts in this book, but also for full-length scripts,*
> *scripts by Aeschylus and Shakespeare — any scripts.*

For more help in how to read a playscript, see the Booklist section on script analysis, page 275.

Study Questions for Individual Script Analysis

As you study your script, seek what is **unique** about your play. Almost all plays show **selfish** characters in **conflict** with each other, and almost all plays keep the audience in **suspense** about what will happen; how is your play different from all other plays? Play analysis is an on-going task. Be prepared, therefore, to learn new things about your play and to change your ideas throughout the rehearsal process.

A. The action of the play

1. In thirty words or less, summarize the story of your play.

2. How are things different at the end of your play than at the beginning? In other words, what changes in the course of the play? (Answer this question in one sentence.)

3. How does the play arouse interest? Sustain interest? Satisfy interest? (Use one sentence for each answer.)

4. What is the primary focus of the play? In other words, what is most important in the script: Telling a story? Depicting a character? Communicating ideas to the audience? Dazzling with spectacle?

B. The characters in the play

1. In twenty-five words or less, describe each character.

2. What is the basic relationship between the characters? For instance, are they lovers? Parent-and-child? Business associates? Total strangers? Master-and-servant?

3. What is the central goal, motive, or desire of each character? (One sentence per character.)

4. What obstacles keep each character from accomplishing his/her goal immediately? (One sentence per character.)

5. What is the central conflict? How does it develop? And what is the result? (One sentence per question.)

C. The style of the play

1. What is the dominant mood of the play? Be as specific as possible. Some samples: hilarious, hateful, frightening, silly, mystifying, cerebral, anxiety-producing.

2. Where does the action occur?

3. When does the action occur?

4. How is the world of the play like the real world?

5. How is the world of the play different from the real world?

D. The plot of the play

1. Divide the play into episodes and summarize each episode in one sentence. A typical romantic play, for instance, might have the following episodes: (1) Alvin asks Jane to marry him. (2) Jane rejects Alvin on account of his name. (3) Alvin wins Jane by changing his name to Elmer.

2. What is the relationship between episodes; how does the plot progress from episode to episode? You will probably need to write a short paragraph to cover this. Some sample plot progressions: (i) Chronological and causal: Episode A **causes** episode B. Episode B in turn **causes** episode C. Episode C concludes the play. (ii) Chronological but not causal: Episodes A, B, and C happen first, second, and third in the time of the story, but the earlier episodes don't really **cause** the later ones. (iii) Non-chronological. Episode B is a "flashback;" in the time of the story, the episodes occurred in the order B, A, C. (iv) Other: some modern plays have no relation to "real" time and arrange their incidents rhythmically, similar to movements in a symphony.

E. The ideas of the play

1. What philosophical ideas or questions does the play suggest? (Use one sentence for each idea or question.)

2. What is the theme of the play? (Limit yourself to one or two sentences.) A theme may be an idea that is repeated until it dominates a play (Technology threatens our humanity); or it may be a topic established by varied but related ideas and questions (How people respond to technology).

3. How important are ideas to the play? (Limit yourself to one sentence.) Answers might range from, "This play exists for the sole purpose of establishing its theme," to "Any ideas found in this play are purely incidental to the main focus on telling

the story."

Further Study:

While the above questions will help you understand your script, they barely scratch the surface of play analysis. To develop your dramatic analysis capabilities, continually read and view plays, and read books such as those listed in the bibliography section titled "Script Analysis," page 275.

Discussion Guide for Group Script Analysis

The following questions are intended to help actors talk productively about their script. It's a good idea to write down a summary of the responses to each question.

1. What happens in this play? Try to summarize the action in one sentence, and then, if necessary, expand on it.

2. Where and when does it happen? Deal first with map-and-clock reality: "It happens on June 6, 1942, in a hospital room in southern California." Then deal with socio-psychological time and place: "It happens immediately after their divorce and before the birth of their child, and it occurs on **his** turf."

3. How are the characters involved in what happens? Who makes it happen? Who profits/loses/changes the most as a result? Who is in control at each moment in the play?

4. How does the plot progress? How many episodes or scenes are there and what is the relation of each scene to the ones that precede and follow it? Can you graph the emotional intensity of each scene?

5. What is the play's style?

Character Analysis Questions

1. What do other characters say about your character? Make a **complete** list. For each statement indicate whether you think the speaker is correct, is mistaken, or is lying.

2. What does your character say about himself/herself? Be complete. Again, indicate whether your character is truthful about each statement, ignorant about himself/herself, or intentionally exaggerating, minimizing or falsifying.

3. What does your character do, and what do these actions reveal about his/her person?

4. What do the stage directions say about your character?

5. What is your character's super-objective? The super-objective is the one thing your character most wants to accomplish in the play. Compose the super-objective carefully.

   a. Start it with a purpose statement: "I want to . . ." or, "I must . . ." or "I have to . . ."

   b. Follow with an **active** verb: "I want **to kill** . . ." or, "I want **to seduce** . . ." or, "I want **to cure** . . ." or, "I want **to tame** . . ." (Avoid static verbs and verbs such as "to show" as in "I want to show I am honest.")

   c. Follow the second, active verb with an object that relates you to others in the play: I want to kill **the king;** I want to seduce **my servant;** I want to cure **my patient;** I want to tame **my lover.**

   d. Be sure the super-objective is specific to the play and at the same time deals with the entire role in the script. In *Oedipus Rex,* for instance, a good statement would be, "Oedipus wants to heal Thebes by punishing the murderer of Laius." An overly broad statement would be: "Oedipus wants to win everyone's admiration." This seems to be a life-long goal of Oedipus but is too general for this single event in his life. A sample of a super-objective that is too small might be, "Oedipus wants to learn his own identity." Actually he doesn't settle on this purpose until well into the play, and after he discovers who he is and blinds himself, the play still goes on for some time.

Sample Character Profiles

To play your character well, you need to know a great many more details about him/her than you will ever share with the audience on stage. Here are three character profile outlines you may use to fill in your character's background. When you add details from your imagination, be sure they fit with the character as portrayed in the script.

Profile 1: Six Traits of Character

This six-trait scheme comes from Sam Smiley's book, *Playwriting: The Structure of Action,* pages 83 to 91.

1. Biological traits: Is the character human or non-human? Male or female?

2. Physical traits: Include here all details about the character's body, voice, costume, manner of walking, and tempo — in other

words everything the audience can **see** and **hear** about the character.

3. Attitudinal traits: What is your character's basic outlook on life? Include such details as characteristic moods and habits.

4. Motivational traits: What are your character's goals, motives, drives, and desires? Also your character's fears and hatreds.

5. Deliberational traits: What does your character think about? How does your character think? To what extent is your character ruled by mind rather than heart (emotions) or belly (desires)?

6. Decisional traits: What, if any, decisions does your character make? How does s/he go about making decisions?

Profile 2: The Bone-Structure of a Character

This three part outline comes from Lajos Egri's book, *How to Write a Play,* pages 36 to 38.

Physiology

1. Sex
2. Age
3. Height and weight
4. Color of hair, eyes, skin
5. Posture
6. Appearance
7. Defects
8. Heredity

Sociology

1. Class
2. Occupation
3. Education
4. Home life
5. I.Q.
6. Religion
7. Race, nationality
8. Place in community
9. Political affiliations
10. Amusements, hobbies

Psychology

1. Sex life, moral standards
2. Personal premise, ambition
3. Frustrations, chief disappointments
4. Temperament
5. Attitude toward life
6. Complexes, obsessions, inhibitions, superstitions, manias, phobias
7. Extrovert, introvert, ambivert
8. Abilities, talents
9. Qualities

Profile 3: Identification of a Character

Jim Cash, film writer and teacher at Michigan State University, developed the following profile for his own use and for his students:

1. Name of character. Male or female.
2. Birthdate and birth place.
3. Education.
4. Occupation.
5. Height, weight, eyes, and hair.
6. Marital status.
7. Children.
8. A significant event that happened at the age of ten.
9. At the age of twenty.
10. At a later age.
11. Ten statements of information about this character — what s/he thinks, feels, cares about, hopes for, believes in, the conflicts and harmonies in his/her life, any kind of information that gives the character dimension.

Constructing a Through Line of Action

1. Go through your script and make a mark at every place where your character changes from one intention to another. The time between each mark is a "beat" or "unit of action."

2. In a notebook, write down two things for each beat: First, write down the intention. Use the same format as for the super-objective *(Page 263).*

   Second, write down what happens to the intention and how it changes to the next one. Typically, intentions are either fulfilled, defeated, postponed, or modified.

3. Don't forget to treat your character's **entrance** as a beat, complete with intention and transition to the next beat.

4. Avoid the following constructions for intentions: "to show . . ."; "to express . . ." **Especially** if what follows is an emotion.

5. Be sure your statement of intentions includes the **why** behind the physical act. **Wrong:** "He wants to sit down." **Right:** "He wants to infuriate the Emperor by sitting down."

6. As much as possible, make your intentions concrete and specific. Avoid vague intentions.

7. Intentions should all differ from each other. This is especially the case when they follow each other in adjacent sequence; it is

also usually the case when two similar beats are separated by several other beats. At the very least, they should build in intensity.

8. Each beat should relate to the character's super-objective. The relationship need not be **stated,** but it should be relatively obvious.

For more details on this technique, see page 276 of the Book List.

Analyzing Your Lines

Every line — every **word** — in your role means something specific to your character. Furthermore, your character wants to accomplish something as a result of every line s/he speaks. These six steps will help insure none of your lines are meaningless or purposeless (in other words, **dead**) when you say them.

1. Look up all words whose definition or pronunciation you are uncertain of.

2. What is the **sub-text** of the line. That is, what does the line mean **to the character who says it?** One way to discover sub-text is to paraphrase the line. Sample: Line: What time is it? Various sub-texts might be: (a) How long until my execution? (b) You are **really** late! (c) I think I missed my wedding.

3. Decide on the **verbal action** of the line. That is, what is your character **trying to accomplish** by saying the line? Sample: For the sub-texts in item #2 above, the respective verbal actions might be: (a) To discover if I still have time to escape from death row. (b) To insult my "friend." (c) To find out if I've avoided a marriage I really didn't want.

4. Conjure up any imagery in the lines. Be sure you visualize, in your mind's eye, what you talk about.

5. Don't skip a line. The point of this exercise is to help you deal with lines you've been ignoring (running them over your lips but bypassing your character's head). The line you are tempted to skip as "obvious" is likely the one that most needs work.

Blocking Checklist

A. Arranging the set.

1. Where is the audience in relation to your set?

2. How many entrances/exits do you need, and where are they? Are they located so that they maximize the effect of important entrances or exits. Up-stage-center doors, for instance, make it difficult for actors to exit without turning their backs on the audience.

3. Where is the furniture? Where are important props such as telephones? Is your set cluttered with unnecessary furniture? Is the furniture arranged so that it shares the play with the audience? The following arrangement, for instance, will make it difficult for the audience to see the face of an actor in Chair"B" and may hide an actor in Chair "A" behind the down-stage actor.

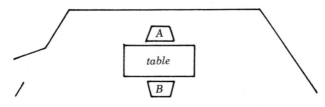

Rearrange the set like this:

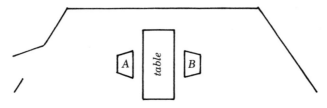

or like this:

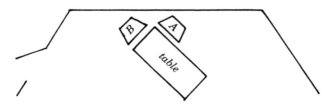

B. Checking the blocking.

1. Does the blocking share the play with the audience? Usually minimize blocking which places the actor's back to the audience or which conceals up-stage actors behind down-stage actors.

2. Does the blocking focus attention on the dominant actor at each moment? In the course of a single scene, the action may belong to one character for awhile, then shift to another; at times, two or three characters may share the scene. The blocking should enhance the focus.

3. Is there an appropriate amount of movement in the scene? Begin with the amount of movement the action would seem to demand in real life, and then heighten this by adding crosses and making them larger (don't forget to motivate each cross). Modify your blocking by considering the characters' relative tempos. In *Streetcar Named Desire,* for instance, Blanche, is likely to move often, quickly, and frenetically while Stella probably moves slowly, less often, more cow-like.

4. Does the blocking symbolize relationship by position and movement? For instance, in a scene where two lovers are "growing apart" the actors might gradually move further from each other. In a scene where one actor "talks down" to another, the persecutor might be standing up-stage of the victim who might be seated or even lying on the floor. In a scene where two apparently equal characters are "sparring," their movement pattern might approximate that of two circling boxers.

For more details on blocking, check the Book List on page 276.

Feedback Sheet: Characterization

Play title:_____

Character:_____ Actor: _____

1. Did the actor concentrate consistently?

2. Was the character believable?

3. Are there moments when the character's intentions need to be clarified?

4. Are there other useful comments?

Observer:_____

Date:_____

Feedback Sheet: Tech and Pacing

Play Title:_____

Character:_____ Actor: _____

1. Should any technical elements be changed?

2. Has the actor made progress in believability?

3. Are there sequences that should be faster, slower, louder, softer, etc.?

4. Were there lapses in line memorization?

5. Are there other helpful comments?

Observer:_____

Date:_____

Final Performance Feedback Sheet

Play Title:_____

Character:_____ Actor: _____

Technical considerations

 Were there memorization lapses?

 Were crosses, pictures, and business effective?

 Was projection adequate?

Character portrayal

 Were given circumstances consistent throughout?

 Were intentions clearly and consistently played?

 Did the actor clearly play the character's changes?

 Was the characterization inventive?

 Was there meaningful variety in the performance?

 Was the energy level satisfactory?

 Did the actor avoid over-acting?

Professionalism

 Did the actor cooperate with fellow actors throughout the rehearsal period?

 Did the actor take responsibility for rehearsal and production processes?

 Did the actor maintain seriousness of purpose?

 What did the actor do to help build cast morale?

 Did the actor display willingness and ability to take direction?

Additional comments:

       Evaluator: _____

       Date:_____

Part IV

Book List

REHEARSAL HELPS

Rehearsing Without a Director

Cohen, Robert. *Acting One*. Palo Alto, CA: Mayfield, 1984. "Studying and Rehearsing," pp. 63-69.

Glenn, Stanley L. *The Complete Actor*. Boston: Allyn and Bacon, 1977. "Rehearsal Discipline," pp. 318-25.

Warm-ups

Berry, Cicely. *Voice and the Actor*. New York: Macmillan, 1973. pp. 18-83, exercises throughout.

Dezseran, Louis John. *The Student Actor's Handbook: Theatre Games and Exercises*. Palo Alto, CA: Mayfield, 1975. "Constructing a Basic Workout," pp. 1-9.

Hill, Harry. *A Voice for the Theatre*. New York: Holt, Rinehart, and Winston, 1985. "Physical Warm-up," pp. 19-22.

King, Nancy R. *A Movement Approach to Acting*. Englewood Cliffs, NJ: Prentice-Hall, 1981. "Warming Up," pp. 18-23; and "Basic Movement Warm-ups," pp. 45-53.

Linklater, Kristin. *Freeing the Natural Voice*. New York: Drama Book Publishers, 1976. "Warm-up," pp. 94-96.

Machlin, Evangeline. *Speech for the Stage,* 2nd ed., New York: Theatre Arts Books, 1980. "The Actor's Practice Routine" and "The Actor's Warm-up Exercises," pp. 239-43.

In addition, the books listed under "Improvisations" all have exercises and games which make excellent warm-up activities.

Script Analysis

Benedetti, Robert L. *The Actor at Work*, 3rd ed., Englewood Cliffs, NJ: Prentice-Hall, 1981. "Dramatic Action and Play Structure," pp. 175-84, and "Scene Structure," pp. 185-91.

Grote, David. *Script Analysis: Reading and Understanding the Playscript for Production*. Belmont, CA: Wadsworth, 1985.

Hayman, Ronald. *How to Read a Play*. New York: Grove, 1977. Entire book. Check first the summary on pp. 93-94.

Hodge, Francis. *Play Directing: Analysis, Communication, and Style,* 2nd ed., Englewood, Cliffs, NJ: Prentice-Hall, 1982. "Characteristics of Dramatic Action," pp. 31-37.

Stiver, Harry E. and Stanley Kahan. *Play and Scene Preparation: A Workbook for Actors and Directors*. Boston: Allyn and Bacon, 1984. "Sample Exercise for the Study of Approach and Style," pp. 7-8.

Improvisations

Dezseran, Louis John. *The Student Actor's Handbook: Theatre Games and Exercises*. Palo Alto, CA: Mayfield, 1975. The entire book is made up of improv ideas.

Hodgson, John and Ernest Richards. *Improvisation,* rev. ed., New York: Grove, 1979. "Stimulating the Imagination," pp. 58-65; and "Building Characterization," pp. 74-89.

Johnstone, Keith. *Impro: Improvisation and the Theatre*. New York: Theatre Arts Books, 1979. The entire book gives insights into improvisational approaches.

Spolin, Viola. *Improvisation for the Theatre: A Handbook of Teaching and Directing Techniques*. Updated ed. Evanston, IL: Northwestern University Press, 1983. "Exercises," pp. 49-273.

Blocking

Cohen, Robert. *Acting One*. Palo Alto, CA: Mayfield, 1984. "Self-Staging," pp. 70-76.

Dean, Alexander and Lawrence Carra. *Fundamentals of Play Direction,* 4th ed., New York: Holt, Rinehart and Winston, 1980. "Basic Technique for the Actor," pp. 32-66; and "The Five Fundamentals of Play Directing," pp. 94-282.

Dezseran, Louis John. *The Student Actor's Handbook: Theatre Games and Exercises*. Palo Alto, CA: Mayfield, 1975. "Using the Language of Direction," pp. 68-79.

Stiver, Harry E. and Stanley Kahan. *Play and Scene Preparation: A Workbook for Actors and Directors*. Boston: Allyn and Bacon, 1984. "Sample Exercise for the Study of Business and Movement," pp. 15-16.

Character Analysis

Dezseran, Louis John. *The Student Actor's Handbook: Theatre Games and Exercises*. Palo Alto, CA: Mayfield, 1975. "Analyzing a Character for Scene Work" and "Charting a Character's Essence," pp. 89-97.

Egri, Lajos. *How to Write a Play*. New York: Simon and Schuster, 1942. "Character: The Bone Structure," pp. 32-43.

McGaw, Charles and Larry D. Clark. *Acting is Believing: A Basic Method,* 5th ed., New York: Holt, Rinehart and Winston, 1987. "Getting into the Part," pp. 129-39.

Smiley, Sam. *Playwriting: The Structure of Action*. Englewood Cliffs, NJ: Prentice-Hall, 1971. "Contrast and Differentiation" (six character traits), pp. 83-91.

Stiver, Harry E. and Stanley Kahan. *Play and Scene Preparation: A Workbook for Actors and Directors*. Boston: Allyn and Bacon, 1984. "Sample Exercises for the Study of Characterization," pp. 23-24, 59-60; and "Sample Exercise for the Study of Dialogue and Language," pp. 31-32.

Constructing a Through Line of Action

Lewis, Robert. *Advice to the Players*. New York: Harper and Row, 1980. "Intention," pp. 52-74.

McGaw, Charles and Larry D. Clark. *Acting Is Believing: a Basic Method*, 5th ed., New York: Holt, Rinehart, and Winston, 1987. "Seeing a Part as Units of Action," pp. 141-45.

Memorization

Cohen, Robert. *Acting One*. Palo Alto, CA: Mayfield, 1984. "Memorizing," pp. 53-62.

Franklin, Miriam A. and James G. Dixon III. *Rehearsal: The Principles and Practice of Acting for the Stage,* 6th ed. Englewood Cliffs, NJ: Prentice-Hall, 1983. "Aids to Memorization," pp. 88-89.

Kahan, Stanley. *Introduction to Acting,* 2nd ed. Boston: Allyn and Bacon, 1985. "Learning Lines," pp. 174-75.

Dealing with Stage Fright

Daly, John A. and Arnold H. Buss. "The Transitory Causes of Audience Anxiety," *Avoiding Communication: Shyness, Reticence, and Communication Apprehension*. John A. Daly and James C. McCroskey, eds. Beverly Hills, CA: Sage, 1984. pp. 67-78.

Hill, Harry. *A Voice for the Theatre*. New York: Holt, Rinehart, and Winston, 1985. "Relaxation — Physical and Vocal Well-Being," pp. 11-22.

Kahan, Stanley. *Introduction to Acting,* 2nd ed. Boston: Allyn and Bacon, 1985. "Stage Fright," pp. 282-88.

OTHER SCRIPTS BY WRITERS
IN THIS ANTHOLOGY

Norman A. Bert

All scripts are available from the playwright, c/o 5704 Nashville Avenue, Lubbock, TX 79413-4601.

The Bottsologuing of Miss Jones. A one-act metaphysical farce. 1978.

Cat Game. A drama about rural Pennsylvania coal miners. 1982.

The Dove, the Hawk, and the Phoenix. A one-act peace play. 1983.

Mixed Doubles. A one-act play about a marriage made in Montana. 1986.

Post Office. A one-act marital comedy. 1981.

Conrad Bishop, The Independent Eye

All scripts are available from the playwright, 115 Arch Street, Philadelphia, PA 19106.

Double Mortgage. Two linked plays about suicide. 1981.

Families. A comic revue about family life. 1980.

Full Hookup. A contemporary tragedy in two acts. 1982.

Medea/Sacrament. A tragedy based on the Greek myth. 1983.

Summer Sisters. A comic fantasy in two acts for three women and a small girl. 1984.

William Borden

All scripts are available from the playwright, R.R. 6, Box 284, Bemidji, MN 56601.

The Consolation of Philosophy. A cynical professor meets a not-so-eager student. 1986.

The Last Prostitute. Two boys come to be initiated by "the best." 1980.

Loon Dance. A serious comedy about a family at a lake. 1982.

The Only Woman Awake is the Woman Who Has Heard the Flute. A romantic comedy. 1983.

Tap Dancing Across the Universe. A romantic comedy. 1981.

Matthew Calhoun

All scripts are available from the playwright, 23-51 19th St. Basement Apt., Long Island City, NY 11105.

Mom. A comedy about an abused mother. 1987.

Plato's Kitchen. A tragicomedy. 1986.

Prayers and Other Problems. A comedy. 1983.

Skits-Ophrenia. A comic revue. 1984.

True Wit. Comic sketches. 1983.

Beverly Creasey

All scripts are available from the playwright, 164 Brayton Rd., Brighton, MA 02135.

Fugue in G. A one-act tragedy about a young woman who thinks she is losing her mind. 1983.

Happy Birthday to Me. A one-act WASP family comedy. 1984.

Heiden Roslein. A full-length stage adaptation of the Schubert song about a careless boy and his comeuppance. 1982.

Mate in Two Moves. A one-act farce about a compulsive chess player and a world out of control. 1985.

Murder Overdue. A one-act spoof of murder mysteries, with audience participation. 1986.

Dale Doerman

All scripts are available from the playwright, 2740 Enslin St., Cincinnati, OH 45225.

The Blind. An 85-minute play without intermission. 1983,

State of the Art. A 35-minute satire.

Tom-Tom. A 55-minute comedy.

Zebra. A 10-minute romantic comedy, a park vignette. 1984.

Stephen R. Grecco

The Bowlers. A one-act play about two couples who metaphorically bowl. In *Yale/Theatre.* New Haven, CT: Yale University Press, winter 1968.

Operatic Arias. A full-length play about Ibsen's Nora as a contemporary New Yorker. 1984. Scripts available from the playwright, 1103 S. Garner St., State College, PA 16801.

The Orientals. A one-act play about the failure of Western rationalism. In *Playwrights for Tomorrow,* vol. 7. Minneapolis: University of Minnesota Press. 1971.

Star-Lite. A full-length realistic drama about a Viet Nam

veteran's inability to survive. 1986. Availeble from the playwright.

The Young Coal Miner and His Wife and a Few of Their Friends. A full-length, naturalistic tragedy. 1981. Available from the playwright.

Billy Houck

All scripts are available from the playwright, 1240 Sage Street, Arroyo Grande, CA 93420.

Birds of Prey. A full-length comedy.

The Day the Flamingos Came Out to Work. A puppet play for lawn flamingos.

Incroyable. A full-length drama about fashion and politics during the French Revolution.

Lobster Tank. A short play for four crustaceans.

Womb Room. A short play for three embryos.

Ben Josephson

All scripts are full-length. They are available from the playwright, 286 East Second Street, Benicia, CA 94510.

What the Light Lights Up. An offbeat comic romance. 1985.

Horace Whirley's Woe. A broad, satiric comedy. 1983.

Never Mind the Wind. A drama. 1979.

Tim Kelly

Destiny. Two acts. Boston: Bakers Plays, 1985.

18 Nervous Gumshoes. Two acts. Colorado Springs: Contemporary Drama Service, 1987.

Lucky Lucky Hudson and the 12th St. Gang. Two acts. Colorado Springs: Contemporary Drama Service.

The Omelet Murder Case. One-Act. New York: Dramatists Play Service, 1984.

Who Walks in the Dark. Two acts. New York: Samuel French. 1987.

Joanna H. Kraus

Circus Home. A full-length play. Rowayton, CT: New Plays, 1979.

The Ice Wolf. A full-length play. Rowayton, CT: New Plays, 1967.

Kimchi Kid. A full-length play. Rowayton, CT: New Plays. 1987.

The Last Baron of Arizona. A full-length play. Tempe, AZ: Pyracantha

Press, 1986, and Rowayton, CT: New Plays, 1986.

The Shaggy Dog Murder Trial. A T.I.E. play. New Orleans: Anchorage Press, 1987.

Wendy MacLaughlin

All scripts are available from the playwright, 1103-B West 47th St., Kansas City, MO 64112.

Chapel. A two-character one-act play adapted for radio. 1986.

Crown of Thorn. The drama of the French priest/scientist Pierre Teilhard de Chardin. 1982.

Mirror/Mirror. A woman's cure of manic depression through right brain contour drawing. 1987.

Secret. A full-length play about a woman Soviet dissident writer. 1983.

Watch Out Little Boy or You'll Fall In. One-act play. 1980.

Patricia Montley

Alice in Collegeland. Comic portrayal of a high school senior in search of a college. Colorado Springs: Contemporary Drama Service. 1986.

Bible Herstory. A feminist satire of Old Testament stories. New York: Samuel French, 1975.

Not So Grim Fairy Tales. A feminist satire of traditional fairy tales. New York: Samuel French, 1977.

Prickly Parables. A feminist satire, in story-theatre style, of gospel parables. 1983. Available from the playwright, Theatre Department, Chatham College, Pittsburgh, PA 15232.

Rosvitha's Review. A full-length musical comedy about the tenth-century nun who was the first woman playwright. Available from the playwright.

William Moseley

Scripts for all of these plays are available from the playwright, 102 Highview Drive, Cocoa, FL 32922.

BLOCKS: An Absurd Play for Young People. 1979.

Duet. A one-act play. 1985.

Jealousy (Two one-act plays: *A Jealous Man* and *A Jealous Woman*). 1981.

The Sound Screen. A one-act play. 1982 (radio) and 1984 (stage).

Winter Funeral. A full-length play. 1980.

Lavonne Mueller

Breaking the Prairie Wolf Code. New York: Dramatists Play Service, 1986.

Collette in Love in *Women Heroes,* Julia Miles, ed. Applause Theatre Book Publishers, 1987.

Killings on the Last Line in *The Women's Project: Seven New Plays by Women*. New York: Performing Arts Journal Publications, 1980.

Little Victories. New York: Dramatists Play Service. 1983.

Oyster Crackers, Undershirts, and Mauve Lemonade. Boston: Bakers Plays, 1975.

Robert Patrick

Big Sweet. A cartoon play with songs. Cincinnati: Dramatics Magazine, 1984 (3368 Central Pkwy., Cincinnati, OH 45225).

Judas. A crucifixion tragedy. 1979. Available from the playwright, 1837 North Alexandria Avenue #211, Los Angeles, CA 90027.

Kennedy's Children. A full-length tragedy about the 60's. New York: Samuel French, 1976.

Mercy Drop and Other Plays. Indescribable pop outpourings. New York: Calamus Press, 1980 (121 Second Ave., New York, NY 10003).

My Cup Ranneth Over. An ironic one-act for two women. New York: Dramatists Play Service, 1979.

T-Shirts. A comic one-act for three men. In William M. Hoffman, ed. *Gay Plays*. New York: Avon Books, 1977.

Christine Rusch

All scripts are available through the playwright's agent, Dan A. Bellaciccio, 6736 Laurel Canyon Blvd., Suite 300, North Hollywood, CA 91606.

Whitewater Rep. The story of a girl who sees what needs to be done and does it.

The Life and Adventures of Sissal T. Hopewell. An exploration of form as Sissy struggles to find her identity.

Kulig! A romantic, carnival-like romp based on the Siege of Stalingrad.

Child of the Wish Winds. A love story concerning child abuse.

Beyond the Blues. An ensemble piece for four black actors based on the life of John Coltrane.

Joel Selmeier

All scripts are available from Joel Selmeier, 2446 Turnberry Dr., Cincinnati, OH 45244.

Absence of Moonlight. Additional scenes between the two characters in *Bug Swatter.*

Numerology. A twenty-minute narrative monolog for a woman.

One Hundred. A short avant-garde one-act for four performers of any age or sex.

Playwright's Intro. A five-minute comic monolog in which a confused playwright introduces the play about to start.

10 W 40. A full-length, single-set, comic drama for two young men and one young woman.

Sam Smiley

Date. A short play about relationships between young people and the very old. New York: Samuel French, 1972.

Hemingway. An anthology. Scripts available from the playwright, 5799 N. Via Amable, Tucson, AZ 85750.

Summer Light. A nostalgic play about a boy and his grandfather. Scripts available from the playwright.

Megan Terry

Calm Down Mother. One-act. New York: Samuel French, 1964.

Ex-Miss Copper Queen on a Set of Pills. One-act. New York: Samuel French, 1963.

High Energy Musicals from the Omaha Magic Theatre. Three full-length works. New York: Broadway Play Publishing, 1983.

Mollie Bailey's Traveling Family Circus; Featuring Scenes from the Life of Mother Jones. Full-length musical. New York: Broadway Play Publishing, 1983.

Sleazing Toward Athens. Long one-act. 1987. Published by Omaha Magic Theatre Press, 1417 Farnam, Omaha, NE 68102.

Janet S. Tiger

All scripts are available from the playwright, 4489 Bertha St., San Diego, CA 92117.

Blind Woman's Bluff. A one-act play about an old woman and a thief. 1983.

One Nightstand. A one-act play about a couple in a motel. 1985.

The Second Battle of Hobson's Choice. A full-length play about a small town that will not reveal a killer's identity. 1982.

Sweepstakes. A one-act play about two brothers — one a sweepstakes fanatic, and the other suicidal. 1985.

The Waiting Room. About decisions made by a Jewish family in Nazi-occupied Vienna. Full-length and long one-act versions. 1980.

Greer Woodward

Don't Sleep Under the Mapou Tree! A participation play for young audiences. Denver, CO: Pioneer Drama Service, 1980.

Tenure Track. Fourteen snapshots of academe, written with Joanna H. Kraus. 1982. Scripts available from Players Press, Inc., P.O. Box 1132, Studio City, Ca 91614-0132.